CATHOLICS CONFRONTING HITLER

Peter Bartley

CATHOLICS CONFRONTING HITLER

The Catholic Church and the Nazis

IGNATIUS PRESS   SAN FRANCISCO

Cover design by Enrique Javier Aguilar Pinto

© 2016 by Ignatius Press, San Francisco
ISBN 978-1-62164-058-5
Library of Congress Control Number 2015948575
Printed in the United States of America ∞

CONTENTS

INTRODUCTION

Hitler's Rise to Power—1919–1933

By 1918, four years of trench warfare had left Germany exhausted and her army facing defeat. Field Marshal Paul von Hindenburg's final offensive in the West had failed, and with American troops pouring into France to reinforce the Allies, he and his chief of staff, General Erich Ludendorff, accepted the inevitable and sued for peace. On 11 November, an armistice was signed between Germany and the Allied Powers at Compiègne in Northeast France, bringing the First World War to an end. Recovering from temporary blindness in a military hospital in Pomerania, Corporal Adolf Hitler heard the news of the German surrender and wept.

Following the emperor's abdication, a German republic was proclaimed with the Social Democrat Friedrich Ebert as president. In the German town of Weimar on the river Elbe, a newly formed coalition government, composed mostly of Social Democrats and Catholic Centre Party members, approved the peace terms that had been dictated by the Allies at Versailles a few weeks before. These events left not only Hitler but also a great many Germans feeling disillusioned and embittered.

A social misfit and sometime vagrant in prewar Vienna, Hitler had served with distinction when war came, earning the highest military decorations his country could bestow.

For a brief time after the armistice, he remained in the army, where he was given political training and assigned to educational duties. In the revolutionary atmosphere of 1919, Hitler was sent to Munich by army intelligence to report on a small left-wing group known as the German Workers' Party (DAP), which had been cofounded in January of that year by Anton Drexler, a toolmaker and labour activist, and Karl Harrer, a journalist. To begin with, the DAP was little more than a debating club, until Drexler raised its political profile and its reputation among those on the fringe of the political spectrum. Embracing a socialist ideology fused with nationalism, xenophobia, and anti-Semitism, the group made an immediate impression on Hitler, whose own ideological development had already taken shape along similar lines. In September 1919, Hitler joined the party. The following year, he changed its name to the National Socialist German Workers' Party, shortly to be abbreviated to Nazi. By 1921, Hitler had wrested control of the party from Drexler.

The party programme was drawn up by Hitler, Drexler, and Gottfried Feder (the group's economics adviser) in February 1920. Its twenty-five principles included the nationalisation of industries on a limited scale and the reform of land ownership. Especially noteworthy was point 24 of the programme, which promised religious freedom, "except for religions which endanger the German race", which could be interpreted to mean almost any religion and did, in fact, portend the dilution of Christianity in the interests of race theory. The programme stressed a preference for "Positive Christianity", without prejudice to denominational interests.[1] Of equal interest, in the light

---

[1] Peter Matheson, ed., *The Third Reich and the Christian Churches* (Edinburgh: T&T Clark, 1982), 1.

of subsequent events, were the first four points of the programme. They were, in short, the union of all Germans in a Greater Germany; the rejection of the Treaty of Versailles, which was regarded as a betrayal of German interests; the demand for additional territories; and the denial of German citizenship to Jews.[2]

When Hitler joined the party, it had fewer than fifty members. By January 1921, the membership had risen to three thousand, and the party had extended its sphere of influence beyond Munich to the rest of Bavaria. Hitler made the difference. Having discovered a flair for a firebrand style of oratory that played upon his listeners' fears and their distrust of Weimar politicians, Hitler drew thousands to his political meetings in the beer cellars of postwar Munich. In impassioned, vituperative tirades, he castigated the enemies of the Fatherland—the capitalists, the Bolsheviks, the traitorous politicians who had stabbed the German people in the back, and, above all, the Jews, "this mortal enemy of our nation and of all Aryan humanity and culture".[3] By 1923, Hitler's National Socialists numbered seventy thousand in Bavaria alone, and the movement had spread to Berlin and to other parts of the country. Many recruits were former Freikorps men, World War I veterans who, immediately after the war, had been drafted into private armies for the express purpose of quashing Communist revolution, a task they performed with matchless brutality. Under the command of Captain Ernst Röhm, Hitler's former comrade-in-arms, they became the paramilitary storm troopers (SA). Fiercely loyal to Hitler,

[2] The Nazi Party programme is summarized in James Taylor and Warren Shaw, *The Penguin Dictionary of the Third Reich* (London: Penguin Books, 1997), 200–201.

[3] Adolph Hitler, *Mein Kampf*, trans. Ralph Manheim (London: Pimlico, 1996), 319.

the SA kept order at his political meetings and engaged Communists in bloodthirsty affrays, settling their differences with the fist and the boot. An entry in Joseph Goebbels' diary recalling a political gathering in Chemnitz gives some idea of the level of violence that was commonplace then: "At the end devastating free-for-all fight. A thousand beer glasses smashed. Hundred and fifty wounded, thirty seriously, two dead."[4] After 1930, Nazis marched to the strains of the "Horst Wessel Song", which commemorated a young SA man who had been killed in a street brawl with Communists. If Hitler is to be believed, by the time the Nazis came to power in 1933, a total of 350 party members had lost their lives in street battles with political rivals.[5]

The year 1923 was a disastrous one for the German economy, and for Hitler also, despite a great upsurge in support for his party. With the economy on the point of collapse, the country was unable to pay the war reparations required under the Treaty of Versailles. In an ill-conceived attempt to enforce payment, the French occupied the Ruhr, Germany's industrial heartland on the west bank of the Rhine. In November, Hitler and Ludendorff conspired to topple the Bavarian government in Munich. The operation, planned in a beer hall, was a botched affair with no hope of success, and the police had little difficulty routing the insurgents. Hitler, Ludendorff, and other leading Nazis were arrested and the SA and the Nazi Party outlawed. Receiving a term of five years' imprisonment for his part in the affair, Hitler was sent to Landsberg Prison

[4] *The Early Goebbels Diaries, 1925–1926*, ed. Helmut Heiber (London: Weidenfeld and Nicolson, 1962), entry for 23 November, 1925.

[5] Hitler to Cardinal Bertram, 28 April 1933, in E. L. Woodward and Rohan Butler, eds., assisted by Anne Orde, *Documents on German Foreign Policy, 1918– 1945*, series C (1933–1937) The Third Reich: First Phase, vol. 1, 30 January–14 October 1933 (London: Her Majesty's Stationery Office, 1957), doc. no. 196.

to complete his sentence. For the nine months of the sentence that he actually served, he was treated indulgently by a fawning prison staff. He received a stream of admiring visitors, posed for photographs, and occupied his time dictating the first volume of his political testament, *Mein Kampf*, to his disciple and collaborator Rudolf Hess before his early release in December 1924.

Albert Speer, Hitler's armaments minister, confessed that he had abandoned the effort to read *Mein Kampf*. Goebbels, on the other hand, thought it "wonderful" and was lavish in his praise of Hitler's political instinct. "Crude", "turgid", and "half-baked" are some of the less-than-complimentary judgements that have been passed upon the book. Where Jews were concerned, ambiguity was not one of its defects; Jews and Bolsheviks alike were hated by Hitler, who made no distinction between the two. Hitler's anti-Semitism had its origin in late-nineteenth-century race theory, especially that which elevated the status of German culture and ascribed to Germans the dominant role in Europe. A special feature of the theory was its emphasis on the purity of German blood.

Exactly when Hitler became an anti-Semite is uncertain. Before his Vienna days, he had read with approval the prose of the composer Richard Wagner, a noted anti-Semite. As a young man in Vienna, he was an admirer of Karl Lueger, the city's anti-Semitic, though popular, mayor. However, a recent biographer, Ian Kershaw, has noted that Hitler showed few signs of anti-Semitism in his Vienna days and that he had several Jewish acquaintances, a fact also alluded to by Hitler's first biographer, Konrad Heiden. By the end of his time in the Austrian capital, Hitler's ideological outlook seems to have been well formed; it then became hardened as a result of his experience of war. By the time he met Drexler in Munich in 1919, Hitler was a political extremist and an undoubted anti-Semite.

Hitler classified Jews negatively: they were non-Aryans, and when describing them he used the language of pathology. Jews were a dangerous admixture; they polluted the German race. Jews, said Hitler, were "spiritual pestilence, worse than the Black Death of olden times".[6] Hitler's appraisal of Marxism reveals it to be a Jewish doctrine conceived for the purpose of world domination. However fanciful that might seem today, it made perfect sense at the time. A common belief, held throughout Western Europe, associated Jews with Bolshevism. Winston Churchill made the connection in an article written in 1920.[7] It is not too difficult to see why. Many leading Bolsheviks, such as Leon Trotsky, Leviticus Kamenev, and Grigory Zinoviev, were Jews, as were Béla Kun and most of his Communist regime in Hungary. So, too, were Rosa Luxemburg and Karl Liebknecht, the leaders of the Spartacist (Communist) movement in Germany, and Kurt Eisner, who in 1919 led a left-wing revolution in Bavaria. As, indeed, was Karl Marx himself. "The relatively high percentage of Jews in the leadership of the Socialist parties on the European continent cannot be denied", wrote Konrad Heiden.[8] But Jewish Bolshevists were later brutally eliminated, to be replaced by non-Jewish leaders. Under Stalin, Communist Russia became tainted with anti-Semitism. And Luxemburg, Liebknecht, and Eisner aside, Jews do not appear to have played any significant role in the growth of German Communism.[9] Jews were, on the other hand, prominent among the supporters of Italian Fascism.

---

[6] Hitler, *Mein Kampf*, 54.

[7] Nicholas Farrell, *Mussolini* (London: Weidenfeld and Nicolson, 2003), 303.

[8] Konrad Heiden, *The Fuehrer* (London: Robinson, 1999), 58.

[9] Paul Johnson, *A History of the Modern World from 1917 to the 1980s* (London: Weidenfeld and Nicolson, 1984), 116.

Hitler, the obsessive anti-Semite, saw Jews behind everything he abominated. Thus, it was impossible for them to escape the odium that was heaped upon them. So the Jews were damned for being capitalists, and they were damned for being Communists. It was held against them that they were overrepresented in the professions and also that they were an inferior race. The Weimar culture that Hitler and the Nazis so despised hardly extended beyond big cities such as Berlin and Hamburg, but the cosmopolitan Jew came to personify in their view every vice of the republic.[10] "What had to be reckoned heavily against the Jews in my eyes", wrote Hitler, "was when I became acquainted with their activity in the press, art, literature, and the theatre.... It is sufficient to look at a billboard, to study the names of the men behind the horrible trash they advertised to make you hard for a long time to come."[11]

Long before the Nazis came to political prominence, their ideology came under attack in the speeches of the papal nuncio Archbishop Pacelli before his recall to Rome in 1929. Years earlier, the Church's position on racialism and exaggerated nationalism had been made crystal clear, and by the highest authority. In the encyclical *Ubi Arcano Dei* of 23 December 1922, Pope Pius XI proclaimed:

> Patriotism ... becomes merely ... an added incentive to grave injustice when true love of country is debased to the condition of an extreme nationalism, when we forget that all men are our brothers and members of the same great human family.[12]

[10] Anthony McElligott, ed., *Weimar Germany* (Oxford: Oxford University Press, 2009), 18.

[11] Hitler, *Mein Kampf*, 53–54.

[12] Anne Freemantle, ed., *The Papal Encyclicals in Their Historical Context* (New York: Mentor Books, 1959), 223.

The following year, anti-Semitism was repudiated in a sermon preached by the archbishop of Munich, Cardinal Faulhaber. At the same time, Faulhaber addressed a letter to the chancellor, Gustav Stresemann, complaining of "the blind raging hatred of our Jewish fellow citizens and other ethnic groups".[13] Letter and sermon coincided with the failed Beer Hall Putsch and brought down on Faulhaber the special loathing of Nazis, who jeeringly designated him "the Jewish Cardinal". At his trial for his part in the putsch, Ludendorff launched into a lengthy tirade directed against the Catholic clergy for the protection they gave to Jews. Stresemann, however, praised Faulhaber for his moral stance.

Nor were these isolated voices. Priests in their sermons and bishops in their sermons and pastoral letters never failed to draw attention to the evils of Nazism. Prominent laymen, such as Dr. Heinrich Held, president of the German Catholic Assembly, also spoke out. Then in 1928 came the Holy Office decree condemning "hatred of the people once chosen by God, the hatred that commonly goes by the name of anti-Semitism". By the end of the decade, German Catholics were left in no doubt that they were endangering their faith if they joined the Nazi Party, and those who did join ran the risk of being denied the sacraments. Uniformed SA men and those carrying party banners could find themselves barred from church services altogether.

Fortunately it was only the minority who were affected by these prohibitions. Of the main confessional groups, Catholics were least inclined to joined Hitler's party, and electoral support for the National Socialists was always

[13] Erich Eyck, *A History of the Weimar Republic*, vol. 1 (London: Oxford University Press, 1962), 271.

lowest in Catholic areas. In Bavaria, the birthplace of Nazism, resistance came from the ever-vigilant Catholic press, from the Catholic Bavarian People's Party (BVP) and its affiliate, the Bavarian Christian Peasants' Association, and from the parish clergy, who were a constant thorn in the side of Nazi propagandists. Catholic priests who joined the Nazi Party were a tiny and generally eccentric minority. The great majority of Catholic theologians were equally unsympathetic, if not actually hostile, although a few looked for "points of contact", especially after 1933 and Hitler's legitimate acquisition of power.[14] The aged Benedictine Abbot Schachleiter paid for his naivety in endorsing National Socialism by being suspended from his order. Abbot Schachleiter was photographed sharing platforms with Nazi speakers. By using renegade priests in this way, the Nazis hoped to persuade Catholics that support for National Socialism was not incompatible with their Catholic Faith.

Hitler was again free to speak in public when, within a year of his release from prison, the ban on the Nazi Party was lifted. In his first public engagement, three thousand supporters packed a beer hall to hear him speak. The police closed the hall two hours before Hitler was scheduled to appear and turned away a further two thousand.[15] Hitler's immediate task lay in rebuilding and uniting a movement that his enforced absence had left in disarray. The North German wing of the movement was led by Gregor Strasser, a social revolutionary who had risen through the ranks of the SA. But Strasser's overt anticapitalist stance did not go down well with Hitler, who had always inclined more to

[14] Robert A. Krieg, *Catholic Theologians in Nazi Germany* (New York: Continuum, 2004), 29.

[15] Dietrich Orlow, *A History of the Nazi Party*, vol. 1, *1919–1933* (Pittsburgh: University of Pittsburgh Press, 1971), 53–54.

the nationalism in National Socialism and who realised the need to attract the support of big business if the National Socialists were to be taken seriously as a future government. Moreover, the failure of the Beer Hall Putsch had taught Hitler an important lesson: he was now convinced that the only way to achieve power was by legal means. That meant that he not only must cast his net wider to attract support but must not risk losing support by tolerating the socialist revolutionary rhetoric of Strasser and his followers on the left of the party.

The stage was set for a showdown when Strasser rescinded the party's twenty-five points and produced his own party programme. At the Bamberg Conference of 1926, Hitler's powerful advocacy prevailed against the Strasserites and so impressed Strasser's lieutenant, Joseph Goebbels, that within a matter of weeks Goebbels changed sides, thereafter committing himself wholly to Hitler. Although Hitler triumphed at Bamberg and emerged as the undisputed leader of the movement, the differences between Strasser and him remained unresolved and were only finally resolved a decade later and in the most perfidious manner.

Nineteen twenty-eight was another bad year for Hitler. With the economy in recovery and the country gaining acceptance within the international fold, there seemed cause for optimism rather than disaffection; thus, the situation was not one that Hitler could easily exploit. In the elections held that year, his National Socialists fielded candidates for the first time but achieved a disappointing 3 percent of the vote, giving them a paltry twelve seats in the Reichstag out of a total of 491.

The good years of the Weimar Republic owed much to the statesmanship of Gustav Stresemann, who had been chancellor briefly in 1923 and who, from 1923 to

1929, proved to be a very able foreign minister. In 1925, Stresemann signed a treaty with France and Belgium at Locarno that recognised existing frontiers and abjured the use of force in international disputes. In the meantime, he oversaw Germany's entry into the League of Nations. He successfully negotiated a reduction in the amount of reparations and was later instrumental in persuading the French to withdraw from the Ruhr.

Unfortunately, Stresemann died unexpectedly in October 1929, and in consequence of the Wall Street Crash of that same month, the country was again plunged into economic chaos. Mass unemployment and widespread panic followed. Seizing his opportunity, Hitler excoriated the politicians of the republic for bringing the country to ruin. He began to stand out as the strong man that the situation demanded—in the eyes of many, the only man capable of restoring order and stability to Germany. All at once, Hitler began attracting support from all sides: from industrialists, landowners, owners of small businesses, the professional class, the military, and the universities. The membership of the Nazi Party quickly tripled. In the elections held the following September, Hitler's National Socialists polled six and a half million votes, giving them a total of 107 seats in the Reichstag. The result propelled them from relative obscurity into the forefront of German politics.

The 1930 election result rang alarm bells within the Church. The issue of Catholic membership in the Nazi Party, which until then had been left undecided, now became a matter of urgency. Towards the end of the year, the senior German prelate, Cardinal Bertram of Breslau, published a statement critical of "false nationalism and the worship of race". He and the other bishops well knew that increasing numbers of Catholics were being drawn to National Socialism, whether out of sympathy with its patriotic appeal or because of its economic aims, while remaining largely ignorant of its fundamentally unchristian character.

The first bishop to prohibit membership in the Nazi Party in his diocese was Ludwig Maria Hugo of Mainz, at the time when the Nazis were jubilant over their success in the Reichstag elections.[16] On 30 October, he publicly defended a priest of his diocese who had come under verbal attack from pro-Hitler Catholics. The following February, Cardinal Faulhaber called a conference of the Bavarian bishops at Freising. In their joint statement the bishops warned against National Socialism "so long as and insofar as it maintains cultural-political views that are not reconcilable with Catholic doctrine".[17] Not wishing to take any action that might precipitate defections from the Church, however, they agreed that Catholics enrolled in the party could still attend church services, though not if parading in Nazi formations, wearing uniforms, or bearing flags. Whether they were permitted to receive the sacraments was left to the discretion of individual priests.

A month later, Bertram, Archbishop Schulte of Cologne, and the bishops of the Upper Rhine publicly associated themselves with the statement of the Freising Bishops' Conference. Bertram, however, appeared to make an about-turn in August when, speaking on behalf of the Fulda Bishops' Conference, he unequivocally prohibited Catholics from joining the Nazi Party. The reason given was Nazism's fundamental opposition to Christianity

---

[16] William M. Harrigan, "Nazi Germany and the Holy See, 1933–1936: The Historical Background of *Mit brennender Sorge*", *Catholic Historical Review* (July 1961): 165. See also Krieg, *Catholic Theologians in Nazi Germany*, 2.

[17] Harrigan, "Nazi Germany and the Holy See", 165; Krieg, *Catholic Theologians in Nazi Germany*, 2.

and to the Catholic Church.[18] Soon the prohibition was extended to all German dioceses. The bishops meanwhile continued to voice their opposition to National Socialism in their published statements.

The pope returned to the theme of the unity of the human race and the false mythology of blood in his Christmas message of 1930 and again in the encyclical *Caritate Christi Compulsi* of 1932. The encyclical appeared only weeks before the July Reichstag elections, when, to the consternation of Church leaders, the National Socialists more than doubled their previous haul, amassing nearly fourteen million votes and gaining 230 seats in the Reichstag. Hitler could not have hoped for more. Suddenly the Nazi Party was the largest political party in Germany; and although the party's share of the vote fell somewhat in the November elections, it made no appreciable difference. The aged President Hindenburg, having been persuaded that the conservative vice-chancellor Franz von Papen would exert a restraining influence on Hitler, agreed to the formation of a coalition government and, on 30 January 1933, appointed Hitler Reich chancellor.

---

[18] Krieg, *Catholic Theologians in Nazi Germany*, 2. For a fuller account, see also Matheson, *The Third Reich and the Christian Churches*, 6–7.

Race and Religion in Hitler's Germany

Hitler Gains Emergency Powers

Less than a month after Hitler's appointment as chancellor, the Reichstag building was destroyed in a mysterious fire. Marinus van der Lubbe, an unemployed and unstable Dutchman of anarchist leanings, was discovered in the charred ruins, half-naked and in a dazed state. He was accused of being a Communist, and it took a special retroactive law to bring him to trial almost a year later, when he was charged with arson, found guilty, and beheaded. Certain prominent Communists who stood accused with him were acquitted.

There was a widespread conviction at the time that the Nazis themselves started the Reichstag fire and that the hapless van der Lubbe was the victim of manipulation. It remains unclear what happened in the Reichstag building that night, but the situation was ripe for exploitation, and the outcome was portentous enough. Nazi warnings of an imminent Communist rising, which were widely believed, persuaded President Hindenburg to invoke article 48 of the constitution and grant Hitler emergency powers.

A relentless course of events now ensued. Even before the Reichstag fire had presented Hitler with an excuse for moving against his political foes, raids had been made by the SA on Communist Party offices, and a decree had been published outlawing all but Nazi Party political meetings. This merely foreshadowed a later decree of mid-July that made the Nazi Party the only legal party, all other political parties having been by that time dissolved.

In March, the Nazis set out to control labour. Communists were expelled from works councils, and many were arrested, along with officials of the Free Trade Unions. Resistance was met with further arrests and imprisonment and, in some cases, murder. An offer by the leadership of the Free Trade Unions to work in cooperation with the regime was spurned. By May, the unions were history. A single authorised union, the Labour Front, was set up under the direction of loyal party member Robert Ley, a coarse-mannered drunk and noted anti-Semite who enjoyed a personal friendship with Hitler.

On 23 March, the Reichstag virtually voted itself out of existence when it passed the Enabling Law. The statute gave permanence to the emergency-powers dispensation under which Hitler had been operating and granted him the right to legislate by bypassing Parliament. On that day, Nazi storm troopers thronged the streets and the legislative chamber of the Kroll Opera House, where the Reichstag now convened, to menace the opposition. Although the Social Democrats resisted the bill, the Centre Party put its trust in Hitler's offer of protection for the Church and gave the bill its support. The outcome was hardly affected. The Enabling Law served merely as a legal façade, and Hitler boasted that he had sought from the Reichstag only what he could have taken anyway.[1]

Meanwhile Hitler and Goebbels proceeded against the Jews when a nationwide boycott of Jewish businesses was

---

[1] Peter Hoffman, *The History of the German Resistance, 1933–1945* (London: MacDonald and James, 1977), 12.

called for on 1 April. Unlike the attack on the Communists, the anti-Jewish boycott appears to have had little popular support. There were excesses in some cities, but on the whole its results disappointed the Nazi leadership. Principled Germans made a point of entering Jewish shops, bravely defying the SA thugs lurking intimidatingly in the doorways. Realizing that the campaign aroused little enthusiasm but rather revulsion, Hitler called a halt to it.

The anti-Jewish boycott provoked anger abroad and drew from the Holy See the first papal note of protest sent to Berlin. Like many subsequent papal notes of protest, it was ignored. According to the writer Sebastian Hoffner, who left a personal account of life in Hitler's Germany, one effect of the boycott was to place the Jewish situation firmly in the public eye. Germans who previously had given little thought to the matter now felt it necessary to have an opinion about Jews. Invidious distinctions came to be made between "decent" Jews and the rest.[2]

While the Nazis were hounding Jews and labour activists, an intense religious struggle was taking place. Priests had their homes searched, Catholic government employees were dismissed from their posts, and a campaign of intimidation was begun against members of Catholic organisations, all within days of the passing of the Enabling Law. The bishops protested these indignities in a letter of 1 April. German Protestantism suffered from being fragmented. Unlike the Catholic Church, which was international and hierarchical, the Protestant church was, as Konrad Heiden, Hitler's first biographer pointed out, a German church to begin with. Hitler's task here was not to lure believers away from their church but to win them back. The Lutheran church generally looked favourably

[2] Sebastian Hoffner, *Defying Hitler: A Memoir* (London: Phoenix, 2002), 117.

on Hitler's new order. The die-hard conservatism of most Protestants made it difficult for them to accept a republic born of a coalition of Socialists and Catholics. Many harboured sentiments of German nationalism, which, for some, sought expression in the movement of German Christians, a pro-Hitler wing of German Protestantism that aimed to adapt Christianity to neo-pagan race theory. Originating in prewar Germany, the movement was energised by the advent of Hitler. Recalling Marcion of the second century, the German Christians aspired to a form of Christianity free of Old Testament influence, the more extreme among them wishing to "Aryanize" Christ.

On 27 May, Hitler instituted the office of Reich bishop. The respected Pastor Friedrich von Bodelschwingh was elected but soon after deposed, as by 23 July the German Christians had gained a majority in the church. Bodelschwingh had made the mistake of protesting the German Christians' determination to exclude non-Aryans from membership in the German church. Ludwig Müller, a former naval chaplain and an ardent supporter of the Nazi regime known for his anti-Semitic sermons, became the new Reich bishop. Müller was a man utterly unfit for high ecclesiastical office, and he alienated many of the faithful by integrating the Evangelical Youth, with its seven hundred thousand members, with the Hitler Youth. The Protestant bishops Wurm of Württemberg and Meiser of Bavaria led a vigorous protest against the action. Müller's reply was the muzzling decree of 4 January 1934, designed to silence opposition. Numerous pastors, those who were not imprisoned, were suspended from office. Bishops Wurm and Meiser were arrested but later reinstated following mass demonstrations by outraged Protestants.

German Protestants of orthodox outlook found themselves at the same time harassed by the state and embroiled in conflict with those of their religious brethren who wished to divorce Christianity from its Jewish roots. A conservative reaction set in. Karl Barth, a Swiss-born theologian, began a theological journal to challenge the views of the German Christians. Pastor Martin Niemöller, joined by a group of like-minded clerics, formed the Pastors' Emergency League (PEL) for the defence of orthodoxy. From the PEL there emerged the Confessional church, to which seven thousand pastors gave their allegiance. There now existed—with the Confessional church, the German Christians, and the remainder, who professed no particular allegiance—a threefold division of the Protestant communion.

In a proclamation read out in Niemöller's parish church at Dahlem, the Confessional church declared the constitution and legally constituted organs of the German Evangelical church destroyed and staked its claim to be the lawful church:

> We summon the Christian communities ... to accept no directives from the present Church Government ... and to decline cooperation.... We summon them to observe the directives of the Confessional Synod of the German Evangelical Church.[3]

The Catholic Bishops Rescind Their Prohibitions

The Catholic Church at first persisted in her opposition to National Socialism. In June the bishops denounced the injustice of an exclusive concentration on race and blood as a condition of citizenship. Catholics were still being encouraged to support the Catholic Centre Party and

[3] Quoted in J. Noakes and G. Pridham, eds., *Nazism 1919–1945*, vol. 2, *State Economy and Society 1933–1939* (Exeter: University of Exeter Press, 1995), 584.

those candidates who, in the March general election, could be counted on to defend the Church and the cause of the confessional schools. Nazi Party members were still being debarred from attending church services if their attendance could be viewed as a public endorsement of National Socialism. The end of March, however, witnessed a change in policy. In a volte-face, the abruptness of which was said to have angered Pacelli, the former nuncio and now the cardinal secretary of state, the bishops of the Fulda Bishops' Conference withdrew their previous prohibitions against membership in the Nazi Party. Two weeks later, the Bavarian bishops did likewise.

The Catholic bishops' reversal of policy was due in no small part to their growing awareness of the popularity of the National Socialist movement. It was not only winning support from all sections of society but was gaining followers at the expense of the Centre Party. Catholics previously had been largely immune to Nazi propaganda. In the historic elections of 1930 and 1932, it was the predominantly Catholic regions that had offered the greatest resistance to National Socialism.[4] But the party was now making inroads into formerly hostile Catholic territory. In Lower Bavaria, for example, the National Socialist vote in the election of March 1933 had more than doubled in less than a year.[5] The problem facing the bishops has been well stated by John Conway: "continued resistance would be very difficult to explain to the Catholic masses, who implicitly accepted Hitler's pledges. Moreover, it appeared likely that the mass appeal of the Nazi campaign might succeed in persuading thousands, even millions, to leave

---

[4] Guenter Lewy, *The Catholic Church and Nazi Germany* (London: Weidenfeld and Nicolson, 1964), 8; J. Derek Holmes, *The Papacy in the Modern World* (London: Burns and Oates, 1981), 102.

[5] Ian Kershaw, *Hitler*, vol. 1, *1889–1936: Hubris* (London: Allen Lane, 1998), 461.

the Church."[6] The bishops were understandably dismayed to learn that Catholic members of the SA, who had been banned from attending services in their own churches, were now frequenting Protestant churches.

Further, it was evident to anyone who gave much thought to the matter that sooner or later the Church would have to reach a modus vivendi with the new regime. Hitler was the legally constituted head of state, a fact that caused many Germans to alter their opinion of him. It was commonly believed that with his elevation to the position of world statesman, Hitler would in future incline to moderation.[7] The legitimacy of his office was no small matter to a people long accustomed to giving unquestioning obedience to its leaders and to a Church that taught that all authority came from God. In a pastoral letter of 10 February, Cardinal Faulhaber reminded the faithful that the respect and obedience owed to the state was a matter of Christian duty, "even when the present form of the state and its system does not please us."[8] Faulhaber reiterated the point in a letter to his diocesan clergy of 5 April, at the same time encouraging them to be forthright in denouncing error.[9] Ernst Helmreich has drawn attention to the dilemma facing both Catholics and Protestants in Nazi Germany who found themselves being against Nazism but not against the government. He writes: "It is easy to decry this dilemma today, it was

[6] J.S. Conway, *The Nazi Persecution of the Churches, 1933–1945* (London: Weidenfeld and Nicolson, 1968), 21–22.

[7] Ian Kershaw, *Making Friends with Hitler* (London: Allen Lane, 2004), 33; R.J.B. Bosworth, *Mussolini* (London: Arnold, 2002), 270.

[8] Quoted in Mary Alice Gallin, "The Cardinal and the State: Faulhaber and the Third Reich", *Journal of Church and State* 12 (1970): 403. See also Ernst Christian Helmreich, *The German Churches under Hitler* (Detroit: Wayne State University Press, 1979), 238–39.

[9] Gallin, "The Cardinal and the State", 392.

much more difficult to see a way out of it in the Germany of that time."[10]

At the end of May, the German bishops met at Fulda in a plenary conference, the first in almost thirty years. Their collective pastoral letter of 3 June, while supportive of the government, raised concerns about the Catholic associations and directed an attack on racial persecution. The bishops emphatically repudiated the claim of the German Christians that non-Aryans could no longer be considered Germans. The exclusive consideration of race and blood they declared to be an injustice. The pastoral ended with a prayer that Germany's leader would offer his protection to the Church.

There were good reasons for thinking that an alliance with National Socialism might benefit the Church. Both were against Communism, liberalism, and Weimar decadence; both stood for patriotism, community, and tradition. Archbishop Gröber of Freiburg and Bishop Berning of Osnabruck were sympathetic to a degree, and became associated with a policy of appeasement. Neither bishop, however, offered the regime his unqualified support. Bishop Gröber insisted that Catholic teaching should always be presented in its entirety; and all the bishops categorically repudiated Nazi race theory.[11]

Those who engaged with Hitler, whether in face-to-face interviews or in written correspondence, were often disarmed by the favourable impression he created. In a cordial encounter with Bishop Berning on 26 April, Hitler professed to be deeply hurt by those who accused him of

---

[10] Helmreich, *The German Churches under Hitler*, 256.

[11] Lewy, a critic of the Church, is nevertheless insistent on this last point. Lewy, *The Catholic Church and Nazi Germany*, 166. See also Hitler's first biographer, Konrad Heiden, *The Fuehrer* (London: Robinson, 1999), 498. Archbishop Gröber is quoted in Peter Matheson, ed., *The Third Reich and the Christian Churches* (Edinburgh: T&T Clark, 1982), 24.

hostility to Christianity. He told Berning that the German state without the Christian Church was unimaginable.[12] Writing to Cardinal Bertram two days later, Hitler appeared reasonable and conciliating. It was, he said, his sincere hope that church and state could work harmoniously together. At the same time, he promised to investigate complaints of priests being attacked, knowledge of which he customarily denied. When Bertram complained of house searches, Hitler expressed sorrow and asked for "more detailed information" and for the names of the individuals concerned.[13]

Defending the decision to lift the ban on Catholic membership in the Nazi Party, Bertram pointed to Hitler's public declaration of respect for the Church and his offer to work with the German bishops. This was a reference to Hitler's speech to the Reichstag of 23 March. Christianity, he had said, was indispensable to the moral renaissance of the German people. It is also likely that Bertram had in mind the radio broadcast of 1 February, when Hitler promised to uphold Christian values. In particular, he extended his offer of protection to the institution of the family. This was more than mere posturing. Hitler very early declared war on the twin evils of prostitution and pornography, which he believed were symptomatic of Weimar decadence. "Grotesque as it seems", writes Ian Kershaw, "Hitler ... continued to be widely regarded as a God-fearing and deeply religious man."[14]

Skilful propaganda successfully distanced Hitler from Nazi atrocities, responsibility for which was always laid at the door of subordinates or extremists in the party. The popular perception of Hitler as a man of reason endeavouring to rein in the wild men in the party owes much to

---

[12] *Documents on German Foreign Policy*, series C, vol. 1, doc. no. 188.

[13] Ibid., doc. no. 196.

[14] Ian Kershaw, *Life in the Third Reich*, ed. Richard Bessel (Oxford: Oxford University Press, 1986), 51.

the genius of the propaganda minister Joseph Goebbels.
The British Foreign Office viewed Goering as the fanatic
of the party and the instigator of Nazi excesses.[15] Cardinal
Faulhaber held the SS to account rather than Hitler personally, and he believed, as did all the bishops, that party
dogmatist Alfred Rosenberg had a baleful influence on
Hitler.[16] But it was not only Germans who were guilty of
misjudgement. The perception of Hitler was a pervading
blind spot with Western democrats. One has only to con-
sult British newspapers of the time to realize how many in
Britain were taken in by him. Writing of the situation in
France, Henri de Lubac, S.J., notes: "The phenomenon of
Hitler was poorly perceived and at times even totally mis-
understood by a number of intellectuals and politicians."[17]
Official representatives from both Britain and the United
States remained convinced of Hitler's peaceful intent; nor
should it be forgotten that as late as 1938 Prime Minis-
ter Chamberlain pledged his faith in the führer's sincerity.
Following the outbreak of war, it was no longer possible
for Hitler to maintain the deception.

The Reich Concordat and Its Aftermath

At the beginning of April 1933, Monsignor Ludwig Kaas,
the leader of the Centre Party, and Vice-Chancellor Papen
were dispatched to Rome by Hitler, charged with the task

[15] Kershaw, *Making Friends with Hitler*, 40.
[16] Gallin, "The Cardinal and the State", 399, 401. See also Ethel Mary
Tinnemann, "Attitudes of the German Catholic Hierarchy toward the Nazi
Regime: A Study in German Psycho-Political Culture", *Western Political Quarterly* 22 (1969): 338–39.
[17] Henri de Lubac, S.J., *Christian Resistance to Anti-Semitism: Memories from
1940–1944* (San Francisco: Ignatius Press, 1990), 17–18.

of sounding out the Vatican on the possibility of arranging a concordat between Germany and the Holy See. Concluding concordats or legal agreements with secular governments enabled the Church to secure her religious privileges while compromising on nonessentials. A concordat did not signify approval of any particular government, as the Vatican newspaper *L'Osservatore Romano* on several occasions made clear. Under Pius XI, the system became the preferred means of regulating church-state affairs.

The extension of the system of papal concordats was made necessary by the changed political situation after 1918. The Austro-Hungarian Empire, which had been the traditional protector of the papacy, became a victim of the dissolution of empires that marked the end of the First World War. Thus, it was only by entering into legal agreements with the new governments of postwar Europe that the Church could protect her vital interests. Generally the system proved successful, even though the Holy See sometimes had to negotiate with regimes in varying degrees hostile to the Church. Throughout his reign, Pius XI concluded ten concordats in all, most of them in the 1920s. They included a mutually beneficent one with Mussolini's Italy, which was incorporated within the Lateran Accord of 1929, and those that the papal nuncio Pacelli negotiated with the German states of Bavaria, Prussia, and Baden.

The initial response to Hitler's overtures was positive though cautious. Cardinal Pacelli had laboured unceasingly, first as nuncio, then as the papal secretary of state, to open negotiations for a concordat with the Weimar Republic, only to encounter opposition from Socialist members of the Reichstag over the issue of confessional schools. Hitler's professed interest in positive Christianity seemed to bode well for the future of the Church. But could Hitler be trusted? Dialogue took place over several weeks. When the German bishops met at Fulda for their plenary sessions of 30 May to 1 June, the Vatican urged that the draft concordat be given priority in their discussions. Hitler's demand was only that the Church should withdraw from party politics. Both the Centre Party and the BVP had a preponderance of clerics holding important political offices, and the bishops at first dug in their heels. But church schools were even now being threatened with closure, and the Catholic associations and youth clubs too were under threat. After all, Hitler was offering generous concessions. Moreover, there seemed a distinct possibility that he might change his mind when, days after the pope approved the text of the concordat, Hitler still had not given his assent.

Why Hitler hesitated at this juncture is unclear. On reflection, he may have wondered if the arrangement with the Holy See would bring him any advantage. The destruction of all but the Catholic political parties was already a fait accompli. What could prevent the Centre Party and the BVP from going the way of the others? The BVP had already suspended its public meetings, due to the growing harassment of its members. Then, at the end of June, Heinrich Himmler's political police, who had dismantled and then swept away the Bavarian police force in March, rounded up and incarcerated almost two thousand BVP members, including 150 priests. Political arrests of Centre Party members were also made.[18] So it hardly seemed necessary for Hitler to enter into a formal accord with the Holy See to get what he wanted. As Pacelli's

[18] Geoffrey Pridham, *Hitler's Rise to Power: The Nazi Movement in Bavaria, 1922–1933* (London: Hart-Davis, MacGibbon, 1973), 316; Frank J. Coppa, ed., *Controversial Concordats: The Vatican's Relations with Napoleon, Mussolini, and Hitler* (Washington, D.C.: Catholic University of America Press, 1999), 132.

private secretary, Father Robert Leiber, S.J., pointed out at the end of June, a promise from the pope to remove priests from party politics was a concession of no value at all. Leiber urged a speedy conclusion to the negotiations.[19]

On 4 July, while Hitler pondered his options, the BVP voluntarily dissolved itself. A day later, the Centre Party did likewise, causing Pacelli to express regret that it should have done so with such haste and without consulting the Vatican. Following these events, Hitler had the political prisoners released from captivity and rescinded local measures to close down Catholic associations. The concordat was provisionally signed on 20 July, Pacelli acting on behalf of the pope and Papen representing the Reich government.

Why, one may ask, did Hitler authorize the signing of the concordat when he already had the Church in Germany at his mercy? Although Hitler desired to see an end to political priests, his main incentive seems to have been his awareness of the international prestige to be gained by entering into a formal agreement with the Holy See. Mussolini had advised him to negotiate for this very reason,[20] and Hitler had been impressed when, in 1929, Mussolini had concluded his own concordat with the Holy See. Additionally, a signed agreement with the Holy See would send a message to the world that the National Socialist State had nothing but the friendliest intentions towards the Catholic Church.

For the pope's part, the demise of the Catholic political parties he considered no great loss; rather, it was consonant with the policy he had been pursuing for a decade. Pius XI had a deep distrust of party politics. In his first encyclical, *Ubi Arcano Dei*, he complained of the discord

---

[19]John Jay Hughes, "The Pope's 'Pact with Hitler': Betrayal or Self-Defense?" *Journal of Church and State* 17 (1975): 72.

[20]Ibid., 69. See also Helmreich, *The German Churches under Hitler*, 256.

caused by political parties, "not really, with all their different views, seeking the public good, but rather their own advantage at the expense of the others".[21] Catholic political parties, led by priests, or including priests in some ministerial role, were a phenomenon of the European political scene from the late nineteenth century until well into the twentieth. They arose from the need to defend Catholic liberties. But Pius XI had begun to dissociate the Church from politics. Early in his reign he banned the Italian clergy from belonging to political parties. Further, he facilitated the fall of the Partito Popolare, the Italian political party theoretically separate from the Church but Catholic in all but name, and which had been favoured by his predecessor, Benedict XV.

Pius XI was instead a strenuous advocate of Catholic Action, relying on its character-forming influence to provide society with leaders. It had been his intention from the outset of his reign to promote its work, as he explained to Cardinal Bertram in 1928.[22] The following year, Catholic Action's continuing independence was written into the Italian concordat at the pope's insistence.[23] Catholic Action, functioning within a framework embracing workers, students, and youth, together with the system of papal concordats, seemed to the pope to be the way forward for the Church.

The Reich Concordat incorporated the earlier concordats concluded with individual German states. According to its terms, Pius XI was granted virtually all he could have wished for. Freedom of worship and freedom in the profession of religious belief were afforded full recognition

[21] Pope Pius XI in A. Keogh, S.J., *The Pope and the People: Selected Letters and Addresses on Social Questions* (London: Catholic Truth Society, 1950), 235.

[22] Pope Pius XI, *The Pope and Catholic Action* (London: Catholic Truth Society, 1935), 5–8.

[23] Peter C. Kent, *The Pope and the Duce* (London: Macmillan, 1981), 14.

(articles 1 and 4), and the clergy was offered Hitler's protection (article 5). Recognition was also extended to the religious orders (article 15) and to the Catholic theological faculties (article 19). Articles 21 through 25 offered guarantees respecting faith schools, an issue high on the Church's list of priorities. Catholic associations with exclusively religious, cultural, or charitable ends were to continue to exist, as were those associations whose members were engaged in social and vocational purposes outside of party politics (article 31). The right of the Holy See to appoint bishops and holders of Church offices was agreed in article 14. No agreement was reached respecting the freedom of the Catholic press, although article 4 permitted pastoral letters and diocesan gazettes devoted to the spiritual direction of the faithful to be published without hindrance. In return for these concessions, it was formally agreed that the Church would stay out of politics. The Holy See signified its commitment to the agreement by accepting the dissolution of the Centre Party and the BVP.[24]

Article 31, which concerned the future of the Catholic associations, proved to be particularly contentious. The task of drawing up lists of mutually acceptable associations was to be undertaken by the Vatican and the German bishops in conjunction with the Reich government. But a consensus was never arrived at, and consequently the Church had to fight doggedly to preserve her associations against a government bent on their emasculation and eventual destruction.

By the agreement entered into with Germany,[25] the Church was henceforth confined to her strictly spiritual

[24] For the complete text of the concordat, see Coppa, *Controversial Concordats*, 205–14.

[25] The concordat was concluded neither with Hitler nor with the National Socialists but with the German Reich. It remained in place long after Hitler's death.

mission of teaching the Faith and administering the sacraments and to such activities as were free of political connotation. In practice, the distinction was not an easy one to make. For instance, the regime's treatment of the Jews was considered a political matter; whereas the hierarchy's strictures on racial theory came under the Church's right to teach the Faith. When Jews were rounded up for transfer to work camps, the bishops made no public protest, although Cardinal Bertram privately, as head of the episcopate, made repeated representations to the Reich chancellery, and several bishops—Bishop Preysing, notably—sheltered Jews. On the other hand, Nazi ideology continued to be denounced in the sermons, lectures, and writings of the Catholic clergy.[26] Yet, despite an appeal for cooperation with the regime by Bishop Galen of Münster, attitudes among many of the clergy and laity remained profoundly hostile. This was borne out in a government memorandum of 21 February 1934 that was sent to all SA leaders in Bavaria.[27]

Cardinal Pacelli had few illusions about Hitler. Fearing that the concordat would come to be disregarded by the regime, Pacelli nevertheless clung to the hope that some, at least, of its provisions would be honoured. In the event, he was proved right. Pulpit denunciations, though they were irritating to the regime and gave rise to complaints, generally went unpunished; and it was no inconsequential matter that the churches remained open throughout the duration of Hitler's rule. In Pacelli's eyes, moreover, the Holy See faced the stark choice either of a negotiated settlement with Hitler or the end of the Catholic Church

---

[26] On the opposition to Nazism by members of the Catholic theological faculties, see Robert A. Krieg, *Catholic Theologians in Nazi Germany* (New York: Continuum, 2004).

[27] Conway, *The Nazi Persecution of the Churches*, 68.

in Germany. A pistol had been pointed to his head: thus Pacelli described his dilemma to Ivone Kirkpatrick, the British minister to the Holy See.

The Reich Concordat strengthened the Church's position by providing a legal basis for future dealings with Hitler, one that defined the status of the Church in the Reich, including her rights and freedoms and those of her members. Crucially, it meant that henceforth what concerned the Catholic Church in Germany concerned also the Vatican. Should the concordat be violated and the pope protest, Hitler could not reproach him with interfering in Germany's internal affairs.

Though not without their reservations, and with some, such as Bishop Preysing, openly critical, the German bishops nevertheless dared to hope that the concordat would herald a new era of church-state cooperation and consequently approved it. The bishops shared in the common desire for order and stability after the street violence and economic chaos that had blighted the Weimar Republic. Few, in truth, had had much sympathy for Weimar; they associated it with modernism. Men such as Faulhaber and Galen, aristocratic representatives of the old order, viewed the new political currents of liberalism and democracy with mistrust. Moreover, the fear of incurring another Kulturkampf was never far from their thoughts. Cardinal Bertram was a youth at the time of Bismarck's persecution of the Church. He had witnessed the subordination of the Church to the state and the imprisonment of priests. The memory of Catholics dying without the consolation of the sacraments was burned into his mind. Hitler's new order held out the promise of fruitful participation by church and state in a regenerated post-Weimar Germany. Of material significance to the hierarchy was the fact that Hitler had ceded to the Church that which the Church held most dear and which Weimar politicians had always resisted—legal guarantees respecting the position of Catholic schools.

Then, Cardinal Bertram was merely echoing the general consensus when he welcomed Hitler's assurances that he would deal with the threat of Communism, the spread of which was feared throughout the West. The end of the First World War had seen the emergence of Communist parties all over Europe. If the Russian experience were to be repeated, it seemed likely that it would happen in Germany. Riots and strikes, organised by left-wing agitators, had taken place in many cities of the Republic. In January 1919, the Freikorps put down a Communist insurrection in Berlin and murdered its leaders, Rosa Luxemburg and Karl Liebknecht. When, three months later, a Socialist Republic of Bavaria was proclaimed in the capital city of Munich, this too was ruthlessly suppressed. For a brief interlude that same year, Hungary became a Communist state under Béla Kun, who, like Luxemburg and Liebknecht, had received his training in revolutionary tactics in Moscow. So Hitler's anti-Bolshevik rhetoric was music to the ears of conservative Germans and Western democrats alike, who both looked to him to provide a bulwark against Soviet incursion. The rhetoric was soothing also to Catholic churchmen, who held strong doubts that a democratic government could offer effective resistance to Communism.[28]

Hardly had the ink dried on the paper of the concordat, however, before the Vatican was protesting its abuses.[29] Catholic schools came under attack, priests were

---

[28] Krieg, *Catholic Theologians in Nazi Germany*, 26. Pius XI held the same doubts. See Coppa, *Controversial Concordats*, 120–21.

[29] Bergen to German Foreign Ministry, telegram, 14 October 1933, *Documents on German Foreign Policy*, series C, doc. no. 501.

thrown into prison, Catholic teachers and civil servants were removed from their posts, and Church property was destroyed in a cynical abandonment of principle that betrayed the contempt in which the Nazi leadership held legal agreements.

Particularly devious was the assault on the faith schools. Party officials visited homes, where parents were required to explain in writing why they wished their children to attend Catholic schools. Under mounting pressure to conform and register their children in state schools, many parents capitulated. When attendances fell as a result, convent teachers were declared redundant and pensioned off. Catholic teachers who refused to promote state schools as the better option faced dismissal. Their courage was applauded by Cardinal Faulhaber in a pastoral letter that was read out in all Catholic schools. On 10 September, the Holy See ratified the concordat at the urging of the Fulda bishops, who believed that only ratification could provide them with the legal foundation on which to base their grievances.

The purging of the radical elements in the Nazi Party took place, accompanied by great brutality, on the night of 30 June 1934, a date infamously recalled as the Night of the Long Knives. Hitler's former comrade-in-arms, Ernst Röhm, and Gregor Strasser, his longtime political adversary, were both callously murdered, along with a great many SA men, in a bloody orgy that shocked the civilised world. In the early street-fighting days the SA had been indispensable to Hitler. Now that the National Socialists were in government, Hitler thought the SA had served its purpose and should give place to the army and the rapidly expanding SS. Röhm, who created the SA, disagreed. Moreover, Röhm's political outlook aligned him with Strasser and the revolutionary arm of the party. Röhm's persistent talk of the need of a second revolution made the Nazi leadership uneasy, and Himmler and Goering had long been urging Hitler to deal with him.

The Röhm purge presented the SS with the opportunity of silencing other troublesome elements, including prominent Catholic laymen who had made themselves objectionable to the regime. Nazi policies had been repeatedly assailed by Erich Klausener, the general secretary of Catholic Action, and by Fritz Gerlich, the editor of *Der gerade Weg*, the largest Catholic newspaper in Germany. Both men were eliminated in the purge; the chief of security, Reinhard Heydrich, had personally added Klausener's name to the death list.[30] Dr. Fritz Beck, a prominent Catholic students' leader, and Adalbert Probst, the national director of the Catholic Youth Sports Association, were additional victims.

Two weeks before the purge, Papen had given a lecture to students of the University of Marburg, during which he injudiciously criticised the regime. Marked for liquidation, he was fortunate to escape with his life and did so only after Goering intervened on his behalf. Soon after, Papen resigned the office of vice chancellor. On 2 August, the aged President Hindenburg died. Hitler then abolished the office of president and had himself proclaimed führer, or leader, of the German Reich and supreme commander of the armed forces. Only at this juncture in German history can it truly be said that Hitler seized power. But to lend legitimacy to his new status, a plebiscite was organised for 19 August, when a majority of 89.93 percent of the electorate was recorded as having voted in favour of the change.

[30] David Alvarez and Robert A. Graham, S.J., *Nothing Sacred: Nazi Espionage against the Vatican, 1939–1945* (London: Frank Cass, 1997), 49.

The Controversy with Rosenberg

In a speech of 13 November 1933, Dr. Krause, the leader of the Berlin faction of the German Christians, called for a second German reformation, from which he hoped would emerge "a church able to accommodate the whole breadth of a racially attuned experience of God".[31] Abolishing the Old Testament was not enough for Dr. Krause, who also wanted the New Testament cleansed of "un-German", especially Pauline, material. This was going too far for some, and there were large-scale defections from the movement.[32]

Krause and the German Christians drew inspiration from the writings of leading Nazi Alfred Rosenberg, the editor of the official Nazi newspaper, the *Völkischer Beobachter*. Estonian born and a fugitive from Moscow, where he had been educated, Rosenberg had been introduced to the infant Nazi Party by the journalist and failed playwright Dietrich Eckart, Hitler's early mentor. In time, Rosenberg became the foremost ideologue of National Socialism, though his writings drew upon earlier works of the kind. In 1930, he published his seminal work, *The Myth of the Twentieth Century*. While serving to underpin Nazi race theory with a quasi-philosophical foundation, the book provided the German Christians with a rationale for their heretical beliefs. It came under immediate attack in the Catholic press and in 1934 was placed on the Index of Forbidden Books by the Holy Office. A difficult and abstruse work that even the Nazi elite had trouble understanding, Rosenberg's *Myth* was deemed "unreadable" by Albert Speer. Goering delivered an even more withering

---

[31] Matheson, *The Third Reich and the Christian Churches*, 39.
[32] Ibid.

verdict on the book, labelling it "junk". Hitler privately complained that it was "stuff nobody can understand".[33] Nevertheless, Hitler was being disingenuous when he disclaimed all responsibility for the book, crediting its sales to attacks made upon it by churchmen. *The Myth of the Twentieth Century* was recommended reading for all Nazi Party members, and Rosenberg's preeminence as philosopher and educator-in-chief of the party was made official in 1934.[34]

Rosenberg called for the formation of a "new-yet-old type of German", who would embody the "old-yet-new values".[35] The old-yet-new values are summed up in the purity of race, which, according to Rosenberg, is the necessary condition of all true art, culture, and civilisation. The first Germans, he explains, were possessed of the highest cultural endowments because they were racially pure. Then disaster occurred. Into the ancient German homeland came Christianity, with its emphasis on love, goodness, and compassion. It was followed by a profound cultural change as inevitable as it was catastrophic. The theory differentiates what Rosenberg calls positive and negative Christianity. The negative kind began with the conversion of the Germans to Catholicism, with consequent racial miscegenation and the legacy of an enduring conflict between Church and race.[36] Positive Christianity, on the other hand, "consciously summons to life the powers of Nordic blood".[37] The fact of Christ's Jewishness

[33] Albert Speer, *Inside the Third Reich* (London: Weidenfeld and Nicolson, 1970), 96.

[34] William M. Harrigan, "Nazi Germany and the Holy See, 1933–1936: The Historical Background to *Mit brennender Sorge*", *Catholic Historical Review* 47, no. 2 (July 1961): 175.

[35] Alfred Rosenberg, *Selected Writings*, ed. Robert Pois (London: Jonathan Cape, 1970), 86.

[36] Ibid., 74.

[37] Ibid., 72.

presents no difficulty at all for Rosenberg, who sub-
scribes to the notion then common among anti-Semites
that Christ was an Aryan because the population of Galilee included Aryans.[38] Despite his emphasis on positive
Christianity, Rosenberg could not by any stretch of the
imagination be accounted a Christian. His belief system
could be described only as pagan and anti-Christian. At
the international military tribunal at Nuremberg, Rosenberg was one of only three Nazi defendants who refused
to attend church services. The mentally unstable Hess and
the arch Jew baiter Streicher also absented themselves.[39]

Rosenberg's fanciful notions came in for trenchant
criticism by a group of Catholic scholars writing under
the auspices of Bishop Galen of Münster. Most famously,
Cardinal Faulhaber took issue with him in his Advent
sermons of 1933, preached with conspicuous courage in
Saint Michael's Church in Munich. Faulhaber was an
Old Testament scholar and a former university professor,
well qualified to debate with Rosenberg and the German
Christians. His Advent sermons appeared in book form the
following year under the title *Judaism, Christianity, Germany* and enjoyed a wide circulation.

In the first of these short discourses, Faulhaber pays
homage to the Jews of the Old Law who, "among all the
nations of antiquity have exhibited the noblest religious
values".[40] The Old Testament conception of God, he says,
is "the noblest conception that the mind of man can con-
ceive".[41] Noting that in its earliest forms, and in the classics of the golden age, German literature is replete with

[38] Ibid., 7, footnote.
[39] From the testimony of Albert Speer, in James Owen, *Nuremberg: Evil on
Trial* (London: Headline Review, 2007), 29.
[40] Cardinal Michael von Faulhaber, *Judaism, Christianity and Germany*, trans.
George D. Smith (New York: Macmillan, 1935), 8.
[41] Ibid., 9–10.

biblical quotations, Faulhaber infers, "[I]f we are to repu-
diate the Old Testament and banish if from our schools
and from our national libraries, then we must disown our
German classics.... [W]e must disown the intellectual history of our nation."[42] Respecting Christ's "forged birth-
certificate", Faulhaber acknowledges that ancient Galilee
included people of mixed-race. However, he points out,
Christ was not born in Galilee but in Bethlehem, the city
of David, in the land of the tribe of Judah; and he was
entered in the official register as a descendant of David.

By disregarding the historical sources, Rosenberg was
able to conjure up a mythical past of cultural excellence
based on the purity of German blood. The reality, as Faulhaber explains, was quite different. The ancient Germans,
as depicted in the *Germania* of Tacitus, were worshippers
of a pantheon of gods, to whom they offered human sacrifice. When not indulging in warfare, they were prover-
bially indolent and given to excessive drinking. They had
no architecture, not even temples, for they worshipped
in woods and lived in wooden huts. It was Christianity
that civilised the Germans, as Faulhaber explains: "It is an
historical fact that this swarm of tribes was first welded
together into stable unity as one nation in consequence
of their conversion to Christianity."[43] Thus, to represent
Christianity as a perversion of all that was good and noble
in the past is to fly in the face of the evidence. "The greatest perversion would be a relapse into the paganism of the
ancient Germans."[44]

Faulhaber's primary objective on the occasion of his
Advent sermons was to uphold the permanent value of the
Old Testament, the German Christians having just passed

[42] Ibid., 17.
[43] Ibid., 104.
[44] Ibid., 93.

a resolution repudiating it. It was no part of his purpose to comment upon the situation then affecting German Jews, as he himself makes clear. His plea that "[a]ntagonism to the Jews of today must not be extended to the books of pre-Christian Judaism" has indeed been held against him, even by those who have praised the sermons. It is likely that he was weighing his words carefully, to avoid the charge of political interference, which, if upheld, could jeopardise future sermons.[45] Even so, perceptive readers will find in these pithy sermons a powerful indictment of Nazi race theory. Who, at that time, could fail to grasp the import of these words? "In this kingdom of Christ on earth there are no pet-children, specially favoured, and no step-children neglected."[46] Faulhaber allows that it is not unlawful to love one's own race; but he insists that love of one's own race must not lead to the hatred of other races. To German Christians, seduced by the pseudo learning of Rosenberg, there is given this reminder: "In the kingdom of God ties of blood are not sufficient.... [W]e are not redeemed with German blood. We are redeemed with the Precious Blood of our crucified Lord."[47] These Advent sermons served merely to reinforce the Nazis' conviction that Faulhaber was no ally of National Socialism but rather its inveterate foe; and soon thereafter he experienced the first of two attempts on his life.

Persecution Intensifies

The end of the year marked a lull in hostilities as Hitler sought to woo the (mainly Catholic) voters of the Saar

[45]Tinnemann, "Attitudes of the German Catholic Hierarchy toward the Nazi Regime", 344.

[46]Faulhaber, *Judaism, Christianity and Germany*, 92.

[47]Ibid., 18, 109.

in the impending plebiscite for the return of that region to Germany. In March 1935, two months after the successful outcome, Hitler renounced the Treaty of Versailles and introduced conscription. About the same time, he announced the formation of the Luftwaffe. In September, the swastika was made the official flag of the nation. The following year, Hitler threw out the Treaty of Locarno, of which Stresemann had been part architect, and German troops entered the Rhineland unopposed. The government was secure and, on the whole, popular. German citizens were reaping the benefits of a strong economy and near full employment.

The one people destined to have no share in the new prosperity were the Jews. In April 1935, a vast multitude of pilgrims assembled at Lourdes heard the cardinal secretary of state, Pacelli, declare that Nazi ideologies were "possessed by the superstition of race and blood". Confirmation of Pacelli's words came at the Nuremberg Rally in September, when Hitler promulgated the Law for the Protection of German Blood and Honour, which prohibited marriages between Aryans and Jews. The legislation came under immediate attack in a pastoral letter of the Catholic hierarchy, which the government tried to suppress.[48] The marriage law was only one of a raft of new laws that stripped Jews of their civic rights and, when progressively expanded over the next few years, proved to be the cause of untold misery to those of their race. By the end of August, seventy-five thousand German Jews had fled Germany for countries abroad.[49]

The Catholic daily newspapers, which had been produced under near-impossible conditions, were suppressed

[48] Tinnemann, "Attitudes of the German Catholic Hierarchy toward the Nazi Regime", 339.

[49] Martin Gilbert, *The Holocaust: The Jewish Tragedy* (London: Collins, 1986), 46.

this year. The diocesan weekly papers alone were exempted from the edict. Cardinal Bertram first, then the bishops in a collective pastoral letter, voiced dismay. Meanwhile Christianity was daily being ridiculed and the clergy defamed in the Nazi press. Hundreds of priests were arrested and thrown into prison, deemed guilty of transgressing a new law forbidding the slander of state and party. The Reich minister of the interior, Wilhelm Frick, accused the Church of "sabotaging the laws of the Reich" for her opposition to the recently enacted sterilisation law.[50] Goering complained that the Church invoked God against the state every Sunday and issued an edict against Catholic pulpit politics. Successive editions of *L'Osservatore Romano* refuted the charges of Frick and Goering, and the refutations were read from German pulpits on the orders of the pope. The Jesuits had to be particularly circumspect in their activities, as they were constantly spied upon. From May that year, the Bavarian police were required to submit monthly reports on Jesuits, and a card index system was compiled on them by the Gestapo.[51]

Acts of violence, even against bishops, were becoming commonplace. Bishops' residences at Würzburg, Rothenburg, and Mainz were attacked and ransacked by Nazi mobs. When Bishop Galen learned that Rosenberg was to speak at a Nazi Party rally in Münster, to be staged in the shadow of the episcopal palace, he sent a letter of protest to the governor of Westphalia. During the course of the rally, which went ahead as scheduled, Nazi hooligans bayed for Galen's blood. From Fulda, where all the bishops now met for their annual conference, a signed statement was forwarded to the führer protesting the religious policy of the regime. The bishops felt that

[50] Harrigan, "Nazi Germany and the Holy See", 186.
[51] Conway, *The Nazi Persecution of the Churches*, 112–13.

the authorities were using the excuse of political Catholicism to persecute the Church. Frick wrote in a memorandum: "Recently half the political police reports have concerned religious matters. We have no end of petitions from all sorts of cardinals, bishops and dignitaries of the Church."[52] Hitler declined to reply to the bishops' protest but used the occasion of a speech at Nuremberg to echo Goering's charge of political Catholicism.

A particular cause of disaffection pertained to the regime's pervasive and, to the Church's way of thinking, noxious influence over the young. Youth movements in all their diversity were an essential part of the German way of life. When Hitler came to power, there were hundreds of youth organisations in existence. The major religions and all political parties had associated youth sections, and there existed numerous other independent youth groups. The Hitler Youth was originally conceived as a junior branch of the SA. Being the only youth organisation sponsored by the state, it was well provided for, enjoying a range of sporting and recreational activities that were denied to other youth groups. In 1933, it was put under the direction of Baldur von Schirach, the former leader of the Nazi student movement and a disciple of Rosenberg. The Hitler Youth enrolled boys between the ages of fifteen and eighteen, who underwent courses of physical and practical training. There was a strong emphasis on drill, as the boys were seen as the future soldiers of Germany, and members were given a certain amount of political indoctrination. Successful aspirants were entitled to wear the Hitler Youth uniform and to carry the "Blood and Honour" dagger. There was a junior section for boys aged ten to fourteen and a separate section for girls. By 1934, the organisation

[52] Quoted in Noakes and Pridham, *Nazism*, vol. 2, 511.

boasted three million members. Regardless of its privileged status, and the many inducements to join, the Hitler Youth was wholeheartedly embraced by only a minority of German youth. As with the parent Nazi Party, enrolment was lowest in Bavaria and other Catholic parts of Germany.[53] Many young people demonstrated their contempt for it, and clashes between members of the Hitler Youth and those of rival, unofficial, groups not infrequently occurred.[54]

By 1936, the only youth movement not proscribed or absorbed into the Hitler Youth was the Catholic Youth movement, which enjoyed the legal protection of the concordat. Its legal status was nevertheless resisted. In 1935, Frick banned members of Catholic associations from wearing uniforms and insignia. Seventeen hundred Catholic Youth members who journeyed to Rome for an audience with the pope had to smuggle their uniforms out of the country. On their return, they were subjected to verbal abuse by German customs officials and had their uniforms confiscated. The Hitler Youth Law of 1 December 1936 had as its objective the integration of all German youth into the Hitler Youth movement, other youth organisations being henceforth outlawed. Intensive efforts were made to coerce Catholics into enrolling, and the ruling prompted an immediate objection from the papal nuncio, Monsignor Orsenigo. The following year, Catholic youth organisations came under a ban in Berlin and in Bavaria, having earlier been banned in Prussia. Membership in the Hitler Youth was finally made compulsory by a law of 25 March 1939, by which time the paramilitary character of the organisation was well established.

---

[53] Daniel Horn, "The Struggle for Catholic Youth in Hitler's Germany: An Assessment", *Catholic Historical Review* 65, no. 4 (October 1979): 569.

[54] See chapter 8.

From May 1936, the Church came under attack from a new side, with the commencement of a series of morality trials directed against religious orders. The trials were accompanied by the most lurid propaganda and brought an instant response from the cardinal secretary of state, who protested to the German ambassador. The Church, and the Jews, enjoyed a brief respite that summer, as sporting representatives from many nations arrived in Berlin for the Olympic Games. Soon after the conclusion of the Games, all the repressive measures of the state were again put into motion. When civil war erupted in Spain, the hierarchy's offer of moral support for the fight against Communism was spurned by Hitler.

The regime did not always have its own way. In November of that year, the Nazis in Oldenburg, a strongly Catholic region, removed the crucifixes from Catholic schools. The action outraged local Catholics, who, with the support of Bishop Galen, united in revolt. Eventually the authorities were forced to reverse their decision and have the crucifixes replaced. As is not unusual in totalitarian states, the repression of religion served only to increase devotion. Mass attendance improved markedly, and participation in religious devotions such as processions and pilgrimages remained especially high throughout the span of the Third Reich. One pilgrimage in Aachen drew close to a million people.

Outwardly, Hitler was still giving a friendly impression, in contrast to leading Nazis such as Martin Bormann and Rosenberg, who made no secret of their hatred of Christianity and of Catholicism in particular. In the month of the Oldenburg incident, Cardinal Faulhaber and Cardinal Schulte met with the führer at his mountain retreat at Berchtesgaden in the Bavarian Alps. Hitler received them cordially enough, and the three had a long conversation.

In their discussion concerning purely religious matters, Hitler appeared accommodating. When, however, Cardinal Faulhaber raised the subjects of the anti-Jewish legislation and the sterilisation law, Hitler's demeanour changed. He became angry and bluntly informed Faulhaber that interference from the Church in such matters would not be tolerated.[55]

The Church Hits Back

Whatever had been the outcome of the meeting at Berchtesgaden, the persecution of the Church continued unabated. A few weeks later, the bishops in Bavaria issued a pastoral letter that detailed some of the injustices arising from the government's attack on religion.[56] The pastoral recalls the bishops' initial sense of gratitude for the National Socialist profession of positive Christianity and their praise for Hitler's Reichstag speech of 23 March 1933. The pastoral then sounds a reproachful note, lamenting that there should now exist in Germany "a hate for Rome". No blame is imputed to the führer. Instead, censure is reserved for those in the Nazi Party who are working in opposition to him. Concluding with a profession of loyalty to the government, and requesting only that the Church's rights and freedoms be recognised, the bishops set forth a principle that would have met with the unqualified approbation of almost every German: "For us, the respect for authority, love of Fatherland, and the fulfilment of our duty to the state are matters not only of conscience but of divine ordinance."

[55] Klaus P. Fischer, *Nazi Germany* (London: Constable, 1997), 362–63. See also Speer, *Inside the Third Reich*, 101.

[56] See Noakes and Pridham, *Nazism*, vol. 2, 587–88, where the pastoral may be read in its entirety.

Unsurprisingly, this latest démarche evoked no response from Hitler; like other pastorals, the innumerable notes and memoranda, Monsignor Orsenigo's representations, and the repeated protests that Cardinal Bertram made to the Reich chancellery, it was ignored. Before the year was out, with their patience strained beyond further endurance, the German bishops appealed to Rome requesting a papal encyclical on the plight of the Church in Germany.

By 1937, the pope's patience with the regime had run out. Accordingly, the secretary of state met with leading members of the German hierarchy in January, when Cardinal Faulhaber was asked to draft the encyclical on the condition of the Catholic Church in the Third Reich. Cardinal Pacelli then made certain additions, which included the opening words by which the encyclical is best known, *Mit brennender Sorge* (With burning anxiety). Written not in the customary Latin but in German, the encyclical was smuggled into the country and distributed secretly by a fleet of motorcyclists without any member of the Nazi Party seeing it or even being made aware of its existence. On Palm Sunday it was read from every Catholic pulpit in Germany. A few passages will suffice to indicate the general tenor of this famous document, and the specific grievances it was meant to address.

Recalling the occasion of the signing of the concordat four years earlier, and the Church's fidelity to "the binding law of treaties", the encyclical proceeds to lay bare the nature of the complaint made against the Hitler government:

> Anyone must acknowledge, not without surprise and reprobation, how the other contracting party emasculated the terms of the treaty, distorted their meaning, and eventually considered its more or less official violation as a normal policy.

The encyclical goes on to accuse the regime of "systematic hostility levelled against the Church", citing as an instance the campaign against the confessional schools, whose freedom of existence had been guaranteed by the concordat.

Turning from the abuses of the concordat, the encyclical goes to the core of Nazi ideology:

> Whoever exalts race, or the people or the State or a particular form of the State ... whoever raises these notions above their standard value and divinizes them to an idolatrous level, distorts and perverts an order of the world planned and created by God.... As God's sun shines on every human face, so His law knows neither privilege nor exception.

There are harsh words for youth organisations, sponsored and directed by the state and in which membership is made obligatory, that manifest hostility to the Church and to Christianity. Patriotism is endorsed as a noble sentiment, but not the misplaced patriotism that precludes loyalty to God and his Church.

The primacy of the natural law over human law is restated; for human laws derive their efficacy from natural law, and this is true "whoever be the lawgiver". Thus:

> Human laws in flagrant contradiction with the natural law are vitiated with a taint which no force, no power can mend.

The primary right in the education of children belongs to the parents, and when the state fails to respect this right, it acts immorally. Catholic parents are given the assurance that the Church would not remain silent

[i]f an education, hostile to Christ, is to profane the temple of the child's soul consecrated by baptism and extinguish the eternal light of the faith in Christ for the sake of a counterfeit light alien to the Cross.

At such time:

It will be everyone's duty to sever his responsibility from the opposite camp, and free his conscience from guilty cooperation with such corruption.

Taken completely off guard, Nazi leaders were enraged beyond measure. *Völkischer Beobachter* fumed against "the Jew-God and His deputy in Rome".[57] Reacting promptly, the Gestapo seized all the copies of the encyclical that it could lay its hands on and prohibited its further publication. Catholic publishing houses that defied the ban were closed down, and their printing presses were destroyed. Reprisals quickly followed. Hundreds of priests and nuns were dragged before the courts on charges of immorality and of dealing in counterfeit currency. The Nazi press reported the trials in prurient detail but evidently alienated readers, as was indicated by a fall in subscriptions.

As well as bringing solace to the Church in Germany, *Mit brennender Sorge* was significant in forming public opinion abroad, especially in the United States. Nazi propaganda had insisted there was no persecution of the Church in Germany. The encyclical nailed that lie and forced Western democracies to confront the reality. From countries across Europe and in the Americas, German ambassadors reported to Berlin complaining of the overwhelmingly

[57]Pinchas E. Lapide, *The Last Three Popes and the Jews* (London: Souvenir Press, 1967), 110.

favourable reception accorded the encyclical.[58] It came like "a clap of thunder" in the words of François Charles-Roux, the French ambassador to the Holy See. The historian Anthony Rhodes has called it "one of the greatest condemnations of a national regime ever pronounced by the Vatican".[59] It was less well received in Britain, which at that time was intent on appeasing Hitler, and in Italy, where the Italian press took a pro-German stance.

The encyclical is unequivocal on the position taken on race. Anti-Semitism is not specifically mentioned, just as there is no specific mention of the Hitler Youth, which also was condemned. Even so, the encyclical drew this comment from one Jewish writer: "Any German or Austrian Catholic who was looking for papal guidance on treating Jews found all he needed in the new decree in order to save, protect or rescue Hitler's victims."[60]

Cardinal Pacelli, who made a material contribution to the encyclical, followed up with an outspoken denunciation of the Nazi idolatry of race before an audience of thousands in Lisieux, France, on 11 July and again two days later to a packed Cathedral of Notre Dame in Paris. The Reich Chief Security Office subsequently classified Pacelli with world Jewry. To cap it all, that summer the pope caused to be inserted in *L'Osservatore Romano* an editorial branding Hitler a man without honour.[61]

The authorities were showing signs of frustration. In the preceding February, Cardinal Faulhaber had preached

[58] Holmes, *The Papacy in the Modern World*, 113; Anthony Rhodes, *The Vatican in the Age of the Dictators, 1922–1945* (London: Hodder and Stoughton, 1973), 206.

[59] Rhodes, *The Vatican in the Age of the Dictators*, 204.

[60] Lapide, *The Last Three Popes and the Jews*, 109.

[61] Camille Cianfarra, *The War and the Vatican* (London: Burns, Oates, and Washbourne, 1945), 102.

a sermon condemning, among other things, the confiscation of pastoral letters, following which the SS invaded his
cathedral and bugged his pulpit. The parochial clergy was
every bit as vociferous in denouncing the evils of Nazism,
and priests evidently observed fewer of the niceties than
their religious superiors. Frick complained to the nuncio
about the extreme and insulting language emanating from
Catholic pulpits and demanded that the guilty priests be
disciplined. The complaint was passed to the cardinal secretary of state, and Frick having quoted many of the coars-
est examples, Pacelli sadly acknowledged that the priestly
language was rather more than intemperate.[62]

The Anschluss with Austria

In the summer of 1934, the chancellor of Austria, Engelbert
Dollfuss, was murdered by Austrian Nazis in an attempted
coup that had Hitler's backing. The object of the coup
was the Anschluss, the union of Germany and Austria,
which was prohibited by the Treaties of Versailles and
Saint-Germain, but which had been Hitler's stated objective from the moment he entered the political arena. On
succeeding Father Seipel in 1932, Dollfuss had proceeded
to apply Catholic social principles to the government of
Austria, especially as set out the year before in Pius XI's
great encyclical *Quadragesimo Anno*. But he was frustrated
in his task in having to face opposition from Communists
on one front and from Nazi supporters of the Anschluss
on the other. The situation was a precarious one and of
particular concern to Mussolini, who supported Dollfuss

[62] Holmes, *The Papacy in the Modern World*, 109–10; Rhodes, *The Vatican in
the Age of the Dictators*, 201–2.

and who wanted Hitler to do so.[63] In the wake of Dollfuss' murder, Austrian Nazis met with resistance from government forces led by the new chancellor, Kurt von Schuschnigg. And when Mussolini, faced with a takeover by Germany of a country bordering his own, ordered four Italian divisions into the Brenner Pass, Hitler withdrew his support for the putsch.

By 1938, however, Hitler was in a stronger position to enforce his demands on Austria. A majority of Austrians favoured union with Germany, and friendly relations had been forged with Mussolini. To placate Hitler, Schuschnigg had been obliged to admit Nazi sympathizers into his administration. In February, the Austrian chancellor journeyed to Berchtesgaden to meet with the führer. In his famously unreliable memoirs, Ribbentrop, who was in attendance, recalls the meeting between the two heads of state as an agreeable occasion, free of pressure. Also present were three German generals: Wilhelm Keitel, chief of staff of the High Command, and von Reichenau and Sperrle, the commanding generals for, respectively, land and air forces of the German-Austrian border. Schuschnigg listened in silence as Hitler outlined his proposals for the nazification of Austria. The Austrian chancellor was given three days to consider them.[64] On his return to Austria, Schuschnigg called for a plebiscite on the Anschluss in a last-minute gamble but backed down when German troops mobilised on the border.

Meanwhile, Nazi-inspired demonstrations took place on cue in Vienna and in other parts of the Austrian Republic. Acting upon Goering's instructions, the Nazi minister of

---

[63] *Documents on German Foreign Policy*, series C, vol. 1, doc. nos. 112, 130.

[64] Milan Hauner, *Hitler: A Chronology of His Life and Time* (London: Palgrave Macmillan, 2008), 127.

the interior, Seyss-Inquart, appealed for help in restoring order. On 12 March, German troops marched into Austria to a rapturous welcome. By the end of the day, the country belonged to Hitler. Executions of opponents of the Anschluss quickly followed. Thousands of Austrians who were spared death were committed to Dachau concentration camp, along with the ill-starred Schuschnigg, who had been forced to resign his office and hand over the reins of government to Seyss-Inquart. Once in control, Hitler announced a plebiscite on the Anschluss, to take place on 10 April.

The Austrian bishops had been outspokenly opposed to Nazi ideology, but after due consideration, they declared themselves in favour of the Anschluss. Austrian Catholics were urged to vote for union with Germany. The bishops' declaration provoked an angry response in Rome. The prospect of Catholic Austria being swallowed up by the Hitler leviathan was viewed with alarm by the pope. An editorial in *L'Osservatore Romano* of 1 April, dictated by the pope, severely rebuked the Austrian hierarchy, and a German-language Vatican Radio broadcast to Austria specifically admonished the archbishop of Vienna, Cardinal Innitzer.[65] When, subsequently, Innitzer ordered church bells to be rung on the eve of the plebiscite, he was summoned to Rome to explain himself. Interviewed by the secretary of state, the Austrian primate revealed that he had received assurances from Hitler and Goering concerning the future of the Austrian Church.[66] The explanation was hardly likely to satisfy the pope and the secretary of state. Pacelli drafted a statement retracting the declaration urging Austrian Catholics to vote for the Anschluss,

[65] Cianfarra, *The War and the Vatican*, 116.
[66] Ibid., 117.

which Cardinal Innitzer, on behalf of the hierarchy, then signed. The plebiscite went ahead under Nazi supervision, and a majority of 99.75 percent in favour of the union was recorded.

With the conclusion of the Anschluss, there began a new wave of assaults upon the Church, and their ferocity paralleled, if it did not exceed, the persecution in Germany. A concord between the Holy See and Austria, agreed and signed in 1934, was declared void. Whatever dubious benefits remained to the Church from the 1933 concordat were denied to the Austrians. Thus Austrian Catholics were left with no legal redress. Religious houses were seized, the Catholic press muzzled, Catholic associations closed down, and nuns and teaching brothers expelled from schools. The Catholic theological faculties in Innsbruck and Salzburg were shut down, and the archbishop of Salzburg, Monsignor Waitz, was arrested. Bishop Sproll of Rottenburg, who had been an outspoken critic of Nazism and the Anschluss, was driven from his diocese following his arrest by the Gestapo, and threats were made against his life. Cardinal Innitzer, who must now have regretted his previous course of action, condemned these outrages in his courageous sermons. As a result, demonstrations were whipped up against him, culminating in the sacking of his episcopal palace by members of the Hitler Youth. When reports of these barbarities reached Rome, Pius XI launched into a personal attack upon Hitler, whom he likened to Julian the Apostate.[67] Hitler replied by forbidding the German press to reprint the pope's speech.

On the night of 9 to 10 November, a planned assault, unprecedented in its fury, was launched against the Jewish people, their homes, and their businesses. The attack was

[67] Ibid., 143.

carried out in reprisal for the murder of a minor German official of the Paris embassy by a disgruntled Jew whose parents had been deported to Poland. Thousands of Jews were arrested; more than seventy were killed or seriously injured. Hundreds of shops and many Jewish homes were destroyed. In addition, almost two hundred synagogues were torched. Because it left behind a vast amount of broken glass, the pogrom became known, infamously, as Crystal Night.

International protests swiftly followed. President Roosevelt denounced the atrocities in a speech of 15 November, the day after recalling the U.S. ambassador to Germany. The Portuguese government officially and Cardinal Cerejeira on behalf of the Portuguese Church both issued strong protests, and German and Austrian Jews living in Portugal were issued visas for their relatives in Germany. Cardinal van Roey, the primate of Belgium, Cardinal Verdier of Paris, and Cardinal Schuster of Milan added their voices to the general protest. Each of them traced the pogrom to the Nazi doctrine of race, which they denounced as heresy. Van Roey branded racial theory a "deadly delusion" and "a doctrinal absurdity". Catholic doctrine, said Schuster, recognizes only "a common blood and brotherhood". Secretary of State Pacelli wrote to all the Catholic bishops of the world with instructions that they do everything possible to ensure that Jews fleeing Germany were granted visas. A shocked and angry Cardinal Faulhaber condemned the profanation of synagogues and sent transport to the chief rabbi of Munich so that religious articles could be conveyed from his synagogue to safety.

Meanwhile, a human tragedy unfolded in Germany that held grave implications for the future. In the winter of 1938, a man named Knauer wrote to the führer from his home in Leipzig requesting that his severely disabled child be destroyed. Euthanasia was contrary to German law. Nevertheless, Dr. Karl Brandt, who was one of Hitler's two personal physicians (Dr. Theodor Morell was the other), was instructed to go to Leipzig and discover whether the father was stating the truth about the extent of his son's disabilities. If so, Brandt was to authorize the doctors who were dealing with the case to carry out euthanasia on the child. Brandt was also to reassure them that if a criminal action were brought against them as a result, the führer would see to it that it was thrown out of court.[68] The Knauer case was a milestone in the history of Nazi eugenics. Subsequently, Hitler authorised Brandt and Philipp Bouhler, who in September 1939 became the head of the euthanasia programme, to proceed in the same way with all cases of a similar kind.

[68] From the testimony of Brandt at the Nuremberg Military Tribunal, in J. Noakes and G. Pridham, *Nazism 1919–1945*, vol. 3, *Foreign Policy, War and Racial Extermination* (Exeter: University of Exeter Press, 1995), 1005.

2

Pius XI, Mussolini, and the Italian Race Laws

The Lateran Treaty of 1929 was the successful outcome of three years of negotiations between Fascist Italy and the Holy See. At the stroke of a pen, it had resolved the long-standing dispute between church and state in Italy and restored to the papacy a temporal sovereignty it had not known for fifty-nine years. Vatican City, under the sovereignty of the pope, was created an independent state, an enclave of the city of Rome under Italian protection. By the terms of a second treaty, a concordat, the Church exacted generous concessions from Mussolini in the areas of marriage law, religious teaching in schools, and the recognition of Catholicism as the official state religion. For its part, the Holy See anticipated the concordat later entered into with the German Reich and withdrew the clergy from active participation in politics.

Although the Lateran Treaty, one of three pacts, proved mutually advantageous, the relationship between pope and Duce worsened subsequently as Mussolini's regime became increasingly totalitarian. A pattern emerged that was to become all too familiar in Nazi Germany, with the suppression of Catholic youth and student groups and attacks made upon church property, all against a background of

violence and intimidation. Catholic Action members were
regularly beaten up by Mussolini's thugs, and at least one
senior churchman suffered physical abuse. Whereas Catholic publications were confiscated and in some cases publicly
burned, the Fascist press remained free to attack Catholic Action, which it accused of being political, contrary to
the laws of the state. Mussolini charged Catholic Action
with having taken the place of the dissolved Partito Popolare. When the pope challenged the Fascist authorities to
produce evidence of political involvement from the documents they had confiscated, they were unable to do so.

They key issue dividing church and state in Italy was
education. Mussolini demanded the total subjection of
Italian youth to the Fascist state, in contravention of the
recently agreed concordat. It was something to which
the pope would never accede. Events culminated in 1931
with Pius XI's forthright denunciation of the totalitarian
state in the encyclical *Non abbiamo bisogno*. The purpose
of Catholic Action was defined in the encyclical as "the
participation and the collaboration of the laity ... with
the apostolic hierarchy". Mussolini, ever distrustful, had
objected to its rival autonomy and to the fact that it was
organised on a nationwide basis. To pacify him, the pope
restructured Catholic Action on a diocesan level, placing
the organisation in each diocese under the jurisdiction
of the local bishop.[1] Furthermore, it was formerly agreed
between the two leaders that Catholic Action would
henceforth restrict its activities to recreational outlets
and to others having religious purposes. A truce of sorts
was observed following the 1931 accord, and the following year, Mussolini paid an official visit to the Vatican,

[1] D. A. Binchy, *Church and State in Fascist Italy* (London: Oxford University
Press, 1941), 498.

his first, to commemorate the anniversary of the signing of the Lateran pacts.

Mussolini's foreign policy was also giving cause for concern. From the mid-1930s, the pope looked on in dismay as Italy seemed progressively drawn towards Nazi Germany. Pius XI was generally well disposed towards Britain and France, though critical of French intransigence over Versailles. Nazi Germany persecuted religion and had an ideology irreconcilable with Christianity and was thus in the pope's eyes essentially no different from Communist Russia, a view shared by his secretary of state, Pacelli.

To begin with, Mussolini had sought alliances elsewhere. He had been the driving force behind the Four-Power Pact of 1933, which committed Britain, France, Italy, and Germany to the cause of peace. But Mussolini grew alarmed over Hitler's repudiation of the armaments-limitation clauses of the Versailles Treaty, and, with the memory of the abortive Austrian putsch still fresh in mind, he aligned himself with Britain and France at the Stresa Conference of April 1935, in a common front against Nazi Germany. The situation changed completely when the invasion of Abyssinia by Italian forces brought down upon Mussolini the opprobrium of the Western democracies and left Italy friendless. Italian intervention in the Spanish Civil War on the side of the Nationalists pushed Il Duce even closer to an alliance with Hitler, who had made a similar commitment in sending the Luftwaffe to the aid of Franco. Like the Italian dictator, Hitler was in need of a friend in Europe.

Hitler had much to gain by achieving an understanding with Mussolini. More so after their mutual foe, France, concluded treaties with the Soviet Union and with the countries of the Little Entente, thereby reviving German fears of a war on two fronts. As early as 1928, Hitler had advocated union with Fascist Italy, believing the arrangement would provide Germany with a natural ally.[2] In fact, Hitler had been an admirer of the Italian dictator since 1922 and had conceived the Munich Beer Hall Putsch a year later in imitation of Mussolini's march on Rome. On 11 April 1933, shortly after taking office, Hitler had sent Goering to Rome to meet with Mussolini. A year later, amid much fanfare, Hitler paid his first state visit to Italy, when he met Il Duce in Venice.

In June 1936, Mussolini appointed his son-in-law, Count Galeazzo Ciano, foreign minister. The pope grew fearful when a state visit to Germany was scheduled for later that year. His fears received expression in *L'Osservatore Romano*, which several times protested the anti-Christian character of Nazism, alas without producing any effect on the Italian dictator. It was after Ciano's state visit to Germany in October that the agreement dubbed by Mussolini the Rome-Berlin Axis was formalised. The following year, Mussolini joined Italy to the Anti-Comintern Pact, which Hitler had forged with Japan in 1936 in an effort to curb the spread of Communism.

Beginning with Goering in January, several high-ranking Nazis journeyed to Rome throughout the first half of 1937 to pay their respects to Il Duce. Then in September Mussolini returned the compliment by paying a two-day state visit to Germany. Two months later, he announced Italy's withdrawal from the League of Nations. When German troops entered Austria the following March, it was with the assent of Mussolini, after Hitler guaranteed that Italy's frontier with Austria would be respected.

To cement the accord between the two countries, Hitler paid a much heralded visit to Rome the following

[2]John Hiden, *Germany and Europe 1919–1939* (London: Longman, 1977), 162.

May. Relations with the Vatican had eased somewhat, although the pope grumbled when painters and decorators began brightening up the city in anticipation of Hitler's visit. *L'Osservatore Romano* conveyed his regret "that there should be raised in Rome a cross which was opposed to the cross of Christ".[3] When the time approached, before departing for his summer residence at Castel Gandolfo, the pope closed the Vatican museums and left instructions that members of the German party be refused admittance to Vatican City. It was an unmistakeable snub, especially as Hitler had expressed a desire to see historic Rome and view the Vatican treasures. Further resentment was occasioned when members of Catholic organisations, most notably university students, absented themselves from the ceremonies honouring Hitler.[4]

Two weeks after the Rome visit, relations between the Vatican and Germany were further soured by the Mundelein affair. The archbishop of Chicago, Cardinal Mundelein, had criticised the Reich government's persecution of the Church, describing Hitler derogatively as "an Austrian paper-hanger". Stung by the insult, the Germans were furious, and the Reich press was almost hysterical in its reaction. Pressure was brought to bear on the pope to discipline Mundelein. Cardinal Pacelli tried to smooth things over; but when, on the contrary, Pius XI made a point of expressing his admiration for the American prelate, he was accused by the Germans of seeking to bring the United States and Britain into a union against Germany.

The rapprochement between Italy and Germany, which had been viewed with increasing alarm by the Vatican,

[3] William M. Harrigan, "Pius XII's Efforts to Effect a Détente in German-Vatican Relations, 1939–1940", *Catholic Historical Review* 49, no. 2 (July 1963): 177, citing *L'Osservatore Romano* of 5 May 1938.

[4] Binchy, *Church and State in Fascist Italy*, 532–33.

resulted in a state of tension, accompanied by a war of words, in the pontiff's relationship with Mussolini. The main focus of discontent concerned the anti-Semitic laws, which, in the wake of Hitler's visit, Mussolini began almost immediately to enforce in Italy. The move caused widespread revulsion. Italian observers, many of whom felt some ideological affinity with the Nazis, had nevertheless been outspokenly critical of Nazi fanaticism on the race issue. Fascist Party members, once they had recovered from their initial dismay, displayed a marked hostility towards the proposed legislation, and efforts were made to obtain exemptions for those Jews who had demonstrated their loyalty to country and party.

Mussolini was not anti-Semitic. He had disdained the discriminatory measures taken against the Jews in Germany, and the pseudoscientific race theory espoused by Hitler and Rosenberg. He had written to Hitler expressing his views on the subject[5] and had instructed his ambassador to Germany to urge Hitler to abandon his racial policy.[6] More than once Mussolini had boasted that Italy knew no anti-Semitism. This was not strictly true. Roberto Farinacci was a senior member of the Fascist Party and a rabid anti-Semite who regularly vilified Jews in the newspaper *Regime Fascista*, which he edited. What is more, the pope had recently put on the Index a book that had sought to popularise anti-Semitism in Italy. Still, it could reasonably be maintained that Italians were the least anti-Semitic people in Europe. Many Jews had been given sanctuary in Italy after fleeing persecution in Germany—as many as eight thousand by 1937,[7] some through the personal

[5] R. J. B. Bosworth, *Mussolini* (London: Arnold, 2002), 270–71.
[6] Nicholas Farrell, *Mussolini* (London: Weidenfeld and Nicolson, 2003), 306.
[7] Binchy, *Church and State in Fascist Italy*, 605.

intervention of Mussolini himself.[8] Moreover, Jews had been prominent in their support for the Fascist Party from the beginning.

Strange as it seems, Mussolini became anti-Jewish without becoming anti-Semitic. Nicholas Farrell, a recent biographer, explains: "Mussolini persuaded himself that the Jews ... had secret loyalties which conflicted with Fascism. Judaism in general was international, it stood against the nation."[9] It was for this reason, evidently, rather than pressure from Hitler, and certainly not because of racial hatred, that Mussolini authorised the so-called Aryan Manifesto of 14 July 1938. Its purpose was to exclude Jews from key positions in Italian life; ultimately it was to exclude them from membership in the Italian race. Once the die was cast, it was not all that difficult for Mussolini to find ways to authenticate the new orthodoxy. The international Jewish press, he noted, had been prominent in denouncing Italy's invasion of Abyssinia in 1935.

The day after the announcement of the new racialist policy, Pius XI addressed a pilgrimage of French nuns, during which he branded the measures "apostasy" and incompatible with Christianity.[10] Farinacci subsequently attacked the pope in the *Regime Fascista*. In several public addresses throughout July, the pope made forceful condemnations of racialism. The Fascist authorities took note and in some districts banned their publication. Early in the year, the pope had asked the cardinals of the United States and Canada to lend their aid to Jewish scholars and professors who had been expelled from Germany and who now sought entry into American universities. He now gave

---

[8] Bosworth, *Mussolini*, 334.

[9] Farrell, *Mussolini*, 304.

[10] Peter C. Kent, "A Tale of Two Popes: Pius XI, Pius XII and the Rome-Berlin Axis", *Journal of Contemporary History* 23, no. 4 (October 1988): 600.

instructions to Catholic professors to refute the errors of racialism in their lectures and in their published writings.

Near the end of the month, the pope delivered a lecture to an audience of Catholic students on the unity of the human race, a theme to which he had returned time and again throughout his pontificate. "There is no room for special races", the pope declared, and he lamented the fact that Italy "should have felt a disgraceful need to imitate Germany".[11] Ciano described the lecture as "violently critical of racialism" and sent for the papal nuncio, who was issued a grave warning.[12] The Anglican *Church Times* praised the pope's statements on racialism as being "of the greatest historical and moral importance".[13]

A countrywide campaign to prevent the adoption of the race laws was promptly undertaken by Catholic Action at the urging of the pope, who appealed for direct action in a speech of 21 July. A propaganda war now raged between Mussolini's supporters and members of Catholic Action, whose successes led the Fascists to resort to violent retaliatory measures. Catholic Action clubs in Milan, Turin, Bergamo, Venice, and many other cities were attacked and ransacked and had their printing presses destroyed by black-shirted mobs. Mussolini accused Catholic Action of being in breach of the concordat by unlawfully engaging in political activity. But the pope was adamant that racialism was a spiritual and religious matter, touching all, a point he made abundantly clear in *L'Osservatore Romano* of

[11] Ibid. See also Pinchas E. Lapide, *The Last Three Popes and the Jews* (London: Souvenir Press, 1967), 95; Farrell, *Mussolini*, 309. Lapide's and Farrell's books both cite *L'Osservatore Romano* of 30 July 1938, which published the pope's lecture in full.

[12] *Ciano's Diary, 1937–1938* (London: Methuen, London, 1952), entry for 30 July 1938.

[13] Quoted in Anthony Rhodes, *The Vatican in the Age of the Dictators, 1922–1945* (London: Hodder and Stoughton, 1973), 214.

24 August.[14] Two months earlier, Ciano had written in his diary: "The Duce is very worked up about the racial question and very angry with Catholic Action. He attacked the Pope violently."[15]

In an addendum, Ciano ventured to suggest that the pope was nevertheless showing "signs of disarming" over the race question. This seems to have been a fairly general impression, if only for a brief interlude, as may be gathered from reports both in the Fascist press and in newspapers abroad. A détente had been arrived at following an agreement between Catholic Action and the Fascist leadership, and this may have led Ciano to infer that the pope's resistance was waning. But Ciano had evidently misread the signs, as his diary entry for 22 August carried yet another complaint: "It seems that the Pope made another disagreeable speech yesterday about exaggerated nationalism and racial ideology. The Duce has summoned Father Tacchi-Venturi [a Jesuit intermediary at the Vatican] for this evening and proposes to deliver an ultimatum to him."

Pius XI was not one to heed ultimatums. Later, students of the Propaganda College, the missionary college only lately founded by the pope himself, heard him deride Mussolini for his fond assumption that Fascism represented a restoration of the Roman Empire. Racism was completely at odds with the noble traditions of ancient Rome, said the pope, who added, "Human dignity consists in the fact that all make up one single family, the human race." The students cheered him to the rafters.[16]

Hitler's ambitions in Europe had reached a critical stage by September. At the behest of Mussolini, British Prime Minister Neville Chamberlain travelled to Godesberg on

[14] Quoted in Binchy, *Church and State in Fascist Italy*, 621.
[15] *Ciano's Diary, 1937–1938*, entry for 8 August 1938.
[16] Binchy, *Church and State in Fascist Italy*, 617 and footnote.

the 22nd to meet Hitler in talks over the future of Czecho-slovakia, but the two leaders failed to reach an agreement. Czechoslovakia was a beneficiary of the breakup of the former Austro-Hungarian Empire. Its racial mix included more than three million Germans, most of whom lived in the Sudetenland, the German-speaking frontier region of the country. A week after the Godesberg stalemate, a conference of the four European powers Great Britain, France, Italy, and Germany opened in Munich and ended with Great Britain and France acceding to Hitler's annex-ation of the Sudetenland to the Reich in return for his assurance that his demands would then be satisfied.

The eight thousand Jewish refugees from Nazi Germany who had only recently made their home in Italy were now persona non grata. In the month of the Munich agreement, all foreign Jews resident in Italy were given six months to leave the country. At the same time, the Council of Min-isters issued a decree excluding Italian Jews from schools and universities, exempting only those who were baptised Catholics. On three occasions in September, the pope spoke out, rebutting Fascist accusations that he was inter-fering in politics and insisting that the deification of the state and the question of race were religious in nature. His statements were given prominence in the *New York Times*.

The proposal to outlaw marriages between Italian "Ary-ans" and members of other races, meaning Jews, became law on 10 November. The ordinance was a clear violation of the 1929 concordat, which accorded civil recognition to marriages validated in canon law. The ordinance provoked the pope to write letters of protest to Mussolini and to King Victor Emanuel. The king responded by promising to give the matter his consideration. Mussolini failed to reply, causing the pope to lodge a formal protest with the government.

The pope's voice was not a lone one. The Italian hierarchy, with the notable exception of Cazzani, the bishop of Cremona, showed itself implacably hostile to racialism. Replying to a lecture that Farinacci had delivered in Milan, Cardinal Schuster labelled anti-Semitism "the myth of the twentieth century". Schuster's outspoken sermon earned him the praise of the pope. From his pulpit in the cathedral of Bologna, Cardinal Nasalli Rocca echoed the oft-repeated dictum of the pope when he stressed the universal brotherhood of men and nations. Even bishops who had looked with favour on the regime were openly critical over the race issue. Priests, too, and laypeople, members of Catholic Action and others, actively opposed the legislation. A campaign urging Catholics to show solidarity with their Jewish neighbours was conducted in many Italian towns, and anti-Semitism was consistently attacked in the Catholic press. All these activities required courage. Dissent led to confrontation with Mussolini's thuggish supporters, and the printed word came under the ever-watchful eye of Farinacci, the self-appointed guardian of Fascist orthodoxy.

In November, the pope dwelt on the incompatibility of anti-Semitism and Christianity when he addressed a group of Belgian pilgrims. The gist of his message was that Jews and Christians had a common father in Abraham. "Spiritually we are all Semites", he told them.[17] In the same month, Vatican Radio condemned racism as a denial of

[17] J. Derek Holmes, *The Papacy in the Modern World* (London: Burns and Oates, 1981), 116. Certain critics have questioned the authenticity of the pope's address. Binchy notes that it was reported in the *Tablet*, but merited only the briefest mention in *L'Osservatore Romano*. Binchy, *Church and State in Fascist Italy*, 617, footnote. Lapide cites the authority of Don Luigi Sturzo, founder of Partito Popolare, and that of an identical report that appeared in the Belgian newspaper *Cité Nouvelle* of 15 September 1938. Lapide, *The Last Three Popes and the Jews*, 114.

Catholic doctrine. The pope was later mocked in a rhyme that appeared in a Nazi publication:

> For all he knows concerning Race
> Would get a schoolboy in disgrace
> Since he regards both Blacks and Whites
> As children all with equal rights,
> As Christians all (what'er their hues),
> They're "spiritually" nought but Jews.[18]

After again repudiating Mussolini's racial policy, this time at a missionary college near Castel Gandolfo, the pope subsequently directed all missionary colleges to offer guidance to seminarians on how best to combat racialism. This drew forth from the Fascist press the accusation that the pope was in league with international Jewry. Mussolini threatened Italian Jews that a worse fate awaited them unless their friends in pulpits ceased to defend them.

The turn of the year found Pius XI firing off complaints to the government when it began excluding Jews from the professions. At the same time, Mussolini instructed Count Bonifacio Pignatti, the ambassador to the Holy See, to convey his displeasure over the clergy's opposition to the race laws. Ciano's diary entry for 2 January read: "I should like to avoid a clash with the Vatican, which I should consider very harmful." Only days later, the authorities became incensed over a sermon that Monsignor Roncalli, who in 1958 would succeed Pius XII as pope, but was then the papal envoy in Turkey, had delivered in Istanbul. "The church does not know the division of humanity into races", he had said.[19] His words were subsequently

---

[18] Quoted in Father Francis Marsden, *Catholic Times*, 9 April 2000, 9.

[19] Owen Chadwick, *Britain and the Vatican during the Second World War* (Cambridge: Cambridge University Press, 1986), 26.

applied to the Italian situation by a writer in a Jewish journal in Istanbul. The Italian government made indignant representations to the Vatican, to no avail. Meanwhile the pope interceded with the ambassadors of the diplomatic corps accredited to the Holy See with the request that they obtain visas for oppressed Jews in both Italy and Germany.

Old and in failing health, the pope received British Prime Minister Neville Chamberlain and his foreign secretary, Lord Halifax, in a private audience in February. The plight of the Jews and the pressing matter of supplying aid to refugees were among the subjects under discussion. It was in the midst of these cares that the pope's health deteriorated; and on 10 February, wearied after an illness lasting several days, he suffered a heart attack and died.

Tributes to Pius XI poured into Rome. Jewish leaders praised him for his work for peace and spoke with gratitude of his uncompromising attitude to racialism.[20] The French Communist newspaper *L'Humanité* applauded the implacable stand he had taken against racialism and Hitlerism. Mussolini at first feigned indifference but out of respect cancelled the meeting of the Grand Council scheduled for the following day. Not all reports of the pope's death were glowing with admiration, but the obituarist in an SS journal got it right when he wrote: "He died the sworn enemy of National Socialism."

[20] Jewish tributes are summarized on pages 115–16 of Lapide, *The Last Three Popes and the Jews.*

3

The New Pope's Peace Initiatives
and the Outbreak of War

Rome now became the centre of worldwide attention as the College of Cardinals sought a successor to the great pope of peace. The election of a pope at such a stage in world affairs concerned not only Catholics but also many outside the Church, particularly the leaders of the Western democracies, who followed events in the Vatican with the keenest interest.

The world seemed to be teetering on the brink of disaster, with Hitler's mounting aggression fuelling fears of another war. While some, the Americans notably, seemed to have little idea that war was impending, the mood of the cardinals gathered in conclave suggested that not many were hopeful that such an eventuality could long be avoided. The Rome-based journalists Reynolds and Eleanor Packard interviewed cardinals of every nationality and noted a conviction among them that some cataclysmic crisis, perhaps war, was imminent.[1]

In 1922, Pius XI had been an unexpected choice as pope, a compromise solution. A different scenario now

---

[1] Reynolds and Eleanor Packard, *Balcony Empire: Fascist Italy at War* (London: Chatto and Windus, 1943), 160. See also Harold H. Tittmann Jr., *Inside the Vatican of Pius XII: The Memoir of an American Diplomat during World War II* (New York: Image Books, 2004), 1.

presented itself. There are times in the election of a pope when one man stands out from the rest as the obvious choice. Although a pope may not nominate his successor, it was well known that Pius XI had greatly admired his secretary of state and had been grooming him for the papal office. He had confided to Tardini, the undersecretary at the Vatican, his conviction that Cardinal Pacelli would be "a magnificent pope". Pius XI had recalled Pacelli from the nunciature in Berlin before appointing him to succeed the aging Cardinal Gasparri as secretary of state. Pacelli proved to be an excellent choice, and Pius XI had to defer to the younger man's judgement on several occasions. Not since the seventeenth century, however, had a pope been succeeded by his secretary of state. Nevertheless, on 2 March, 1939, Cardinal Eugenio Pacelli was elected pope in the shortest conclave for three hundred years, and one of the shortest in history. He chose the name Pius XII.

News of his election was greeted with approval by leaders of the free world. Pacelli had been the preferred choice of both Britain and France, and President Roosevelt, whom Pacelli had met when he had visited the United States as secretary of state, was a personal friend and admirer. German and Italian commentators were not so welcoming. The Nazi paper *Berliner Morgenpost* succinctly summarised official German opinion: "The election of Pacelli is not favourably accepted in Germany, since he has always been hostile to National Socialism."[2] Some German papers were more sanguine in their reporting of the event. It was noted with satisfaction in German diplomatic circles that the new pope was much more of a diplomat than his fiery and outspoken predecessor. Ciano sounded a hopeful note by pointing

[2] Quoted in Pinchas E. Lapide, *The Last Three Popes and the Jews* (London: Souvenir Press, 1967), 121.

out that Pacelli had in the meantime improved relations with Germany. Mussolini declared himself satisfied with the result of the election and promised "to send the pope some advice on how he can usefully govern the Church".[3]

Most press reports mentioned the pope's opposition to racialism, in which he had been of one mind with his illustrious predecessor. The Jewish oracle *The Palestine Post* commented: "The cordial reception accorded the election, particularly in France, England and America—and the lukewarm reception in Germany—are not surprising when we remember the large part he played in the recent papal opposition to pernicious race theories."[4] Indeed, one of the first official acts of the new pope was to establish within the Vatican Information Office a special department for the welfare of Jews.

Foremost in Pius XII's mind, however, was how the suffering of the Church in Germany might be alleviated. After consulting with the three German cardinals, Bertram, Faulhaber, and Schulte, the pope set up a committee headed by three German bishops who were charged with the task of improving relations with Germany. He also sent a personal message to Hitler notifying him of his accession to the papacy.[5] It was a courteous gesture recalling Leo XIII's friendly overture to Emperor Wilhelm I on the former's election to the papacy in 1878. But a reciprocating gesture on Hitler's part was not forthcoming; and the German episcopal committee came to nothing.

Nevertheless, Pius XII's goodwill on this occasion marked the beginning of a more conciliatory tenor in

---

[3] *Ciano's Diary, 1939–1943*, ed. Malcolm Muggeridge (London: William Heinemann, 1947), entries for 2 and 3 March 1939.

[4] Quoted in Lapide, *The Last Three Popes and the Jews*, 122.

[5] E. L. Woodward and Rohan Butler, eds., assisted by Anne Orde, *Documents on German Foreign Policy 1918–1945*, series D, vol. 6, *The Last Months of Peace, March–August 1939*, doc. no. 28.

Vatican policy towards the Reich. Years of protests, culminating in the encyclical *Mit brennender Sorge*, had failed to
improve the situation of the Church in Germany. Nor had
Pius XI's frequent thunderbolts hurled against Mussolini
and his racial policies achieved very notable success. The
new pope early decided that a détente with Germany might
be possible if public criticism of the regime were to be
muted. Accordingly, *L'Oservatore Romano* was instructed
to desist in its attacks on the German government.[6]

To be sure, there were signs of a desire for more cordial
relations coming out of Germany. The German press had
generally taken a positive attitude in its appraisal of the late
pope's achievements. Government buildings had flown
their flags at half-mast to mark his passing, and a Requiem
Mass held for the pope in Berlin had been well attended
by government officials. Sadly, the situation deteriorated
rapidly in the summer of 1939, with renewed attacks on
the religious orders and Catholic associations, prompting the Holy See to protest the outrages in a lengthy note
to the government.

On 11 March, ignoring opposition from Germany, Pius
XII appointed the experienced Cardinal Luigi Maglione
as his secretary of state. The appointment was favourably
reported in the democratic press. Four days later, Hitler
calmly dismembered Czechoslovakia, annexing the provinces of Bohemia and Moravia to the Reich and making
Slovakia an independent state subservient to Germany.
Meanwhile, Hitler demanded the return to Germany of
the free port of Danzig on the Baltic and of the Polish
Corridor, the strip of land dividing East Prussia from the
rest of Germany, which had been ceded to Poland by
the Treaty of Versailles.

[6] Ibid.

In April, Mussolini infuriated Hitler by invading Albania without consulting him. Mussolini's action, following close upon the spoliation of Czechoslovakia, alarmed President Roosevelt. Appealing directly to the two dictators, the president requested a pledge from both not to engage in armed aggression against the countries of Europe and the Middle East for a period of ten years; at the same time, he called for the opening of peace talks. Roosevelt petitioned the pope to support his appeal; but while the pope expressed his appreciation of the president's initiative, he regretted that he was unable to support it at the time. The British government endorsed Roosevelt's appeal in a communiqué to the press.[7]

The Vatican's reserve in this matter proved the wiser reaction. President Roosevelt's entreaty served only to arouse the ire of the German government, which viewed it as transparently biased; and Hitler lectured the American president at length on the history and geography of Europe. The German ambassador to the Holy See, Diego von Bergen, called President Roosevelt's appeal "naive, even childish". He elaborated in a confidential report to the German Foreign Ministry:

> Pius XII has ... during the short time since his enthronement spoken repeatedly in the cause of peace.... In all his pronouncements, however, without expressly addressing any specific states, he has confined himself to invoking peace on the basis of justice, thereby making it so to speak a matter of conscience for all concerned. Roosevelt, on the other hand, has made the mistake of only addressing

---

[7] E. L. Woodward and Rohan Butler, eds., assisted by Anne Orde, *Documents on British Foreign Policy 1919–1939*, 3rd series, vol. 5, 1939 (London: Her Majesty's Stationery Office, 1952), doc. no. 188.

two specific Heads of Government, and in addition of making public this entirely one-sided appeal.[8]

Pius XII continued to devote his energies to preserving the peace in Europe. Throughout the summer of 1939, he made repeated diplomatic representations, personally and through his appointed representatives, to that end. On 21 April, the pope approached Mussolini with a proposal for a five-power conference, to be attended by the representatives of the heads of state of Great Britain, France, Italy, Germany, and Poland, aimed at averting war. Mussolini, whose ambitions in North Africa were at that moment being fiercely contested by the French, was nevertheless amenable. Consequently, on 3 May, the pope communicated his proposal to the five powers through the papal envoys in London, Paris, Rome, Berlin, and Warsaw. The papal nuncio, Archbishop Orsenigo, informed Hitler of the plan during a visit to the führer's mountain retreat at the Berchtesgaden. Hitler said he would get in touch with Mussolini, but he did not think there was any danger of war. He blamed Britain as being the chief danger to peace, in stirring other countries against Germany.[9] The pope's proposal was coolly received in Paris.[10] But from Berlin, Sir Neville Henderson wrote to Lord Halifax: "Personally, I can see no other possible arbitrator than the Pope, and it is a hopeful sign that Hitler apparently did not turn down the suggestion out of hand."[11] The British delegate in Warsaw, Sir H. Kennard, informed Halifax that the Poles did not look with favour on the idea of a conference but were willing to accept the pope as a mediator.[12]

[8] *Documents on German Foreign Policy*, series D, vol. 6, doc. no. 240.

[9] Ibid., no. 331.

[10] *Documents on British Foreign Policy*, doc. no. 434.

[11] Ibid., doc. no. 487.

[12] Ibid., doc. no. 426.

The official replies, received within the week, were not encouraging. The representatives of each of the five nations thanked the pope for his interest, and all stressed the wish to avoid war. They appeared unwilling, however, to compromise where their respective interests were concerned. Sumner Welles, the U.S. undersecretary of state, praised the pope for his efforts to keep the peace, which he said were of "the utmost value", and lamented that they had failed to achieve the desired result.[13]

What particularly dismayed the pope was the attitude of the Poles. In an attempt to facilitate discussion, Pius XII had asked President Mościcki, through the nuncio, Monsignor Cortesi, to halt the attacks on Germany that were regularly appearing in the Polish press and to open negotiations with Hitler. In that event, the pope said, he was willing to act as intermediary if the two parties should request it. Alas, Mościcki was intractable. Poland would not give in to German pressure, he said.[14]

On 10 May, the pope decided not to press the matter of the proposed conference, largely as a result of assurances received from Hitler and Mussolini that there was no immediate prospect of war. He made it clear that his proposal could be taken up at a later date should the circumstances warrant it. Lord Halifax wrote to Sir D'Arcy Osborne, the British envoy to the Holy See:

> Although His Holiness's soundings may not have produced the full result for which all lovers of peace may have hoped, we are confident that knowledge, throughout the world, of interest which he has evinced will not fail to exert powerful moral influence for good.[15]

[13] J. Derek Holmes, *The Papacy in the Modern World* (London: Burns and Oates, 1981), 122.

[14] Camille M. Cianfarra, *The War and the Vatican* (London: Burns, Oates, and Washbourne, 1945), 171.

[15] *Documents on British Foreign Policy,* doc. no. 487.

Less than two weeks later, Mussolini joined Hitler in the Pact of Steel, an alliance forged in the event of war. Amidst general alarm, the pope informed British minister Osborne of his willingness to work out a basis for agreement between Germany and Poland. The British Foreign Office, however, rejected the idea, thinking the pope was trying to conciliate Hitler. Then on 22 August, it became known that Germany was about to sign a pact with Russia. This would secure Hitler's eastern perimeter and was widely viewed as a portent of war. Owen Chadwick observes wryly: "That day Lord Halifax telephoned Osborne asking him to persuade the Pope to do what the Foreign Office had been trying to stop the Pope doing for three months—to try and bring Germany and Poland to the negotiating table, and to issue a 'last appeal to reason'."[16]

The result was the pope's appeal for peace that was broadcast to the world on Vatican Radio on the evening of 24 August, the day after the signing of the German-Soviet nonaggression pact. In the broadcast, the pope declared, in his most memorable passage, "Empires not based on peace are not blessed by God.... Nothing is lost by peace. Everything can be lost by war." The British foreign minister, Lord Halifax, and King Leopold of Belgium sent messages of appreciation to the Vatican. The day after the pope's broadcast, Mussolini told Hitler that he was unable to engage in a European war unless Germany supplied the necessary weapons and raw materials that Italy lacked. Hostilities were subsequently postponed, as Hitler delayed his planned invasion of Poland.[17]

---

[16] Owen Chadwick, *Britain and the Vatican during the Second World War* (Cambridge: Cambridge University Press, 1986), 73.

[17] Milan Hauner, *Hitler: A Chronology of His Life and Time* (London: Palgrave Macmillan, 2008), 147. Hitler had planned the invasion for either the following night or the night of the 26th. See Pierre Blet, S.J., *Pius XII and the Second World War according to the Archives of the Vatican* (Herefordshire: Gracewing, 2003), 21–22.

Intense diplomatic activity ensued. On 29 August, the pope commended Mussolini for his part in seeking a peaceful solution to the crisis and asked him to redouble his efforts. Pius thought Mussolini could be a useful ally in bringing his influence to bear on Hitler. Two days later, the pope made a last-ditch attempt to avoid war. His idea for a diplomatic solution based on a revision of the Treaty of Versailles was communicated to the five powers directly concerned. At the same time, he urged Germany and Poland to observe a fifteen-day truce so that an international conference could be called to consider the plan.[18] Lord Halifax informed German Foreign Minister Ribbentrop of the British government's strong support for the pope's proposal and conveyed the same information to Warsaw.

This latest effort on the Holy Father's part directed to the cause of peace was, alas, overtaken by events. That same day, a number of German convicts were released from prison, dressed in Polish uniforms, and instructed to attack a German radio station in Silesia on the border with Poland. Affecting moral outrage at this unprovoked act of Polish aggression, Hitler ordered German troops into the Polish Corridor. Early next day, the papal nuncio in Berlin, Monsignor Orsenigo, telephoned the Vatican with the news. Hitler, it seems clear, did not believe that Britain and France would go to war over Poland. When, therefore, he was given an ultimatum to withdraw his troops from Polish territory, he ignored it, thinking that, as in the case of his previous demands, Britain would back down. Great Britain and France consequently honoured the guarantee each had given to Poland and declared war on Germany.

Although, in the end, war could not be averted, Pius XII's efforts to preserve the peace in Europe are deserving

---

[18] Cianfarra, *The War and the Vatican*, 186.

of the highest praise. Sir D'Arcy Osborne commented: "We are in a position to state that His Holiness, up to the last moment, has unceasingly tried to prevent hostilities, not only through the initiatives already known to the public, but also through more confidential steps."[19] Camille Cianfarra was the *New York Times* correspondent in Rome from 1935 to 1942. In his book *The War and the Vatican*, he paid the pope this tribute:

> His work to save Europe and the world from the ravages of war, although it was not successful, will undoubtedly remain as one of the outstanding contributions to peace given by a single man in our century.[20]

Having seen all his efforts to avoid war come to nought, Pius XII now sought ways and means of limiting the suffering that would inevitably follow, just as he had done during the First World War when, as a young monsignor, he had put into operation the welfare and rescue plans of his pope, Benedict XV.[21] At the beginning of hostilities, he appealed to the countries involved to observe international agreements on the humane conduct of war. His Pontifical Relief Commission, with bureaus in many European countries from the Baltic to the Balkans, organised the distribution of food, clothing, and medical supplies to the innocent victims of the conflict. Every Catholic diocese throughout the world was asked to help collect funds. Archbishop Roncalli, the future Pope John XXIII, took charge of operations in Greece and the Balkans with half a million lire given him by the pope to get him started. Working closely with the pope, Roncalli later succeeded in

[19] Quoted in Anthony Rhodes, *The Vatican in the Age of the Dictators, 1922–1945* (London: Hodder and Stoughton, 1973), 232–33.

[20] Cianfarra, *The War and the Vatican*, 176–77.

[21] John Frain, *The Cross and the Third Reich: Catholic Resistance in the Nazi Era* (Oxford: Family Publications, 2009), 314.

persuading the Allies to lift the blockade of Axis-occupied countries so that food shipments could get through to the starving Greeks.

The Vatican Information Bureau was another of Pius XII's initiatives. The service provided for the gathering and exchange of information, and through it many thousands of people were put in touch with family members who were missing or were being held as prisoners of war. Beginning in 1939 with a staff of two, by 1943 the bureau employed six hundred people, who dealt with requests for help in tracing more than two million displaced persons. From his base in Istanbul, Roncalli was successful in tracing prisoners of war and concentration-camp inmates when efforts by the International Red Cross had met with failure. The Catholic Refugee Committee, which was established by the pope under the direction of Father Leiber, enabled thousands of European Jews to enter the United States by providing them with baptismal certificates and money.[22]

On 20 October, Pius XII promulgated the first encyclical letter of his reign, *Summi Pontificatus*, known also as *Darkness over the Earth*. It had been awaited with great interest, by those outside the Church as well as those within. In the encyclical, the pope set forth a Christian ideal of society and inveighed against contemporary errors that threatened the peace. Of these, two receive particular attention.

> The first, disastrously widespread in our day, consists in losing sight of that kinship and love which ought to bind human beings to one another. Such love is called for by our common human origin; it is called for by our common

[22] Mary Ball Martinez, "Pope Pius XII in the Second World War", *Journal of Historical Review* 13, no. 5 (September–October 1993): 2–3, available at Institute for Historical Review, accessed 28 August 2015, http://www.ihr.org/jhr/v13/v13n5p26_Martinez.html.

possession, whatever race we belong to, of the reasoning
faculty by which man is distinguished.

The dignity that rationality gives to all men arises from
this fact—namely, that "God crowned the work of creation which he had begun by making 'man in His own
image'." Further, the unity of the human race reaches
its perfection in Christ's sacrifice of Redemption. Thus,
echoing the apostle to the Gentiles, "there is neither Gentile nor Jew, neither circumcision nor uncircumcision ...
but Christ is all things and in all things."[23]

There are distinct echoes of *Mit brennender Sorge* where
the encyclical touches the subject of patriotism. Love of
one's country, a noble thing in itself that ought to be
encouraged, nevertheless "must not interfere with, must
not take precedence over the commandment to show
Christian charity towards all men". And there is a scathing
condemnation of those who regard signed pacts "as written in water". For peace between nations, "there must be
general persuasion that an oath given will be kept sacred
by both parties."

And what of the second error?

It is the error of those who impiously endeavour to dissociate the civil authority from any connection at all with
the Divine Being; forgetting that the community quite
as much as the individual depends upon Him as its first
author and its supreme governor.

Should anyone have doubted that the pope is here direct-
ing attention to the danger posed by totalitarian regimes,
even more unmistakeable was this warning:

[23] Col 3:11.

Whoever considers the state to be the end towards which all is directed, to which all must bow, is of necessity an enemy and an obstacle to all true and lasting progress among nations.

Summi Pontificatus closes with some consoling words for Catholic Poland, which even then lay trampled under the Nazi jackboot:

The blood of so many who have been cruelly slaughtered, though they bore no military rank, cries to heaven especially from the well-loved country of Poland. Poland, imperishably crowned in the pages of history by the long record of her loyalty to the Church and her services to Christian civilization, should claim from all eyes a brotherly, a human tear.

The encyclical met with a mixed reception, although it was well received in the democratic West. The exiled Polish primate Cardinal Hlond professed his gratitude for the sentences about Poland, the only country specifically mentioned. The British praised the encyclical unstintingly, as did the French, and the French Air Force dropped eighty-eight thousand copies of it over Germany. The *New York Times* proclaimed on its front page: "Pope Condemns Dictators, Treaty Violators, Racism; Urges Restoring of Poland". Reviewing the encyclical for the same newspaper, Anne O'Hare McCormick commented: "The dictatorship of today is not simply a form of government; it is a form of life, a usurpation of every human and divine right."[24] And she likened the totalitarian dictatorship to an abnormal growth, a tumour afflicting the whole social body.

[24] Anne O'Hare McCormick, editorial, *New York Times*, October 30, 1939, 16.

Official reaction in Germany was predictable. Although the pope had confined himself to a statement of principles and had refrained from condemning by name any government or party, nevertheless Reinhard Heydrich, head of the Reich Security Office, wrote to the chief of the Reich chancellery, Hans Lammers: "The encyclical is directed exclusively against Germany, both in ideology and in regard to the German-Polish dispute." The encyclical was attacked for being antiracialist, and though it was read out in churches without hindrance, further publication was prohibited. When the BBC broadcast the contents of the encyclical, it brought a complaint to the pope from the German embassy in Rome. In a footnote to *Summi Pontificatus*, Pius XII told Haiti's new black ambassador to the Holy See, "[T]here is an equality among all men, based upon the unity of mankind; no race is inferior."

In September 1939, Josef Müller, a German lawyer and a prominent Catholic, approached the Vatican on behalf of the resistance circle in the Abwehr (German military intelligence) with a daring proposal. The German opposition was keen to make contact with the British in order to explore the conditions for a peace treaty once the Hitler regime had been removed. Müller wanted to know whether the pope would agree to act as intermediary, even though by doing so he would be compromising Vatican neutrality. Nevertheless, Müller was put in contact with Pius XII's private secretary, the Jesuit Father Leiber. Information was subsequently passed to Osborne, who would then communicate it to London. When Osborne heard from the Foreign Office, the reply would be sent through Father Leiber to the German Resistance.[25]

[25] David Alvarez and Robert A. Graham, S.J., *Nothing Sacred: Nazi Espionage against the Vatican, 1939–1945* (London: Frank Cass, 1997), 25.

From the start, the British attitude was sceptical. The Foreign Office was also put off by the German opposition's reluctance to abandon German territorial claims. The pope, for his part, was emphatic that decentralisation and a plebiscite in Austria, matters raised by the British, would not be a barrier to peace if there were agreement on other points. Regime change in Germany and an avowal of Christian morality were, he said, the primary matters of concern. The British insisted that Hitler must first be removed before peace talks could commence. The cloak-and-dagger operation went completely unnoticed by German embassy officials at the Vatican. Müller's secret mission was eventually uncovered by Hermann Keller, a Benedictine monk and Nazi agent, whose report on the matter was sent to Admiral Canaris, the head of the Abwehr. Canaris, however, was himself a leading figure in the German opposition to Hitler. He therefore took no action on Keller's report. The so-called Roman Conversations ended in May 1940, when the Holy Office was made aware, through the German opposition, of Hitler's imminent offensive in the West. The pope immediately contacted Brussels and the Hague, and communicated the intelligence to British, French, and Belgian representatives at the Vatican.[26]

On 10 May, the same day that Churchill replaced Chamberlain as British prime minister, Hitler invaded the Low Countries. Pius XII responded by sending telegrams of moral support to the Queen of Holland, the King of Belgium, and the Grand Duchess of Luxembourg, lamenting the fact that each country should have been invaded "against its will and right". Camille Cianfarra called this action "the most courageous decision of his

Pontificate".[27] The action angered Mussolini, who protested through Dino Alfieri, his ambassador to the Holy See. On the other hand, the Allies thought the pope's response to the German assault on the Low Countries was inadequate. This was to become a familiar refrain, for whereas the Axis powers constantly complained that the pope favoured the Allies, the Allies were always keen to exploit the moral authority of the pope for propaganda purposes. The Allies' lukewarm attitude on this occasion prompted the pope's assistant Monsignor Domenico Tardini to retort that what they wanted to see was plain enough to anyone "who knows how to read telegrams."[28]

Beginning in September 1939, the pope made repeated diplomatic approaches to Mussolini, directed to keeping Italy out of the war. This was also the concern preoccupying President Roosevelt. In February 1940, Mr. Myron C. Taylor was sent to Rome as Roosevelt's personal representative to "his old and good friend" Pope Pius XII, "in order that our parallel endeavours for peace and the alleviation of suffering may be assisted".[29] From 1940 until the end of 1944 the two men carried on a correspondence, as Mr. Taylor journeyed between Washington and Rome. The idea had been put to Roosevelt by the U.S. secretary of state, Cordell Hull, who had pointed out to the president the desirability of gaining access to the Vatican's multifarious sources of information—information that the U.S. government lacked. Mussolini, however, grew more hostile to the Allies as time wore on. According to Ciano, Il Duce was consumed with thoughts of war and remained

[27] Cianfarra, *The War and the Vatican*, 224–25.

[28] Chadwick, *Britain and the Vatican during the Second World War*, 111.

[29] Roosevelt to Pius XII, 23 December 1939, in Myron C. Taylor, *Wartime Correspondence between President Roosevelt and Pope Pius XII* (New York: Macmillan, 1947), 19.

convinced that the Allies would meet with defeat. His admiration for Hitler, Ciano said, increased with the führer's every military success.[30]

President Roosevelt had proposed that the pope, Mussolini, and he should join forces in a common effort to restore peace in Europe. Later, in a letter delivered by hand to Il Duce by Undersecretary of State Sumner Welles, Roosevelt appealed to Mussolini to remain a nonbelligerent.[31] The pope was deeply appreciative of these initiatives and expressed the hope that the president's immense authority in world affairs would have some influence for good. The pope addressed his own appeal in writing to Mussolini on 24 April. The British, too, were doing their utmost to restrain Il Duce and limit the war to the campaign against Nazi Germany. But Mussolini remained noncommittal, even though Roosevelt made seven separate appeals to keep Italy neutral. Pius XII and Welles, who was in Europe at the time, were agreed that the cause appeared lost. So it was. On Tuesday, 11 June, Mussolini took Italy into the war on the side of Nazi Germany.

The pope, as head of a neutral enclave, now became host to a throng of diplomats stationed in Rome, who moved from what had now become unfriendly or, in the case of the British, enemy territory, into the living quarters made available for them in the Vatican. After Italy's entry into the war, the pope addressed two further appeals to Mussolini. But the position was hopeless. By this time, neither the Axis nor the British would entertain talk of peace any longer.

---

[30] *Ciano's Diary, 1939–1943*, entries for 25 February, 8 March, and 18 March 1940.

[31] Tittmann, *Inside the Vatican of Pius XII*, 9–10.

4

The Well-Loved Country of Poland

German forces quickly overwhelmed the Poles, who were greatly outnumbered and inferior in both air and land capability. Within a week of the German invasion, the medieval capital of Cracow was taken. It took only another forty-eight hours before the Germans were at Warsaw. Days later, the Russians moved into Poland from the east. The government fled the country for Rumania before eventually taking up abode in Britain.

It now befell Catholic Poland to be carved up by two godless regimes. The western part of the country, containing 340,000 ethnic Germans, was annexed to the Reich and became known as the Warthegau, taking its name from a river of that region. Russia regained her former territories in the east, which had been ceded to Poland by the Treaty of Riga in 1921. What remained of the country, roughly the middle third, fell under direct German rule and was designated the General Government.

The Poles did not take the invasion lying down but fought back bravely. More than 150 Polish resistance groups sprang up throughout the land. Resistance ranged from activities such as the distribution of propaganda leaflets and clandestine publications to sabotage and armed struggle, and it involved all age groups. Boy Scouts reported military information to the Resistance, and schoolchildren distributed underground newspapers.[1] Most resistance groups eventually were subsumed under the Union of Armed Struggle, which had been set up by senior army officers and which later became the Home Army. Remnants of the Polish army and air forces fought in France in 1940; and Poles fought alongside the British in virtually every World War II campaign.

At the beginning of the Nazi occupation, the governor general Hans Frank bluntly spelled out his policy for Poland. The Poles, he boasted, were to be the slaves of the Greater German Reich, and the land would be plundered for food for Germany. Frank was echoing Himmler, who had recommended that Poland be turned into a nation of slaves. Frank's subordinate, the brutal Arthur Greiser, was appointed Reich governor of the Warthegau, including the districts of Poznan, Lodz, and part of Warsaw. Greiser's chief responsibility related to the evictions, which began almost immediately. Poles were abruptly removed from their dwellings before being sent to labour camps in Germany. Their departure made way for the resettlement of the country by Germans, who, by early 1941, were coming to live in Cracow in increasing numbers and were bringing their families with them.[2]

Transports in lorries and cattle tracks from eastern Poland to Russia began in the winter of 1939 to 1940. Having been banned from entering Russia, priests were regularly smuggled aboard the conveyances to accompany their people. One priest was Father Tadeusz Fedorowicz, a canon of the Catholic chapter in L'vov, who felled trees in a forest in Kazakhstan while secretly ministering as a priest.

[1] David G. Williamson, *Poland Betrayed: The Nazi-Soviet Invasion of 1939* (Barnsley, UK: Pen and Sword, 2009), 161–62.

[2] Countess Karolina Lanckorońska, *Those Who Trespass against Us: One Woman's War against the Nazis* (London: Pimlico, 2005), 61.

By early February 1940, about one million Polish peasants had been deported from eastern Poland to Russia. A quarter of the total number were Jews, out of a Jewish population of three million. By August of the following year, half a million Poles had been deported from the Ukraine alone. Many of those who had fled before the advancing Germans and who now found themselves trapped between two armies of occupation were compelled to join the rest of the deportees. The activities of the Russians were not so well known in the West, as the radio broadcasts were full of the atrocities committed by the Nazis. An eyewitness of the Russian deportations observed grimly: "With the Russians people disappeared like stones in water; nobody could ever find out anything about them."[3] Many Poles, both Jewish and non-Jewish, fled to Hungary, where they were greatly assisted by the Hungarian government. The International Red Cross, Catholic Action, and various Polish relief organisations also lent assistance. The Hungarian Red Cross received support from sympathizers in England and the United States and especially from the pope, whose envoy, together with representatives from neutral countries, made regular visits to the refugee camps.[4]

Meanwhile, the persecution of the Church, which had been the hallmark of Nazi rule in Germany, Austria, and Czechoslovakia, was now, with even greater severity, extended to Poland. In the first month of the war, the Germans executed more than two hundred priests and imprisoned a thousand others. Many priests and several bishops were exiled, together with the primate, Cardinal Hlond, who was branded an enemy of Germany. The

[3] Ibid., 64.
[4] Nicholas Kallay, *Hungarian Premier* (London: Oxford University Press, 1954), 334.

former nuncio in Warsaw, Archbishop Cortesi, remained in Rumania to direct papal relief efforts from there. The leadership of the Polish Church, now that Hlond had been banished abroad, fell upon the shoulders of the courageous archbishop of Cracow, Prince Adam Sapieha. But Sapieha was, at all times, under the scrutiny of the Gestapo. Polish intellectuals, many of them priests, met their end in mass shootings or were sent to the concentration camp at Oranienburg. The Jagiellonian University in Cracow, one of the oldest in Europe, was shut down, and two hundred members of its staff banished to Sachsenhausen concentration camp, which eventually incorporated Oranienburg. The order had gone out from Hitler that the Polish intelligentsia, the nobility, and the clergy were to be eliminated, to forestall resistance that might be formed around them, a measure known euphemistically as "political housecleaning".[5] Frank, who was given to boasting, contended that if posters were to be put up to register the killings, there would not be enough forests in Poland with which to make the paper.[6]

By the end of October, of almost 700 priests of the diocese of Gnesen-Posen, 451 were in prison, 36 were missing or in exile, and 74 had either been shot or were confined to a concentration camp. Of almost 500 churches in the diocese, only 30 remained open.[7] In the diocese of Chelmno-Pelplin, a mere 20 of its 500 priests were still active in November. Of the remaining clergy, some had been murdered; others were

[5] From the testimony of Erwin Lahousen, Abwehr officer, given at Nuremberg, in James Owen, *Nuremberg: Evil on Trial* (London: Headline Review, 2007), 52–54.

[6] Quoted in ibid., 115.

[7] J. Noakes and G. Pridham, *Nazism*, vol. 3, *Foreign Policy, War and Racial Extermination* (Exeter: University of Exeter Press, 1983), 956, citing a contemporary church report.

exiled, in prison, or in hiding.[8] A concentration camp was opened in Bojanowo exclusively for nuns; in 1941 about 400 sisters were interred there.[9] Nuns in the eastern part of the country were, until 1941, deported to Russia, in some cases to Siberia, where they were put to manual work.[10]

For several days after the invasion of Poland, Pope Pius XII observed what Harold H. Tittmann has called "a prudent reserve". Mr. Tittmann was assistant to Myron Taylor, President Roosevelt's personal representative to Pius XII. He thus had an unrivalled insight into Vatican affairs. Tittmann suggests several reasons for Pius' initial silence on Poland, two of which were believed to be uppermost in the pope's mind. At the time, Mussolini was trying to broker a peace deal by bringing representatives of the governments of Great Britain, France, Germany, and Poland to the conference table. Although sceptical, "the Pope felt that, with the peace of the world at stake, he should take no steps, such as denouncing Nazi aggressions, which might interfere with any progress toward ending the war."[11] The pope also feared that such a denunciation would only bring greater affliction to the Polish population. In the event, his fears on this score proved to be well founded.

But factual information that could not long be ignored was coming out of Poland, conveyed to Rome by exiled Polish priests. When a report detailing evidence of German

---

[8] Pierre Blet, S.J., *Pius XII and the Second World War according to the Archives of the Vatican* (Herefordshire: Gracewing, 2003), 72–73.

[9] J. S. Conway, *The Nazi Persecution of the Churches, 1933–1945* (London: Weidenfeld and Nicolson, 1968), 325.

[10] Eva Fogelman, *Conscience and Courage: Rescuers of Jews during the Holocaust* (London: Victor Gollancz, 1996), 173.

[11] Harold H. Tittmann Jr., *Inside the Vatican of Pius XII: The Memoir of an American Diplomat during World War II* (New York: Image Books, 2004), 111.

atrocities committed against Poles and Jews was submitted to the Holy Father by Cardinal Hlond, Vatican Radio
was authorised to broadcast its contents. On 21 January
1940, the full extent of Poland's torment was revealed to a
shocked public worldwide.

Vatican Radio broadcasts were made in English,
French, Portuguese, German, and Polish. Other radio stations relayed the news, and newspapers gave the story mass
coverage. The *Manchester Guardian* of 24 January editori-
alised: "Tortured Poland has found a powerful advocate
in Rome." The same day, readers of the *New York Times*
were told, "It is now clear that the Papacy is throwing the
whole weight of its publicizing facilities into an exposé of
conditions."[12] As a result of the publicity, attitudes towards
Germany hardened, especially in Britain, where the
broadcasts were being exploited for propaganda purposes.
A high-level German army memorandum expressed the
concern that had taken hold in Germany over the broadcasts; at the same time, it betrayed some idea of the true
scope of the terror: "It is true that what the foreign radio
stations have broadcast so far is only a tiny fraction of what
has happened in reality."[13]

Alert to the fact that the Allies were reaping the benefits
of anti-German feeling, Hitler made angry representations
to the Holy See and threatened reprisals unless the broadcasts were brought to an end. In fact, reprisals were already
taking place. Soon Archbishop Sapieha of Cracow and the
Polish bishops were beseeching the pope to refrain from
speaking out. Vatican Radio was making matters worse,
as every broadcast brought in its wake terrible retaliations.

[12] Anthony Rhodes, *The Vatican in the Age of the Dictators, 1922–1945* (London: Hodder and Stoughton, 1973), 238; J. Derek Holmes, *The Papacy in the
Modern World* (London: Burns and Oates, 1981), 129.

[13] Quoted in Noakes and Pridham, *Nazism*, vol. 3, 938–39.

Fearing also a worsening of the situation in Germany if he did not comply, the pope yielded to Polish entreaties and the Nazi ultimatum and suspended the broadcasts.

In his Christmas message of 1939, the pope condemned the invasion of Finland, which Hitler had conceded to Stalin, among other territories, in a secret addendum to the Nazi-Soviet Pact. The pontiff went on to deplore the complete disregard for life, liberty, and human dignity, and specifically crimes committed against noncombatants, refugees, women, children, and the aged. Such acts, said the pope, "cry for the vengeance of God".

The pope protested the treatment of Poles and Jews when Ribbentrop visited Rome the following March; and the German foreign minister was handed a list of German atrocities committed in Poland. The pope was told he was meddling in politics. Ribbentrop then produced a list of his own, containing alleged atrocities committed by Poles against Germans. When the pope sought permission to send a papal delegate to Poland, Ribbentrop dismissed the request with the weak promise that the matter would be looked into. Ribbentrop's visit to Rome was represented by the German-controlled press in Poland as a sign of cooperation between the Holy See and Germany.[14]

Hoping to destroy both Churches in the Warthegau, Polish and German, Greiser issued a decree in September 1941, reducing them to private associations. The maintenance of monasteries, convents, and seminaries was henceforth prohibited, and Church charities were transferred to the Nazi Welfare Office. Two weeks later, the majority of what remained of the clergy was removed to Dachau. Only one bishop remained in the Warthegau, his activities

---

[14]Robert A. Graham, S.J., *The Pope and Poland in World War Two* (London: Veritas Foundation Publication Centre, 1968), 34.

severely hampered by the Gestapo. Monsignor Orsenigo's complaint to the Reich chancellery went unanswered. Deep concern was being expressed about the spiritual welfare of Catholics in the Warthegau, as the majority of priests had been murdered or were in prison.

Since the Vatican refused to recognize German sovereignty in the occupied territories, those territories did not come under the protection, dubious as that was, of the Reich concordat. Vatican representatives, consequently, were denied event the right of access to them. The Polish bishops were compelled to communicate with the Holy See via Orsenigo at the Berlin embassy. Protests were useless, as the annexed territories were deemed to lie outside Vatican jurisdiction, a point reiterated whenever Orsenigo raised the matter of the spiritual welfare of Catholics living there. Von Weizsäcker of the German Foreign Office believed the fanatical anti-Catholic Martin Bormann was responsible for this policy.[15]

Poles condemned to forced labour in Germany faced the cruelest discrimination. Prohibited from attending German churches, they remained confined to camps, where services were conducted by their own priests. German priests befriended the Poles but were not allowed to minister to them. The outstanding piety of the Poles made a great impression on German Catholics, who openly sympathised with them. The papal secretary, Maglione, on behalf of the pope asked Cardinal Bertram to intervene for them, but the pleas of Bertram and other German bishops having already been disregarded, there was nothing further to be done. The pope repeatedly petitioned the German bishops to defend the human rights of Poles, regardless of race or religion. Bishops Galen and Preysing in particular

---

[15] *The Memoirs of Ernst von Weizsäcker* (London: Victor Gollancz, 1951), 269.

each made a robust defence of their human rights. The regulations were eventually relaxed, but Polish-language services in German churches remained under a ban; not even the confessional was exempted.

In the summer of 1941, Cardinal Hlond raised the matter of the pope's supposed silence over Poland. In reply, Maglione pointed out that the pope had already spoken out on three occasions that year, first in an Easter message, then in a message addressed to the Eucharistic Congress in Saint Paul, Minnesota, and, finally, on the occasion of the feast of Saints Peter and Paul. Not confining himself to Poland, the pope had spoken out more generally on the subject peoples of the German occupation. Tardini thought a resounding public protest on behalf of Poland unnecessary. What is more, he said, it would simply inflame German sensibilities and would surely be exploited by the Allies. Further, an explicit protest would bring in its train inevitable reprisals against the already beleaguered Poles, and, crucially, would seriously jeopardize the Holy See's charitable work in Poland and its contact with the Polish bishops.[16]

By sponsoring a concert in 1942 given by the Polish pianist Mieczyslaw Horszowski, Pius XII affirmed his solidarity with the Polish people and contributed indirectly to the relief of Polish war victims, who were the beneficiaries of the proceeds from Horszowski's tour. The concert took place at the Pontifical Institute of Sacred Music. Afterwards, the pianist was received in audience by the pope, an event that was given maximum publicity in *L'Osservatore Romano*. In his Christmas message for that year, the pope again raised his voice on behalf of those "who without any fault on their part, sometimes only

---

[16]Blet, *Pius XII and the Second World War*, 87, quoting Tardini. See also Graham, *The Pope and Poland in World War Two*, 36–38.

because of their nationality or race have become con-
signed to death or slow decline". The German ambassador to the Holy See lodged an immediate protest, but the
Polish ambassador, Casimir Papée, thanked the pope pro-
fusely for his Christmas message and for all he had done
for the Polish nation.

Curiously enough, only weeks before, Wladyslaw
Raczkiewicz, the Polish president in exile, had ventured
to suggest that the pope should provide "words that
would clearly and distinctly indicate where the evil was
to be found, words that would stigmatize the authors of
the evil".[17] The pope replied, in effect, that ever since the
beginning of hostilities he had done just that. Unfortunately, papal messages of support to Poland only rarely
reached their destination, as the Germans sought to persuade the Poles of the pope's indifference to their situation. Pius' letters were usually confiscated by the Gestapo
and forwarded to Berlin. Copies of *Summi Pontificatus* were
falsified to give a pro-German slant, and forged reports circulated claiming papal support for Germany. Thus, a sense
of isolation was created among the oppressed population,
who did not know of the pope's refusal to recognize German sovereignty in Poland and who also were kept in
ignorance of the numerous diplomatic protests that passed
between Rome and Berlin. Weizsäcker confessed that of
the nuncio's many grievances, those regarding the spiritual
welfare of Polish prisoners and the fate of the Polish clergy
gave him the most trouble.[18]

In March 1943, Cardinal Maglione sent the Reich
government in Berlin a long and exhaustive letter of protest summarizing the Nazi persecution of the Church in

---

[17] Blet, *Pius XII and the Second World War*, 83.
[18] *The Memoirs of Ernst von Weizsäcker*, 282.

Poland. The Germans refused to accept the letter, and it was returned by Weizsäcker, but not before it had been studied by Ribbentrop. After the war, the document was used in evidence at the International Military Tribunal at Nuremberg.[19] A month earlier, Cardinal Maglione had proposed that Archbishop Sapieha make public some of the letters sent by the pope to the bishops in Poland. In this way, Maglione hoped to allay the complaints emanating from the Polish government in London. Sapieha's own idea was for the pope to write another letter, one that would summarize the contents of all his previous letters. The pope decided on a more direct approach. In an address to the College of Cardinals, but intended for a wider audience, Pius XII spoke out about the situation in Poland more forthrightly than previously. He recalled Christians to a consideration of all that he had said in the past, so that their judgements might be made in the light of a well-formed conscience. At the same time, the pope indicated his solicitude for those who were enduring persecution solely because of their nationality or race, and he condemned the Nazi policy of extermination.

The address was broadcast on Vatican Radio, and despite the severe penalties incurred in circulating printed matter without permission, fifty thousand copies were distributed secretly throughout Poland. Hlond and Sapieha were effusive in their praise; both described the address as "historic". The pope's words evidently contented those such as the exiled Bishop Radonski, President Raczkiewicz, and the Polish ambassador to the Holy See, Papée, who had previously expressed dissatisfaction with the pope's response to the plight of the Poles. Undersecretary Tardini thought

---

[19]Graham, *The Pope and Poland in World War Two*, 56–60. For a more detailed account, see Blet, *Pius XII and the Second World War*, 87–90.

them ungrateful, considering "everything the Holy See did and does for the Poles".[20]

It seems clear that the exiles in London had no more than an imperfect understanding of conditions in their homeland and were less informed than the pope. Lacking firsthand knowledge of the German occupation, Radonski's criticisms of the pope were based on false reports.[21] Unlike Cardinal Hlond, who had fled abroad, Radonski had been abroad when the Germans invaded and was refused reentry to the country. Papée was taking his instructions from the Polish government-in-exile in London. His representations to the Holy See, Harold Tittmann has noted, were at odds with those of the Polish bishops on the spot, who, fearing harsh German reprisals, did not wish the pope to make flaming protests.[22]

The Italian ambassador to the Holy See, Alfieri, seems to have been more appreciative of the need for caution. In May 1940, he observed: "We ought to speak words of fire against the atrocities in Poland, and the only thing which restrains us is the knowledge that words would make the fate of those wretches even worse."[23] Even Bishop Radonski admitted that he refrained from writing to his own diocesan clergy for fear of exposing them to certain persecution.[24] Archbishop Sapieha, it is true, had written to Maglione late in 1941, requesting a strong protest against the Germans. However, when almost a year later

[20]John Lukacs, "The Diplomacy of the Holy See during World War II", *Catholic Historical Review* 60, no. 2 (July 1974): 277. See also Graham, *The Pope and Poland in World War Two*, 40.

[21]Graham, *The Pope and Poland in World War Two*, 41–42.

[22]Tittmann, *Inside the Vatican of Pius XII*, 115.

[23]Quoted in Dan Kurzman, *A Special Mission: Hitler's Secret Plot to Seize the Vatican and Kidnap Pope Pius XII* (Cambridge, Mass.: Da Capo Press, 2007), 126.

[24]Graham, *The Pope and Poland in World War Two*, 46.

the pope wrote him a letter full of encouraging words, Sapieha replied regretting that he was unable to communicate its contents to his people, as such an act would be bound to provoke reprisals. Instead of petitioning the pope for "words of fire", which they knew would be followed by severe repercussions, Polish bishops and priests contented themselves with requests for material aid and for papal intercessions on behalf of Polish workers in Germany and priests in Dachau.

The Vatican had responded promptly to the need to supply food and clothing to Poland but had been frustrated in its efforts by German intransigence. The Germans later relented, and money and essential supplies were able to be sent to Poland through the agency of the American Commission for Polish Relief. There were several such agencies. Jews in particular benefitted from the work of the Special Commission of Assistance created by the Home Army in 1942 and code-named Zegota.

A major figure in the provision of relief was the Austrian-born Countess Karolina Lanckorońska, who was a close acquaintance from childhood of Archbishop Sapieha. Countess Lanckorońska was a volunteer nurse with the Polish Red Cross while secretly participating in the Polish Resistance. In 1941, the Main Council for Relief entrusted to her care all prisoners in the German-occupied territory. In this role she was successful in organizing extra food, and in the distribution of parcels and other forms of assistance, for approximately twenty-seven thousand prisoners. Many lives were saved as a result of her efforts. Countess Lanckorońska later suffered interrogation and was transferred from one place of detention to another. As an inmate of the women's concentration camp at Ravensbrück, she nursed the sick and the dying, among whom were women who had been made the unwilling victims of medical experiments. In Ravensbrück they were known as "rabbits".

An associate, Father Michael Rekas, was a professor at an underground Catholic seminary and chaplain to a hospital near L'vov when he founded a relief organisation known as the Apostolate of the Sick. With the assistance of Countess Lanckorońska, he arranged for the feeding of Poles, Jews, and Ukrainians and for the medical care of refugees. As a member of the Resistance, Countess Lanckorońska came into contact with the Jewish Committee, which regularly supplied her organisation with foodstuffs for imprisoned Jews. Those Jews who managed to avoid imprisonment were herded into ghettos in Polish cities, where they experienced the most serious privations and the most abominable treatment. The excessive nature of the cruelties enacted against the Jews aroused in many Poles feelings both of deep disgust and profound pity. Cardinal Hlond thought the brutality of the Nazis exceeded that of the Russians.

Any Pole caught sheltering or feeding Jews could expect a death sentence. Most cases were summarily dealt with, retribution taking the form of public executions. Typical was the fate of the citizens of Stary Ciepielów, who were suspected by the SS of sheltering Jews. Twenty-three villagers—men, women, and children—were herded into a barn, which was then set alight. All were burned alive. The following day, ninety-six men of the nearby village of Bialka were shot for aiding Jews.[25] Several Jews were publicly hanged in the town square of Lodz. Hanged with them were the Christian couple and their children who had given them shelter.[26] Rescue work entailed fearful risks,

[25] Martin Gilbert, *The Holocaust: The Jewish Tragedy* (London: Collins, 1986), 504.
[26] Fogelman, *Conscience and Courage*, 30.

for it was official Nazi practice to take reprisals against the families of those who were caught aiding Jews. Eva Fogelman, a historian of the Holocaust, observes:

> Yet remarkably, thousands of people continued to hide Jews. Attics, cellars, sewers, ditches, pigsties, haystacks, brothels, closets, pantries, space behind double walls, monasteries, convents, orphanages, schools and hospital quarantine rooms were converted into temporary shelters and long-term hideouts.[27]

In August 1942, when Jews by the thousand were being transported to the death camps of the General Government, the head of the Ukrainian Uniate church in Galicia, Metropolitan Andreas Szeptycki, was approached by two rabbis who asked if he would find a sanctuary for some Jewish children. He and his brother, Father Clement, the head of the Uniate monasteries, and their sister, Josepha, who was the mother superior of the Uniate nunneries, were successful in hiding 150 Jewish children. Rabbi Kahane, one of the men who had applied to Szeptycki, was among 21 Jews who found a refuge in the Uniate archbishop's residence. Twenty-eight others were hidden in the monastery of Saint Basilius disguised as monks.[28] Elsewhere, the Capuchin monastery in Cracow also provided a refuge for fugitive Jews. Approximately 200 convents, chiefly in and around Warsaw and in eastern Galicia, sheltered Jewish children.[29] Very often the rescuers were themselves the victims of persecution.

All told, Archbishop Szeptycki is credited with saving the lives of several hundred of his Jewish fellow citizens.

[27] Ibid., 30–31.

[28] Gilbert, *The Holocaust*, 410; Pinchas E. Lapide, *The Last Three Popes and the Jews* (London: Souvenir Press, 1967), 186.

[29] Lapide, *The Last Three Popes and the Jews*, 186–87; Fogelman, *Conscience and Courage*, 173.

Not to be outdone, his Latin Rite opposite number, Archbishop Boleslaw Twardowski of L'vov, sheltered Jewish families in his archbishop's palace.[30] In churches, monasteries, and convents throughout Poland, fugitive Jews found sanctuary and were fed and clothed. A priest of the Ostra Brauma Church in Vilna even set aside a room in his residence to serve as a synagogue. Karol Wojtyla, the future Pope John Paul II, was a student in an underground seminary who combined his studies with daytime work in a chemical factory. A leader in the Resistance, he was kept continually under German surveillance but was protected by Archbishop Sapieha. A former school friend recalls him rescuing many Jewish families from city ghettos and providing them with safe houses and new identities.[31] The Jewish historian Pinchas Lapide wrote:

> Hundreds of righteous priests, monks and nuns ... saved at least 15,000, but perhaps as many as 50,000 Polish Jews during the blood-stained years from 1940 to 1945.[32]

One of the most remarkable rescue operations conducted by an individual came to general notice as recently as 1999, when four Kansas schoolgirls began researching the life of Irena Sendler for a school project. Irena Sendler was the daughter of a Catholic doctor whose patients were mostly poor Jews. Posing as a sanitary worker, she rescued Jewish children of the Warsaw ghetto, smuggling them out to safety. Most of the children found a safe home with Catholic families and in convents, where, for their

[30] Lanckorońska, *Those Who Trespass against Us*, 315.

[31] Quoted in Mary Craig, *Man from a Far Country: A Portrait of Pope John Paul II* (London: Hodder and Stoughton, 1979), 49.

[32] Lapide, *The Last Three Popes and the Jews*, 187. See also Adam Zamoyski, *Poland: A History* (London: Harper Press, 2009), 322.

protection, they were given non-Jewish names. No one ever refused to take a child from her. Eventually captured, this courageous woman was cruelly tortured before being condemned to death. Her life was spared when the German officer in charge of the firing squad accepted a bribe. Even this experience did not deter Sendler from continuing her rescue efforts. She is believed to have saved the lives of some 2,500 children.[33]

More widely known after he was made the subject of a Stephen Spielberg film is Oskar Schindler, a German Catholic businessman of somewhat shady business dealings whose Cracow factory became an asylum for Jews. Schindler had Jews transferred from the nearby Plaszow labour camp to make up his workforce. They were well treated, and Schindler did all within his power to protect them. As the war drew to a close, he effected the removal of more than a thousand Jews—Schindler's List—to Moravia and safety.[34]

Rescue networks came into being through the labours of church and political groups and through concerned individuals. They were brought together under the umbrella of the Council for Aid to Jews. The organisation had been founded in Warsaw in December 1942, when many thousands of Jews were being taken from the Warsaw ghetto to the gas chambers at Treblinka. Numerous groups dedicated their efforts to the saving of Jewish children. One of the problems encountered in this type of rescue work arose from the reluctance of parents to give their children up if their destination was a Christian sanctuary. Some nuns evidently thought their duty required

[33] See the article "Just a Thought: She Saved 2,500 Children from Death", in *Alive* (September 2008).

[34] Biographical note on Schindler in James Taylor and Warren Shaw, *The Penguin Dictionary of the Third Reich* (London: Penguin Books, 1997).

them to save not only Jewish lives but their souls too.[35] But most seemed to have respected the children's Jewish faith. Priests taught children the Old Testament and arranged for visits by rabbis. Although efforts were later made to restore Jewish children to their rightful parents, this was not always possible. Inevitably, many children were orphaned by the war. Surrogate parents who had grown attached to their charges were sometimes reluctant to give them up, and in some cases, the real parents had to sue to get their children back.[36]

According to the historian Emanuel Ringelblum, thousands of Poles played a part in saving thousands of Jewish lives, in the Warsaw ghetto and countrywide. Ringelblum was executed in the latter part of the war, together with his wife and children and the Polish gardener who had given him shelter.[37] Yet, the courageous individuals who risked their lives for their Jewish neighbours accounted for only a small proportion of the total population— 1 percent at most, thought Ringelblum. And there was a darker side to the story. In Poland, as elsewhere under the Nazi yoke, the situation of Jews was exploited by the unscrupulous. Some individuals were only too eager to separate Jews from their property. Many did not scruple to betray Jews to the authorities, sometimes for money, but for other reasons too. Revenge attacks took place against Jewish Communists who had collaborated with the Soviets, and, in 1945, Jews were killed and had their synagogues burned in a pogrom by Polish militia.[38]

[35] Fogelman, *Conscience and Courage*, 216.

[36] Ibid., 348.

[37] Gilbert, *The Holocaust*, 661.

[38] Zamoyski, *Poland*, 340–41; also Lapide, *The Last Three Popes and the Jews*, 182–83.

By the end of the war, more than six and a quarter million Poles, a quarter of the total population, had been murdered, of whom three million were Jews. Of the 2,579 Catholic clergy detained in Dachau, nearly 70 percent were Polish; and Poles accounted for more than 80 percent of the 1,034 clergy who died there. Of the Catholic priests who either were shot out of hand or who perished in the concentration camps of the Third Reich, the majority were Poles.[39]

[39] Ernst Christian Helmreich, *The German Churches under Hitler* (Detroit: Wayne State University Press, 1979), 357–58.

5

Christian Witness in Occupied Western Europe

France

After the fall of France and the end of the Third Republic, the French National Assembly convened at the spa town of Vichy in the unoccupied zone and, by a majority of 569 votes to 80, granted full powers to the prime minister, Marshal Henri Philippe Pétain.

Pétain was then in his eighties; a World War I hero, he was arguably the most revered man in France. "Pétain is France, and France, today is Pétain", the archbishop of Lyons, Cardinal Gerlier, had enthused when the marshal paid a visit to Lyons in 1940. Neither Gerlier nor any of the bishops countenanced collaboration with Germany. At least some of them supported the leader of the Free French, General Charles de Gaulle, who, from his London exile and by courtesy of the BBC, was the voice of French resistance. The bishops nevertheless endorsed the Vichy government as being the duly constituted government of France. In fact, Vichy was widely endorsed, and even after the Germans partitioned the country and Vichy France became progressively the puppet of its German masters in the northern, occupied zone, Pétain's personal standing in the country remained high.

Even before the Germans overran northern France, French hostility to Hitlerism found an outlet in print. The journal *Etudes* published several critical pieces by Father Jules Lebreton, S.J., in early 1939. Afterwards, publications inimical to the new order perforce went underground, where they became one of the main foci of resistance. The tract *33 Conseils à l'occupé* (33 hints to the occupied) was in circulation in Paris at least as early as August 1940.[1] Clandestine newspapers—the work, in part, of trade unionists—began appearing in Paris in the autumn of 1940, shortly before the emergence of *Liberté*, the first underground newspaper of the unoccupied zone.[2] Some little time later, the texts of Vatican Radio broadcasts and letters of the German bishops were duplicated and distributed by a group of Paris students under the direction of Father Michael Riquet, S.J. The journal *La Question d'Israel* brought its publisher, Théomir Devaux of the Fathers of Notre-Dame-de-Sion, to the attention of the Gestapo in 1940.

A tract written by the left-wing poet Jean Casson, *La Vichy fait guerre* (Vichy wages war), achieved a wide circulation with the help of a group of the author's friends, who called themselves the Free French in France. The tract was the forerunner of the group's newspaper, *Resistance*, which appeared from December 1940 to late March 1941. The first editorial proclaimed: "Resist! In our anguish at the disastrous fate that has befallen our nation, this is our heartfelt cry." Advice was offered on how to build up groups and networks of resistance workers.[3] *Resistance*, and all similar publications, were distributed at considerable risk, as was

[1] Agnes Humbert, *Resistance: Memoirs of Occupied France* (London: Bloomsbury Publishing, 1946), 14.

[2] Julian Jackson, *France: The Dark Years, 1940–1944* (Oxford: Oxford University Press, 2001), 403.

[3] Humbert, *Resistance*, 309.

shown by the fate of Paul Petit, who distributed articles under the title *Résitance Spirituelle* until his arrest and imprisonment. He was subsequently beheaded on Hitler's orders.[4]

In November 1941, the Jesuit theologians of Lyons under the leadership of Father Pierre Chaillet, S.J., began to offer a more substantial critique of National Socialism in their underground journal, the *Cahiers du Témoignage Chrétien* (Notebooks of Christian witness). Warning of Nazi evils, in particular racialism, the essays appealed to the moral conscience of Christians and drew inspiration from papal and episcopal teaching as well as from Protestant sources. Not only Jesuits but other Christian writers contributed articles to the series, which continued to appear right up to the eve of the Liberation.

The progress of the *Cahiers*, and of much other underground literature, forms the subject matter of the book *Christian Resistance to Anti-Semitism* by the French Jesuit Father Henri de Lubac, who was himself a diligent coworker in the enterprise. With the covert support of parish priests and laypeople, the *Cahiers* found their way into all parts of France and even to countries abroad. The articles were read with approval by the pope and Cardinal Maglione and were warmly, though of necessity secretly, endorsed by members of the hierarchy in both zones of France. The first issue featured the cautionary article "France, Be Careful Not to Lose Your Soul", by Father Gaston Fessard, S.J., who concluded that collaboration with Pétain's government amounted to collaboration with Nazism.[5] But not everyone drew that conclusion. Pétain remained popular and continued to find support even among the Resistance.

[4]Henri de Lubac, S.J., *Christian Resistance to Anti-Semitism: Memories from 1940–1944* (San Francisco: Ignatius Press, 1990), 117.

[5]Jackson, *France: The Dark Years*, 418.

La Voix du Vatican (The voice of the Vatican), in the words of Father de Lubac "the true elder brother of the *Cahiers*", reproduced the pope's allocutions, especially his strictures on racialism and the Nazi superstition of blood. Published first in Avignon, where it was typed and mimeographed, it later issued forth from the printing press of Jules-Xavier Perrin of Marseilles. *La Voix du Vatican* enjoyed a wide circulation in the unoccupied zone.

In the early years, resistance was limited to a few individuals and small groups. It was very much low-key and hardly ever confrontational, the most notable exception being the Communist-led miners' strike of May 1941 in the occupied zone. Espionage was an important aspect in the north, where some networks forged links with de Gaulle's Free French in London and with British Intelligence. The Press and Information Bureau was set up in Lyons in Vichy France in 1942 and later transferred to Paris; it was largely concerned with propaganda, a matter that absorbed the Resistance in both zones of France. Christian Democrats, Socialists, Communists, and trade unionists all had underground publishing outlets. Not all were anti-Vichy, and only the Communists had links to a political party. French politics, according to H.R. Kedward, was the politics of resistance.[6] Membership in the Resistance never became the subject of episcopal prohibition. Indeed, Catholics were significantly represented from the outset and were in many cases its leaders.[7]

Communists who took part in the Resistance did so by flouting Communist Party policy, which was Stalin's policy. Taking its orders from Moscow, which had a treaty of

---

[6] H.R. Kedward, *Occupied France: Collaboration and Resistance, 1940–1944* (Oxford: Basil Blackwell, 1987), 57.

[7] Ibid., 48; de Lubac, *Christian Resistance to Anti-Semitism*, 230; Jackson, *France: The Dark Years*, 418.

friendship with Hitler and recognised the Vichy regime, the Communist Party in France remained docile during the first year of the occupation. It was only after Hitler's military offensive against the Soviet Union in June 1941, which put an end to the embarrassing Nazi-Soviet pact, that the French Communist Party abandoned its official passivity and henceforth devoted its resources to opposing the German occupation.

The military contribution of the Maquis was, as Julian Jackson has said, "infinitesimal". The British valued the Maquis chiefly as a source of information and were reluctant to arm it. Only after D-day, when the Germans were in retreat, did the Maquis offer any very significant military contribution to the struggle for liberation, though it did have other areas of concern. In the last stages of the occupation, it was engaged in a virtual civil war with France's collaborationist police force, the Milice.

In the general confusion following the fall of France, the situation of the Jews gave no immediate cause for alarm. There were no death squads employed in mass shootings, as in Poland; even the first anti-Jewish law, promulgated in October, occasioned little concern. The decree excluded Jews from public office, although it permitted exemptions in the case of those who had rendered exceptional service to France. An edict of the following June, superseding the previous one, increased the number of occupations barred to Jews and brought forth protests from the papal nuncio and from Cardinal Gerlier.[8]

In May 1942, French police in the occupied zone began to arrest foreign Jews, mostly Poles and Czechs. Wholesale arrests continued until August, the largest roundups

---

[8] Pierre Blet, S.J., *Pius XII and the Second World War according to the Archives of the Vatican* (Herefordshire: Gracewing, 2003), 233.

occurring on 16 and 17 July. The victims—men, women and children—were deported from France during the course of the year, most from the camp at Drancy in the southwest of the country. Several intercessions made on their behalf by the papal nuncio, Archbishop Valerio Valeri, came to nought. On 22 July, Cardinal Suhard of Paris and the cardinals and bishops of the occupied zone responded with an "anguished appeal" addressed to the head of state, Marshal Pétain:

> Profoundly shocked by the mass arrests and the inhuman treatment meted out to the Jews, we cannot stifle the outcry of our conscience. In the name of humanity and Christian principles, we raise our protest.[9]

Four weeks later, Catholic and Protestant church leaders met with Marshal Pétain to voice their concern. Clearly upset, Pétain explained that the arrests had been made in response to German demands. As the principal spokesman for the Catholic hierarchy, Cardinal Suhard continued to speak out, although Jewish leaders requested that he not do so, as they feared reprisals would more than likely be made against Jewish families still in hiding. Infuriated by the fact that Jews were evading capture, in August the Germans ordered the arrest of all Catholic priests suspected of sheltering them. Of those arrested, one, a Jesuit, had personally saved eighty Jewish children from deportation.[10] Many thousands of foreign Jews found a haven. It was not only churchmen who assisted them; an honourable minority of French men and women from all walks

[9] Quoted in Pinchas E. Lapide, *The Last Three Popes and the Jews* (London: Harper Press, 2009), 191.

[10] Martin Gilbert, *The Holocaust: The Jewish Tragedy* (London: Collins, 1986), 437.

of life came to their aid. The Young Christian Workers (Jocists) were deeply involved in rescuing Jews. Parish priests combined with their parishioners in setting up rescue networks. Jewish children were concealed in Catholic schools and orphanages and given false names, an arrangement attributable in large part to Cardinal Suhard. The houses of religious orders, including nunneries, not only sheltered Jews, but became factories for the production of false identity papers and work permits. Protestants, a minority in France, also provided outstanding examples of help in every aspect of rescue.

When the roundup of the Jews of Vichy France began on 2 August, it was protested by the pope on two occasions through his envoy, Archbishop Valeri. The papal protest, which the Vichy press was forbidden to publish, was rejected by the foreign minister, Pierre Laval. It did, however, find its way onto Allied radio and to the French underground press.

On 17 August, Grand Rabbi Jacob Kaplan described to Cardinal Gerlier the harrowing scenes taking place at the railway station and communicated the intelligence that Jews were being deported, not to Poland for "ethnic regrouping", as was commonly supposed, but to Germany to be exterminated. Kaplan said the information was reliable, and he revealed its source to be the grand rabbi of France, Isaiah Schwartz.[11] Profoundly disturbed by the news, Gerlier got in touch with Pastor Boegner of the Council of the Protestant Federation, with whom he was in regular contact. The two churchmen agreed to send, independently, a written protest to the head of state, Gerlier on behalf of the archbishops of the unoccupied zone, and Boegner on behalf of the Protestant Federation.

[11] De Lubac, *Christian Resistance to Anti-Semitism*, 149–60.

Although sympathetic, Pétain intimated that matters were beyond his control and subsequently attempted to justify his passivity to Rome through Leon Berard, Vichy's minister to the Holy See, citing the "difficult circumstances" that beset him. Maglione rebuffed him, however.[12]

The first deportations from the unoccupied zone were made from the diocese of Archbishop Jules-Gérard Saliège of Toulouse. Saliège was an old man and in such a reduced state of health that he was unable to walk. He nevertheless was able to mount a robust defence of moral values. He had early made known his position on "the new heresy of Nazism". In the diocesan bulletin of Toulouse for 12 April 1933, he wrote:

> Catholicism cannot agree that belonging to a specific race places men in a position of inferior rights. It proclaims the essential equality of all races and all individuals.[13]

Now, from the pulpit of his cathedral in Toulouse, into which he had been borne on a stretcher, Saliège denounced the roundup and deportation of Jews. He ordered his protest to be read from the pulpits of his diocesan clergy, and the pope had it broadcast on Vatican Radio.

Letters of protest by other members of the Vichy hierarchy quickly followed. Although the archbishop of Toulouse had provided the lead, there had been prior agreement about the course of action to be taken. Bishop Théas of Montauban responded a week later with what was generally considered to be the strongest letter. Those of Cardinal Gerlier and Bishop Delay of Marseilles followed on 6 September. Bishops Moussaron of Albi and Vanstenberghe of Bayonne issued their protests on 20 September.

[12] Ibid., 161–62.
[13] Ibid., 148.

Excerpts from the letters of Gerlier and Théas were broadcast by the BBC. On 4 October, the protest of the National Council of the Reformed Church was read out in all Protestant churches.

Pius XII indicated his approval of these actions in a personal message relayed to Marshal Pétain by the nuncio, who petitioned Pétain to intervene in the interests of the Jews. But Pétain was weak and ineffectual, rapidly becoming no more than a background figure. Laval was the prime enforcer of German demands, and he was adamant that the Jews must leave France. When Laval ordered the deportation of twenty thousand Jews, he was attacked on Vatican Radio.

On 9 September, it was reported in the *New York Times* that a rift had opened up between the Vichy government and the Church, as a result of Catholic priests' continuing to shelter Jews in defiance of the order requiring them to hand the Jews over. The Jesuit order provided hiding places for several hundred children; and, all told, more than 120 priests were deported east for the crime of hiding children in their presbyteries. Cardinal Gerlier scorned Laval's edict by offering his protection to the children of Jews who had been evicted and who now were being sheltered in Catholic homes.

Meanwhile, in the occupied zone, Cardinal Suhard of Paris appealed to Catholics to offer their assistance to fugitive Jews. The response was overwhelming. "Every Catholic family shelters a Jew", complained the pro-Nazi journalist Jacques Marey.[14] "A declaration of war by several Princes of the Church" was how the Nazi journal *Au Pilori* described the situation in the two zones, and it demanded the head of Gerlier, "the raving Talmudist".[15]

---

[14] Lapide, *The Last Three Popes and the Jews*, 193.
[15] Ibid.

The great roundup of 1942 led to the growth of organisations whose sole purpose was to rescue Jews. One concern, operated by Varian Fry, an American citizen based in Marseilles, devoted itself principally, but not exclusively, to the rescue of intellectuals and political opponents of Hitler. The writers Thomas Mann and Franz Werfel made their escape with the assistance of Fry. Groups that had been formed, for the most part, to meet the needs of refugees who came flooding into France were adapted to the new situation. The Protestant organisation Cimade, which had confined its activities to the welfare of inmates of internment camps, not only Jews but all refugees from Nazism, now, with the cooperation of willing pastors, found safe homes for Jewish children. Father Chaillet, who had been the principal inspiration behind the *Cahiers*, acted as secretary to the Lyons-based Council of Assistance for Refugee Christians, which had Cardinal Gerlier and Pastor de Pury as patrons. This became the Council of Assistance for Émigrés, to contend with the large numbers of Jews seeking help. With the active support of Gerlier, Chaillet was able to hide more than two hundred children in the region of Lyons. This was only a fraction of the eighteen hundred Jews that Chaillet is thought to have rescued.

The main Jewish network was the Children's Relief Organisation (OSE), which was initially entrusted with the task of improving the conditions of children in the camps. The organisation had legal status. Organisations devoted to welfare, such as the Quakers, the Unitarians, the French Red Cross, and the Secours Suisse, came under the umbrella of the Nîmes Committee, a collaborative Christian / Jewish endeavour of which Donald Lowrie of the YMCA was president and organizer. But soon the OSE was engaged in the illegal work of rescuing and hiding children. Obliged to quit its Paris headquarters after the German occupation, the OSE had moved south into the unoccupied zone, becoming established in Montpelier. Here, the organisation was greatly assisted by Archbishop Saliège and Bishop Théas, who directed their diocesan convents and religious houses to open their doors to Jewish children.[16]

Five hundred children found a haven in various schools and religious houses through the rescue operation established in Nice by Moussa Abadi, a Syrian Jew, and with the authorisation of the local bishop, Monsignor Paul Rémond. Abadi was able to call on help from various sources, Catholic, Protestant, and Jewish. His base of operations was a room set aside for him in the house of Bishop Rémond. Abadi was able to come and go as he pleased in his capacity as inspector of independent education, a bogus office and title invented by Rémond.

An escape network in the region of Lyons was organised by Georges Garel, a Jewish engineer, who, in collaboration with Saliège, succeeded in rescuing about sixteen hundred children. Garel had earlier taken part, with Abbé Alexandre Glasberg and OSE agents, in the daring rescue of around a hundred children who were being interned in a disused barracks near Lyons. The children were hidden in Catholic homes and religious houses through the efforts of Amitié Chrétienne (Christian Friendship) operatives. Religious networks, working closely with Jewish groups, were successful in saving some seven thousand Jewish children living in France.[17] Garel was generous in acknowledging the help he received: "In every department or diocese there was a religious or lay, public or

[16]Eva Fogelman, *Conscience and Courage: Rescuers of Jews during the Holocaust* (London: Victor Gollancz, 1996), 339–40.
[17]Ibid., 209.

private charity or institution which involved itself in the protection of our children."[18]

Nice was an important centre of Vichy resistance. It was the location for an underground printing press, which, while it was operational, produced around 2,000 false identity cards, 1,230 false birth certificates, and almost 1,000 false baptismal certificates, in addition to other useful false documents.[19] Similar work was undertaken in Lyons, where the forging of false identity papers became a specialty of the nuns of the order of Notre-Dame-de-Sion. Their confreres in the Paris convent of the order specialised in procuring families willing to take in Jews. In this way, they were instrumental in rescuing hundreds of children.

Amitié Chrétienne was, like the OSE, a legal body that engaged in illegal undercover operations. Indeed, it is thought to have been the first welfare body to have broadened its scope to embrace the illegal activity of rescue. A coalition of Catholic, Protestant, and Jewish workers, Amitié Chrétienne was the inspiration of a Protestant, Gilbert Beaujolin, and a Catholic, Olivier de Pierrebourg. Father Chaillet and Abbé Alexandre Glasberg were involved in the work, which was sponsored by Gerlier and Boegner. Amitié Chrétienne operated throughout the whole of Vichy, where it maintained formal links with Jewish groups. Its overt legal purpose was related to the welfare of refugees, but its raison d'être found expression in its opposition to anti-Semitism and in its underground work in helping Jews evade arrest and transportation.

Jean Weidner, a Dutch Seventh-day Adventist who ran a textile business in Lyons, was a friend of Gilbert

---

Beaujolin. Weidner joined Amitié Chrétienne and, with the Dutch diplomat Arie Sevenster, created an escape network for Dutch refugees known as the Dutch-Paris network. Salomon Noach, a Dutch businessman living in Lyons who joined the organisation, was particularly effective in raising funds and in procuring false identity papers. After 1942, Weidner expanded the scope of his operations to create a network devoted to helping refugees cross the border into neutral Switzerland. Family members, friends, local farmers and traders, and staff from the Seventh-day Adventist College at Collognes on the border with Switzerland all immersed themselves in Weidner's rescue work.[20] Providing escape routes into neutral Switzerland engaged many, especially in the border region, where churches, monasteries, Protestant parsonages, and private homes undertook the risk of hiding refugees until such time as they could be safely transferred out of the country. Mostly young people, often Jewish and Christian Boy Scouts, acted as guides. The operation cost lives, as the danger of betrayal was ever present.

In November 1942, the Germans occupied the southern zone of France, and early the following year, Amitié Chrétienne was closed down after the Gestapo raided its premises. One of the directors, Joseph Rovan, bravely defied the curfew to retrieve key documents, including a stash of false identity papers, before the Gestapo could lay hands on them. Other papers linking Amitié Chrétienne to the Resistance were secreted on the person of Father Chaillet, who, while in detention, managed to eat them without arousing suspicion.[21]

---

[20] Bob Moore, *Survivors: Jewish Self-Help and Rescue in Nazi-Occupied Western Europe* (Oxford: Oxford University Press, 2010), 58–60.

[21] De Lubac, *Christian Resistance to Anti-Semitism*, 133–34.

Compulsory labour service for Germany (STO) came into force in France in February 1943, voluntary recruitment having fallen short of demand. The service originated in the need to supply for Germany's depleted industrial reserves and to free German industrial workers for military service. Attitudes to the STO differed markedly. It was protested by Cardinals Suhard, Gerlier, and Lienart, and although the remaining bishops did not condemn it, neither did they condemn its evasion. Some young men fled to the woods and hills to avoid being conscripted. Some felt constrained by duty to go; still others left in a spirit of adventure. Church authorities shared in the widespread fear that if men refused to leave for labour service, women would be taken instead.[22] Albert Speer was of the opinion that the STO was largely counterproductive, as French armaments workers went into hiding to avoid the possibility of being conscripted, thus leaving the French factories seriously undermanned.[23] Nevertheless, thousands of young men went off to work in Germany, not all unwillingly, and about two hundred priests volunteered to go with them as chaplains.

A quite different form of foreign service was inspired by the German offensive against Russia in the summer of 1941. The crusade against Bolshevism, as some saw it, evoked a response in certain Frenchmen whose support for Pétain's authoritarian regime owed more to their fear of Communism than to anything else. Such a man was the aged Cardinal Baudrillart, rector of the Catholic Institute in Paris, and a vociferous supporter of the French Legion (LVF), the volunteer force recruited to fight for Germany

[22] Richard Vinen, *The Unfree French: Life under the Occupation* (London: Allen Lane, 2006), 258.

[23] Albert Speer, *Inside the Third Reich* (London: Weidenfeld and Nicolson, 1970), 309.

against the Communists in Russia. None of the bishops, apart from Baudrillart, lent their support to the legion, which was not allowed to have chaplains. Neither did Pétain support it.

Cardinal Baudrillart's speeches and writings aroused much controversy. Father Graham, S.J., relates how a delegation of diocesan priests told Cardinal Suhard they would refuse to send students to the Catholic Institute if the rector continued in the same vein.[24] Suhard wanted the pope to silence Baudrillart but was told that since he, Suhard, was archbishop of the diocese, the responsibility rested with him. The learned Baudrillart was by no means pro-German. He inveighed against Nazi atrocities in Poland and had denounced Hitler and his anti-Semitic ideology in an article written two years before the occupation of France. His death on 23 May 1942 spared the French Church further embarrassment.

The same month that the STO came into force saw the resumption of the deportations. But the French police, who had experienced few scruples about rounding up foreign Jews, now displayed a stubborn reluctance to take part in the arrest of French Jews. The work was carried out by German police with the cooperation of the collaborationist Milice. The head of the Jewish Evacuation Department, Adolf Eichmann, demanded that the operation be speeded up, so the arrests proceeded with even more than the accustomed ruthlessness. Protests soon followed. The clandestine journal *Courrier Français du Témoignage Chrétien* (French mail of Christian witness) was founded this year. *Courrier* number 4 warned of "the progressive invasion of the Hitlerian poison into French souls" and reminded its

---

[24]Robert A. Graham, S.J., *The Vatican and Communism during World War II* (San Francisco: Ignatius Press, 1996), 91.

readers of the Catholic Church's position on the persecution of Jews:

> The judgement has been pronounced: they [deportations]
> are contrary to the law; they are unjust; no one is bound
> by conscience to submit to them.[25]

Then, in a broadcast beamed to France, Vatican Radio
pronounced:

> He who makes a distinction between Jews and other
> men is unfaithful to God and is in conflict with God's
> commands.[26]

Jews fleeing persecution found a haven in the southeast
of the country, where the Italians were in control. More
than once, the Italian military resorted to force to frus-
trate the Vichy police. As a result, Jews flocked into the
Italian zones. The Italian authorities were under pressure
from Berlin to hand over Jews and from the Vatican to
spare them. Some thirty thousand Jews were transferred
to the Italian zone through the mediation of Father Pierre
Marie-Benoît, a Capuchin friar from Marseilles. When
the Gestapo came to carry out arrests, the Italians refused
their cooperation, and the planned evacuation of the area
was obstructed by Italian troops. In vain did Ribbentrop
complain to Mussolini. Il Duce consistently refused German demands for the deportation of Jews but ordered his

---

[25] Quoted in de Lubac, *Christian Resistance to Anti-Semitism*, 40.

[26] Monsignor Stephen M. DiGiovanni, H.E.D., "Pius XII and the Jews:
The War Years as Reported by the *New York Times*", no. 48, citing a Vatican
Radio broadcast as reported in the *New York Times*, in *Rutgers Journal of Law
and Religion*, accessed 31 August 2015, http://lawandreligion.com/.

generals in the Italian zone to save Jewish lives regardless of their nationality.[27]

Father Marie-Benoît, with the aid of his associates, who were many and eminent, conducted an important rescue mission from his monastery in Marseilles, churning out hundreds of false passports and identity papers and organizing underground escape routes, which took Jews, Allied airmen, and other fugitives from Nazism out of the country and into neutral Spain and Switzerland. Constantly on the run from the Gestapo, Father Marie-Benoît turned up in Rome, where he continued his clandestine operations, providing false papers for hundreds of Jews while working for the Jewish Emigrants Aid Society (DELASEM). His scheme to evacuate all the Jews of southern France to Allied-controlled North Africa had the backing of the pope and the British government, but Italy surrendered to the Allies on the eve of the planned evacuation, after which the Germans overran the Italian zone.

The precise number of French citizens who offered their protection to Jews in this dark period of history will never be known. The scale of some rescue operations was astonishing. Father Marie-Benoît and his helpers are a case in point. No less remarkable was the collaborative effort of the villagers of the Protestant region of Le Chambon-sur-Lignon. Led by their pastor, André Trocmé, they were successful in hiding several thousand Jews during the occupation. Sometimes there was a price to be paid. The Portuguese consul in Bordeaux, Aristides de Sousa Mendes, aided by his wife and sons, issued thousands of signed entry visas, contrary to the orders of his government. It was mostly Jews who benefited, but other fugitives from Nazism also

---

[27]Nicholas Farrell, *Mussolini* (London: Weidenfeld and Nicolson, 2003), 366. See also Gilbert, *The Holocaust*, 531, 543.

received help. Portuguese consuls in Toulouse, Bayonne, and Marseilles issued visas without authorisation. The official in Marseilles and the consul in Luxembourg were both relieved of their posts. Mendes' personal and professional reputation suffered as a result of his humanitarian work. On his return to Lisbon, he faced disgrace and eventual ruin.[28] "The acts of courage and devotion were innumerable, and many will never come to light", wrote Pinchas Lapide of the French occupation. They bore much fruit; for more than two hundred thousand Jews, three-quarters of those living in France when the Germans invaded, outlived the occupation.

Belgium

Unlike most German armies of occupation, the military administration of Belgium and northern France was noted for its humanity. The military governor, General Alexander von Falkenhausen, was a professional soldier whose associates included Germans who plotted to overthrow Hitler. Not surprisingly, he was kept under Gestapo surveillance.[29] Although Falkenhausen, in obeying orders, authorised the removal of Jews from Belgium, it is incontestable that many Jews owed their lives to his protection.[30]

The Belgian government had created an extensive relief organisation to ease the situation created by the influx of refugees. Seventeen thousand German Jews were included

---

[28] Moore, *Survivors*, 247; also Fogelman, *Conscience and Courage*, 200–1.

[29] Ger van Roon, *German Resistance to Hitler: Count von Moltke and the Kreisau Circle* (London: Van Nostrand Reinhold, 1971), 209–10.

[30] See Falkenhausen's entry in Robert S. Wistrich, *Who's Who in Nazi Germany* (London: Routledge, 2002).

in their number. The Communists had an organisation in place to help all refugees, whereas the Committee for the Defence of Jews (CDJ) confined itself exclusively to assisting Jews. The Catholic bishops ordered monasteries and convents to open their doors and provide shelter to Jews. The CDJ located hiding places, warned of imminent arrests, and provided Jews with money and false documents. The primate, Cardinal van Roey, opened an account in his own name with the National Bank of Belgium, which enabled the Jewish Aid Committee to deposit funds required for its operations. As in France, welfare and rescue operations involved Jewish and non-Jewish groups working together. But there was a good deal of cooperation all round, and Catholics worked in conjunction with Communists. A Communist, Hertz Jospa, led the Independent Front (FI), whose members were recruited from across the political spectrum.[31]

Van Roey vehemently repudiated Nazi race theory when it was introduced into Belgium. His protest received the approbation of the pope, who ensured that it was reproduced in *L'Osservatore Romano* and transmitted on Vatican Radio. Van Roey was also forthright in his denunciation of the Rexists, the Belgian Fascist Movement, whose leader, Léon Degrelle, was excommunicated in 1943. When several Jewish leaders, including the acting chief rabbi, Salomon Ullmann, were thrown into prison, van Roey was successful in obtaining their release. He intervened, alas without success, when on 18 December 1942, Jews were arrested for transportation east. For his pastoral letters, van Roey drew inspiration from the Holy Father's Christmas messages. Publication of the pope's words was forbidden in Belgium, and the numerous diplomatic representations

[31] Moore, *Survivors*, 175.

of the Holy See in the interests of Jewish deportees and prisoners of war were not generally known.

Hundreds of Jewish children and some adults found sanctuary and protection through the network created by Bishop Kerkhofs of Liège in collaboration with the Catholic lawyer Albert van den Berg and through the active cooperation of the bishop's many associates, both religious and lay. Bishop Kerkhof's contacts included those from among the German military authorities, and his numerous interventions on behalf of Jews sometimes paid off. There was no kind of resistance activity that the network declined to undertake. His diocesan priests rallied to his support, immersing themselves in rescue work of one sort or another. More than a hundred were arrested, and a third of these died in captivity.[32]

Belgian resistance was marked by a high degree of clerical participation and by the cooperation established between the clergy and their congregations. Many clergy formed what has been called a "secret association" of priests dedicated to the rescue of Jews, while others acted in their own behalf. Regular contact was made with the CDJ and the umbrella organisation L'Aide Chrétienne aux Israelites (ACI). Some priests involved their close relatives in their secret undertakings. Father Emile Boufflette died in captivity in 1943 at age thirty-three, after a lengthy involvement in various forms of resistance. Assisted by family members, he is believed to have rescued around a thousand Jews. His coreligionist Father Joseph Peters arranged for four hundred fugitives to be given sanctuary and provided with false papers. He too paid with his life when he was executed in Liège on 31 August 1943. Fathers Boufflette and Peters are merely representative of many priests

[32] Ibid., 196–97.

who cannot be named for reasons of space.[33] Unlike other countries of the German occupation, the penalty in Belgium for hiding Jews only rarely led to a death sentence but, due to the comparative leniency of General Falkenhausen's military administration, might entail no more than a few weeks in prison.[34]

Most rescue networks in Belgium, being geared to the need to save children, were overwhelmingly female in membership and often headed by women. Andrée Guelen Herscovici, a schoolteacher, was a resourceful operative working with the CDJ who persuaded Jewish parents to part with their children, found them safe homes, and kept secret the records of their hiding places.[35] Jewish families were more inclined to part with their children if they could be entrusted to the care of women, which partly explains the success of Andrée Guelen Herscovici. The Belgian queen provided an inspirational role model for women by taking an active part in the work. It was due to the intervention of Queen Elizabeth that the Nazi authorities at the Malines deportation centre were induced to spare children under the age of six. The children were subsequently placed in orphanages, and adult Jews over sixty-five were found places in homes for the elderly. In the quest to save Jewish lives, the nuns of the order of Notre-Dame-de-Sion deserve special mention. The activities of their coreligionists in Paris and in Lyons have already been noted; in Belgium the sisters were responsible for carrying out the audacious rescue of two hundred Jewish children from trains destined for the east. The children were subsequently found hiding places in various convents throughout Belgium.

[33] Ibid., 197–98.
[34] Ibid., 202.
[35] Fogelman, *Conscience and Courage*, 340–41, footnote.

Jewish parents were understandably fearful lest their children lose their Jewish identity, although their fears appear to have been largely without foundation. Pinchas Lapide recounts the case of Abbé Louis Celis, who took in four Jewish children and cared for them for three years until the end of the war, when he helped them emigrate to Israel. The children, two boys and two girls, were raised as Jews. Abbé Celis heard their prayers, taught them Hebrew and the Torah, and even arranged a Bar Mitzvah for one of the boys.[36] Many children survived owing to the combined efforts of Abbé Joseph André and the bishop of Namur, Monsignor Charue, who were materially assisted by the Jesuit fathers and the Sisters of Charity. The children's material welfare was provided for, and Abbé André himself ensured that they received a sound Jewish education.[37] Father Celis and Father André were not exceptional but rather representative of many Christian clergy who behaved rightly towards their Jewish charges.

Before the Germans invaded, there were about ninety thousand Jews living in Belgium, of whom only 10 percent were Belgian citizens. Most of the others were from Eastern European countries, with a predominance of Poles. Three-quarters of the total number, some sixty-five thousand persons—men, women and children—survived. Citing Jewish sources, Pinchas Lapide attributes the survival of so many of Belgium's Jews to two reasons: (1) the protection afforded many of them by Falkenhausen at the instigation of the queen and Cardinal van Roey and (2) the role of Belgium's bishops in actively promoting the rescue efforts of their clergy.[38] The Belgian hierarchy

---

[36] Lapide, *The Last Three Popes and the Jews*, 207–8.

[37] Ibid., 207. See also Fogelman, *Conscience and Courage*, 249.

[38] Lapide, *The Last Three Popes and the Jews*, 204.

was greatly heartened by the unwavering support of Pope
Pius XII. Paul van Zeeland, a former Belgian prime minister, commented:

> We have always found in the acts and messages of the
> Pope and of our princes of the Church, the moral con-
> demnation unqualified and implacable, which the iniqui-
> tous treatment of the Jewish people deserved.[39]

The Netherlands

Jews in prewar Holland comprised about 11 percent of the
population. They enjoyed an equality with their fellow
Dutch citizens, not least in Amsterdam, where most Jews
lived. There was a Dutch National Socialist Party, but it
remained largely ineffectual. As early as 1934, Catholics
were warned by their bishops that they faced stiff canon-
ical penalties if they joined it. The National Socialists
made modest progress in the provincial elections of 1935,
when they gained 8 percent of the vote. Significantly, this
was halved two years later, after the party endorsed anti-
Semitic policies.

The persecution of the Jews followed immediately
upon the German subjugation of the Netherlands in 1940,
and, contrary to general practice, no distinction was made
between Dutch Jews and those of foreign extraction. The
Catholic bishops lodged a formal protest as soon as race
laws were introduced into the country. When in October public-sector workers were compelled to reveal their
racial origins, the measure was protested by the Dutch
Reformed church. The ordinance was merely a preamble

---

[39] Quoted in ibid., 206.

to a later one requiring the forcible removal of all Jews from teaching and civil-service posts.

The Dutch police for the most part collaborated willingly with the Reich authorities. The ranks of the force were swelled by Dutch Nazi Party members and further complemented by the addition of German military police. A callous indifference to suffering and an unconcealed anti-Semitism accompanied many police acts.[40] There were some notable exceptions, however. In the autumn of 1941, and again in the spring of 1943, police officers declined to cooperate when ordered to seize Jews. A separate incident in February 1943 involved six Catholic police officers who refused to comply with orders, taking inspiration from directives set forth in a pastoral letter that had been read out in church the previous Sunday.[41] Policemen gave warning of imminent raids, and many an officer turned a blind eye to suspicious-looking documents.[42]

Police collaboration with the Reich was impacted most crucially in Amsterdam, where most of Holland's Jews were concentrated. To facilitate matters, the mayor and the chief of police were removed from office by the Gestapo, which administered the country after the withdrawal of the Wehrmacht. Gestapo nominees filled the void. Removing politically suspect officials was a Nazi policy that was sometimes extended to the working population. New regulations restricting the movement of Jews became a daily occurrence. First theatres and cinemas became off-limits; then bicycles had to be handed over, and Jews were forbidden to buy petrol. In the autumn of 1941, it became

[40] Benno Gitter, *The Story of My Life* (London: Weidenfeld and Nicolson, 1998), 57–58.
[41] Bob Moore, *Victims and Survivors: The Nazi Persecution of the Jews in the Netherlands 1940–1945* (London: Arnold, 1997), 200.
[42] Ibid. See also Gitter, *The Story of My Life*, 58.

mandatory for Jews to wear the yellow Star of David. At the same time, a curfew was imposed from eight in the evening until eight the following morning.[43]

The Jews fought against these measures, forging alliances with Gentile sympathizers. Fierce riots broke out in the capital in February 1941. Posters appeared blazoning, "Don't Touch Them!" and "Even If They Are Dirty Jews—They Are Our Jews!"[44] A general strike was called in Amsterdam in a demonstration of solidarity with the Jews, which quickly spread to other parts of the country. As railways, shipyards, and armaments factories were hit, hundreds of Netherlanders were arrested. In the end, the strike did nothing to improve conditions but rather made matters worse as anti-Jewish regulations were enforced with even greater severity.

The following February, officials of the Catholic and Reformed churches presented Seyss-Inquart, of Austrian notoriety, now the Reich commissioner for the Netherlands, with a joint protest regarding the treatment of Holland's Jews. After the evictions commenced later that year, a second protest letter found its way onto Seyss-Inquart's desk. To soothe matters, the Reich commissioner's office gave assurances that exemptions from deportation would be made in the case of baptised Jews and Jews of mixed marriages. The Reich authorities dragged their feet, however, and the baptised Jews and Jews who were married to Christians were left languishing in prison. Following a suggestion from officials of the Reformed church, Protestant and Catholic bishops agreed that the last protest letter, which had been addressed to Seyss-Inquart through

---

[43] Jews who survived the persecution in the Netherlands and have written about their experiences include Benno Gitter and Johanna-Ruth Dobschiner, author of *Selected to Live.*

[44] Gitter, *The Story of My Life,* 65.

internal channels, should now be made public. Informed of the plan, the deputy Reich commissioner, Fritz Schmidt, warned of dire consequences should the letter be read out in Christian churches, as was the intention.

Despite the warning, the Catholic hierarchy went ahead as planned, and the parochial clergy were directed to read the letter of protest from their pulpits. This was done on Sunday, 26 July. The letter expressed the bishops' concern that Jews in the Netherlands were being excluded from participation in the normal life of the nation. It noted with horror that entire families were being shipped to Reich territory and subject territories. It pointed out that such measures were in conflict with the moral consciousness of the Dutch people; and it beseeched the Reich authorities, as a matter of urgency, not to put them into effect.[45]

Seyss-Inquart took his revenge a few days later by ordering the arrest of all Jews who were baptised Catholics; they were then deported east from Westerbork transit camp. About a hundred people were affected. They included the saint and philosopher Edith Stein, a nun of the order of Discalced Carmelites, who, like the other deportees, died in Auschwitz. The Dutch Reformed church took a different line and, in refraining from making a public protest, undoubtedly saved lives, if only for a time. Dutch Jews of the Protestant faith were eventually deported in September 1944.[46]

Resistance in the Netherlands took diverse forms and was not at first directed to the rescue of Jews. An initial show of defiance was manifested in activities such as pamphleteering, civil disobedience, and even armed

---

[45] Guido Knopp, *Hitler's Holocaust* (Stroud, UK: Sutton, 2004), 243; Moore, *Victims and Survivors*, 127–28.

[46] Moore, *Victims and Survivors*, 129.

resistance, which some thought the only effective means of contending with the enemy. Networks with specific aims grew up from among students, church members, pacifists, and anarchists. One course of action focussed attention on the STO, the compulsory labour force recruited for work in Germany. The French reaction to the STO had been ambivalent; on the other hand, it was condemned unequivocally by the Belgian hierarchy. In the Netherlands, organisations existed for the specific purpose of helping young men evade it. As the situation of the Jews worsened, however, opposition groups and wider networks directed to the business of rescue became the hub of resistance. The mass roundup of July 1942 lent impetus to movements devoted to the rescue of children. Finding safe homes for children was the main work of the Amsterdam Student Group, a complex web of students and their wider contacts. The organisation was funded by members of the network and, in part, by the Catholic Archdiocese of Utrecht. Students circulating reports on the arrests and transportations found that the initial reaction to the news was sometimes one of disbelief.

Bob Moore, a historian of the Dutch Resistance, has drawn attention to the disproportionate role played by Dutch Calvinists in rescue work. Calvinist networks reached throughout the country but were most densely concentrated in Amsterdam and the surrounding area, where, it is estimated, they maintained many hundreds, perhaps even thousands, of hiding places. Beginning from a nucleus of family members and friends within the local congregation, Calvinist networks reached out to other congregations throughout the Netherlands, eventually embracing members of the Dutch Reformed and Catholic churches.

The case of the Calvinist pastor Johannes Bogaard and his sons was typical. They began by hiding Jews in their farm buildings before expanding their rescue work to form a network. They seem to have operated with little concern for their personal safety. The farm buildings were searched on several occasions, and although Jews were found there, the family was treated with remarkable leniency. The father, Johannes Sr., suffered two brief spells of imprisonment.[47] A similar disregard for personal safety attended the labours of Haarlem's ten Boom family, who created an escape network, hiding Jews at home before finding them secure places with farmers. Eventually the whole family was arrested, although most were later released.[48] There appears to have been a lack of consistency in the punishments meted out, and others were not so fortunate. The network created by Joop Westerweel of the Plymouth Brethren sect managed to smuggle 150 Jews out of the country and to hide many more before Joop was arrested and executed in the summer of 1944.[49]

Mass arrests recommenced in February 1943, provoking an immediate Catholic response. Drawing inspiration from the pope's most recent Christmas broadcast, the hierarchy delivered a joint pastoral letter that was read out in all Catholic churches. Catholics were urged to acts of civil disobedience rather than become complicit in the roundup of Jews. A pastoral letter of May branded the deportations "an injustice that cries to Heaven".[50] A week later, a strong note of protest endorsed by both Protestants and Catholics was forwarded to Seyss-Inquart, after mixed Aryan-Jewish marriages were threatened with forced sterilisation. The measure was described as "so monstrous that it is impossible for us to refrain from

[47] Ibid., 230.

[48] Ibid., 227.

[49] Ibid., 64–65.

[50] Anthony Rhodes, *The Vatican in the Age of the Dictators, 1922–1945* (London: Hodder and Stoughton, 1973), 322.

addressing you in the name of Our Lord".[51] In the same month, German religious leaders came under attack in the Dutch Nazi Party press for their opposition to the regime in Germany.

A document of the German Foreign Office in the Netherlands of 25 June 1943 reported that 100,000 Jews out of 140,000 had been deported.[52] The figure had risen to 110,000, or 79 percent of the Jewish population, by the time the Netherlands was liberated, according to Lapide. The Netherlands provides a stark contrast to France and Belgium in the survival rate of Jews. Despite the example of the churches, despite the sympathy strikes and the praiseworthy efforts of members of the Resistance, it would seem that the populace, in large part, displayed a regrettable indifference to the fate of Dutch Jews. Eva Fogelman, a historian of the Holocaust, has noted that in Belgium there were fewer denunciations by neighbours, whereas in the Netherlands betrayal was commonplace. Jew hunters are believed to have uncovered 8,500 Jews, most of them in Amsterdam.[53] Although church leaders in the Netherlands were vociferous in defence of the Jews, their protests availed them little. Writing of the role of the Catholic clergy, Pinchas Lapide notes sorrowfully that while they protested "more loudly, expressly and frequently against Jewish persecutions than the religious hierarchy of any other Nazi-occupied country, more Jews ... were deported from Holland to death camps; more than anywhere else in the West".[54] In contrast, the Catholic bishops in Belgium made no thundering protest but otherwise directed their energies to the rescue of Belgium's

[51] DiGiovanni, "Pius XII and the Jews", 6.
[52] Knopp, *Hitler's Holocaust*, 164.
[53] Moore, *Victims and Survivors*, 231.
[54] Lapide, *The Last Three Popes and the Jews*, 202.

Jews, of whom three-quarters were saved from the extinction planned for them by Hitler.

Norway and Denmark

Norway and Denmark were invaded in the same month in 1940. Both countries had prospered in the 1930s under progressive Social-Democratic governments, though both included significant numbers of Nazi sympathizers among their populations. Shortly after their occupation, Himmler established a "Viking" division of the Waffen-SS composed of Danish and Norwegian volunteers. Norway and Denmark were mostly Lutheran, and neither country had a very substantial Jewish population.

Norwegian resistance held out for several weeks after the Wehrmacht launched its surprise attack in the spring. After the subjugation of the country to German rule, Vidkun Quisling, the founder of the Norwegian Fascist Party and arch collaborationist, was appointed president of the new puppet state. The Evangelical Lutheran church had been outspoken in condemnation of Nazism, and Bishop Berggrav of Oslo most particularly. Ecclesiastical protest was fomented when the nazification of the state began to impact Norwegian youth. After verbal protest was disregarded, the pastors of the state church protested with their feet by resigning their offices and quitting their official residences.[55] The judges of the Norwegian Supreme Court also resigned their offices in protest. Something similar to what had earlier transpired in Germany followed, with the creation of a German-sponsored Protestant church leadership.

[55] Van Roon, *German Resistance to Hitler*, 203.

The harassment of Jews conformed to the usual pattern, with the confiscation of property and the dismissal of Jews from public office. Arrest and internment came next. When the German Reichskommissar, Josef Terboven, demanded their expulsion, Quisling's government readily complied, and local police carried out the orders. Plans to deport Jews from Oslo in November 1942 were fiercely protested by the Protestant bishops. "God does not differentiate between peoples", they declaimed. Several hundred Jews were nevertheless expelled from Oslo that month, Auschwitz being their destination.

Norway had at most two thousand Jews, the majority being concentrated in the cities of Oslo and Trondheim. Some escaped capture by going into hiding in the country. More than half the number of Jews fled Norway for neutral Sweden. Most of these received assistance from an escape organisation that operated on the border and had been set up by an ex-policeman, Alf Tollef Petersen.[56] Rescuing Jewish children became a particular vocation of the Quakers.

The German occupation of Denmark met with little resistance to begin with. Like Vichy France, Denmark retained its own government, and this enjoyed considerable autonomy in the conduct of internal affairs. The Germans set great value on cooperation with the local inhabitants, as Denmark was such an important source of food for the Reich. When the Danes dug in their heels over the mistreatment of Jews by refusing to see them confined to ghettos or made to wear the Star of David, the Germans backed down.

The Jews of Denmark were a mixed population. Many were refugees from Germany and the Greater Reich;

---

[56] Moore, *Victims and Survivors*, 79–80.

many more were in mixed Aryan-Jewish marriages. Almost half the total number lived in the capital Copenhagen. The appearance of anti-Semitic propaganda and other abuses was condemned by the Catholic bishops in a note to the minister of justice, Thune Jacobsen. Otherwise the Jews were left pretty much alone until the summer of 1943. In August that year, the country was paralysed as a result of anti-Nazi strikes and demonstrations, causing the Germans to declare a state of emergency.

When persecution came to the Jews, it prompted a protest letter from the country's Lutheran bishops, which was then read from Protestant pulpits. Inspired by the example of King Christian, who set his face defiantly against the forces of occupation, Danes from all walks of life played an exemplary role in protecting their Jewish fellow citizens. Unlike other countries of the occupation, there was hardly any organised resistance in Denmark, and rescue had to be improvised. Danes took Jews into their own homes and hid them in places of relative security, such as hospitals and nursing homes, as the Norwegians had done. In October 1943, a prominent member of the German opposition, Helmuth Count von Moltke, gave warning that Danish Jews were soon to be rounded up and transported to concentration camps in the east. The precise nature of Moltke's information enabled the Danes to evacuate by sea almost all of their seven thousand Jews, an expeditious rescue effort that Fogelman has called "the most famous network operation of the war".[57]

---

[57] Fogelman, *Conscience and Courage*, 205.

6

Efforts to Rescue the Jews of Central and Eastern Europe

Slovakia

The racially mixed Republic of Czechoslovakia had been created in 1918 out of the former Austro-Hungarian Empire. Notwithstanding the asset of a sound economy, social integration was impeded by discord engendered by the predominance of the Czechs over the other peoples of the republic. This internal discord suited Hitler's purpose, as by November 1937 he had made plain his designs on Czechoslovakia.[1]

Having already lost the Sudetenland to Germany, in March 1939 the Czech government played into Hitler's hands by placing Slovakia under martial law. Using the same intimidating tactics that he had used on Schuschnigg over the Anschluss, Hitler summoned Emil Hácha, the Czechoslovak president, to Berlin, where, in the presence of Goering, Ribbentrop, and Keitel, he called on him to surrender his country. Hácha, who was elderly

[1] Hitler outlined his plans in a high-power meeting in November of that year. See James Taylor and Warren Shaw, *The Penguin Dictionary of the Third Reich* (London: Penguin Books, 1997), s.v. Hossbach Memorandum.

and in poor health, at first demurred. When Goering grew impatient with him and threatened to bomb Prague, Hácha fainted with fright and had to be revived by Hitler's doctor.

After a sleepless night fending off Hitler's demands, Hácha finally capitulated and signed the surrender at four o'clock on the morning of 15 March. Hours later, German troops overran Czechoslovakia. Hitler then annexed the Czech provinces of Bohemia and Moravia to the Reich. Slovakia became autonomous for the first time in its history, although remaining under German protection. Jozef Tiso, a Catholic priest and leader of a Catholic Slovak party, became the first (and last) president of the newly formed Republic.

Slovakia adopted the Nuremberg racial code on 9 September 1941 by government decree and without holding a debate in Parliament. The papal nuncio in Bratislava, Monsignor Giuseppe Burzio, lodged an immediate protest before alerting the Vatican to the changed situation. Burzio was instructed by Secretary of State Maglione to address a written protest to the Slovakian government while the Vatican pondered the provisions of the new legislation. At the urging of the nuncio, the Slovakian bishops collectively protested the anti-Semitic legislation to President Tiso, describing it as a violation of natural law and freedom of conscience.

Tiso was sympathetic and promised to help, but he wielded only limited influence. The real power in Slovakia lay with the prime minister, Vojtech Tuka, who revealed himself to be an eager collaborator in Nazi racial policy. On 12 November, Karol Sidor, the Slovak minister at the Vatican, was handed an official note of protest expressing Pius XII's "deep pain" that a country almost wholly Catholic should enact racial legislation in complete contravention of Catholic principles.[2] Sidor was directed to deliver the protest to his government in Bratislava.

When, early the following year, it became clear that the government was preparing to deport Jews to labour camps in Poland, Monsignor Burzio conveyed news of the "atrocious plan" to Rome. Their deportation, he said, was equivalent to a death sentence. Maglione responded with an instruction for the nuncio to intervene. But having already gone in person to intercede with the prime minister, Burzio knew there was no satisfaction to be gained from that quarter. Tuka was quite open about the matter and professed to see nothing inhuman or unchristian in evicting Jews.

Five days after receiving this latest intelligence, the Holy See submitted a second note of protest to the Slovakian government in which it deplored the "painful and unjust measures against persons belonging to the Hebrew race". Such measures, the note said, were an abuse of their human rights.[3] The Holy See rejected the claim that shipping Jews from Slovakia was to satisfy the need for labour service in the Greater Reich, alleging that the end awaiting them was something altogether more sinister—namely, annihilation. Sidor was instructed to intercede with his government in the name of the pope, with a view to calling a halt to the evictions.

That spring, all protests having been set aside, the first of Slovakia's ninety thousand Jews, many of them Catholics, were rounded up by the local police and transported to Poland. An estimated twenty-four thousand obtained

---

[2] Pierre Blet, S.J., *Pius XII and the Second World War according to the Archives of the Vatican* (Herefordshire: Gracewing, 2003), 169.

[3] Pinchas E. Lapide, *The Last Three Popes and the Jews* (London: Harper Press, 2009), 139.

asylum by fleeing across the border into Hungary.[4] On the prompting of the pope, the Slovakian hierarchy issued a pastoral letter condemning the iniquity and ordered it to be read in all Catholic churches. The measure gained a momentary respite, as the deportation plans were deferred. Yet only days later it was learned that the government proposed to expel ten thousand men and an equal number of women from among the Jewish population. The pope sent for the Slovak minister, Sidor, who was dispatched to Bratislava with instructions to intercede with Tiso and Tuka. The nuncio in Bratislava was given identical instructions. Tuka, as ever, was unhelpful. Not mincing words, he spelled it out to Burzio that the Holy See was meddling in politics. President Tiso was more understanding, having already intervened to ensure that a deportation order for four thousand Jews was cancelled. Two weeks later, the Slovakian bishops released another pastoral letter that, although censored, received a wide circulation in the Catholic press. While averring that Slovakian Jews were a pernicious influence in society, the bishops condemned their brutal treatment and demanded that they be dealt with in a humane fashion.

In May, the government, which until then had ignored all papal protests, at last gave its reply. It did little to allay Vatican fears. Slovak Jews, it said, were to be deported to Lublin, where, the Reich authorities had solemnly promised, they would be treated humanely. Exceptions were to be made in the case of Jews baptised before 1939 and Jews who had contracted marriages to Aryans before September 1941. Authorisation for the transports, which departed from Bratislava and from other parts of the country, came

---

[4]Nicholas Kallay, *Hungarian Premier* (London: Oxford University Press, 1954), 325.

from the interior minister, Alexander Mach, after Tiso refused to sign the expulsion orders. It seems the Slovakian government was unaware of any plan for the systematic murder of the deportees, for, three months later, it was petitioning Berlin to allow representatives to visit the "workers" in Poland.[5]

Further intervention by the Vatican and an official protest by the hierarchy in August evidently made an impression on the government, which suspended all deportations for six months. Jews still remaining in Slovakia, believed to number about thirty-five thousand, were offered the protection of exemption orders. By February 1943, however, it was learned that Mach was making preparations for their expulsion. The hierarchy addressed a letter of protest to the government, and seven bishops made an additional appeal in a pastoral letter. No one, they said, should be deprived of his liberty unless his guilt be proved, and no one should suffer injury just because he is a Jew.[6]

Informed of the changed situation, the pope addressed a personal plea to the government. But neither Tiso nor Prime Minister Tuka was able to guarantee protection of Slovakia's remaining Jews. Tuka was adamant that the band of evildoers, as he called them, must be expelled from the land, and he would suffer no argument on their behalf.[7] This latest démarche on the part of the Holy See was backed up by another note of protest in which Maglione demanded an end to the expulsions. The note was handed

[5] From the evidence of Dieter Wisliceny, SS major and adviser on Jewish matters to the Slovakian government, given before the military tribunal at Nuremberg. James Owen, *Nuremberg: Evil on Trial* (London: Headline Review, 2007), 81.

[6] Ethel Mary Tinnemann, "The Silence of Pope Pius XII", *Journal of Church and State* 21 (1999): 273.

[7] Blet, *Pius XII and the Second World War*, 173–74.

to the Slovak minister at the Vatican. Later, Burzio was able to report that the deportations, which were already in preparation, had been suspended. Yet, even though the immediate peril had receded, in 1944 disturbing reports reached Rome of a census being taken of the survivors. These were later confined to a ghetto.[8]

Events in Slovakia took a dramatic turn in August 1944, when the army rebelled in support of the approaching Russians. The Wehrmacht promptly invaded, and within forty-eight hours, the country was under German control. Although Tiso warned the German ambassador to expect difficulties from the Vatican if action were taken against the Jews, a further thirteen thousand were quickly rounded up for transportation. Dismissing Vatican entreaties, the Germans defended the expulsions as a necessary security measure in the light of the army rebellion.

From 1941, when Slovakia's race laws came into force, to August 1944, when the Wehrmacht took control of the country, the Holy See sent a total of six letters of protest to Tiso's government. To these must be added the many oral representations of its envoy. Contemporary German documents credited the survival of nearly twenty-five thousand of Slovakia's Jews, a quarter of the total number, to Vatican pressure. The six-month moratorium, beginning in the summer of 1942, was decisive, in that it enabled many Jews to seek asylum in churches and monasteries and in houses and farm buildings throughout the country.

It may be wondered why a Catholic country with a priest as president and several priests in Parliament should have offered such slavish obeisance to Hitler. As a Reich protectorate, Slovakia's sovereignty was no more than tenuous; yet it was a new experience of sovereignty, and

[8] Ibid., 175.

Slovaks evinced a patriotic determination to hang on to it. Tiso's commitment to the cause of independence was never in question. But it was probably the fear of Communism more than any other reason that accounted for Slovakia's collaboration with the Nazis. Repugnant as it was, Slovakians felt that Nazism represented the most formidable obstacle to Communist expansion. "Just as the fear of Communism put him in power, so it tended to keep him there", Paul Johnson wrote of Hitler.[9]

Controversy continues to surround the tragic figure of Father Tiso. Pius XII had disapproved of Tiso's appointment as president of the new republic. Like his predecessor, he thought that priests should be above politics. Moreover, Tiso was apparently persuaded that Christianity and Nazism were not entirely incompatible, a view that caused him to be regarded with suspicion at the Vatican.[10] In a moment of anger, the undersecretary of state, Tardini, described Tiso and Tuka as "lunatics". That Tiso should thus be bracketed with Tuka is perhaps unfair. For whereas the former might not have been above reproach, the latter's abrogation of moral responsibility was greater.

Tiso's dilemma has been well stated by Owen Chadwick: "You are an official of an immoral state. Do you resign because you cannot bear it, which clears your conscience but stops you from helping? Or do you put up with horrors because you can make them slightly less horrible by staying where you are?"[11] After the war, the Americans handed Tiso over to the Communists, who exhibited him

[9] Paul Johnson, *A History of the Modern World from 1917 to the 1980s* (London: Weidenfeld and Nicolson, 1984), 354.

[10] John Frain, *The Cross and the Third Reich: Catholic Resistance in the Nazi Era* (Oxford: Family Publications, 2009), 124.

[11] Owen Chadwick, *The Christian Church in the Cold War* (London: Penguin, 1993), 62.

in a vengeful show trial. It was revealed at his trial that he had considered resigning but had been persuaded to remain in office so as to help Jews avoid deportation and that he had undoubtedly saved Jewish lives. His accusers had their way in the end. Acclaimed as a hero by many of his countrymen, Tiso was hanged by the Communists on 18 April 1947.

Rumania

Of all the countries that fell within the orbit of Nazism, none oppressed its Jews with greater enthusiasm than Rumania—so much so that even the Germans complained of the brutality of Rumanian methods. Yet despite commonplace massacres, the survival rate of Jews was unusually high, higher than in any other German satellite country.

The country had strong economic ties with Germany, and its dominant political party, the Iron Guard, was pro-Nazi. Although little more than 10 percent of the population was Catholic, a concordat governing relations between the Holy See and Rumania had been in place since 1927. The papal nuncio, Archbishop Andrea Cassulo, was thus provided with a statutory basis on which to conduct negotiations with the Antonescu government. The precariousness of their situation led many Jews to seek the legal protection of the concordat by asking for baptism. Concessions had indeed been granted to baptised Jews when the first racial laws were promulgated in 1940. Growing suspicious of the excessive number of conversions, however, the government instructed the Rumanian minister at the Vatican to raise the matter with Cardinal Maglione. In 1941, in a clear breach of the concordat, the government passed a law prohibiting Jews from changing

their religion. The Holy See lodged an immediate protest, the first of several, and the government momentarily
backed down. But the following year, in an act of under-
handedness that augured no good for Jewish citizens,
Church archives were raided by Rumanian police, and the
names of all converts from Judaism were taken.

When the regime came to expel its Jews, neither the SS
nor the Gestapo took any part in the operation, as Rumania
was not under German military control. And Rumanian
Jews were deported not to Poland but to Transnistria, a
former Russian province annexed by Rumania after it
had joined with Germany in the attack on the Soviet
Union in 1941. Transnistria has been variously described
as a penal colony for Jews, and, more graphically, as the
Rumanian Siberia.

In the autumn of 1942, Alexander Safran, the chief rabbi
in Rumania, asked his close friend Cassulo to intercede
with the authorities on behalf of his people. It appeared
to be a last throw of the dice for Safran, because Cassulo
had already, on numerous occasions, protested the government's anti-Jewish policy. His protests had resulted
in occasional successes in the case of baptised Jews, but
his appeals on behalf of the Jewish community in general
almost invariably fell on deaf ears.

Without holding out much hope, Cassulo nevertheless acceded to Rabbi Safran's request and made further
representations to various government ministers. All were
rebuffed. At this point, Safran handed Cassulo an intimate
dossier recounting the full extent of the Rumanian persecution, with the request that it be taken to Rome and
laid before the pope. Armed with the incriminating document, Cassulo left for Rome in September. He returned
in November, bringing with him a lengthy memorandum containing the official response of the Holy See to

the plight of the Rumanian Jews. The memorandum was submitted to the Antonescu government, which promptly suspended the deportations. Despite relentless German pressure, they were never restarted.

The harrowing conditions of the Jews in Rumania proper continued to cause concern. Cassulo was instructed by Maglione to do what he could to help. Alas, the nuncio's task was not an easy one. Government promises to abide by the terms of the concordat were not always adhered to. Under orders from the Vatican, Cassulo requested, and eventually was granted, permission to visit the concentration camps in Transnistria, for which purpose the pope put at his disposal a large sum of money. Throughout 1943, the nuncio ranged over the whole area of Transnistria, visiting camps and distributing material comfort to Jewish inmates and prisoners of war.

Of particular concern to the nuncio was the welfare of Jewish children, many of whom were orphans. Working closely with Rabbi Safran and Dr. Wilhelm Filderman of the Jewish community, and in regular communication with Cardinal Maglione at the Vatican, Cassulo put in motion an audacious rescue operation. The object was to transfer the children from Transnistria to Rumania proper, and from there via one of the Black Sea ports to Palestine. But the scheme required the cooperation of the authorities. Would they be amenable? After much procrastination on the part of the government, the scheme eventually was blessed with success. Notwithstanding the indignant protests of the mufti of Jerusalem, Amin el-Husseini, several thousand Jewish children and a considerable number of adult Jews arrived safely in Palestine.

Early 1944 brought a new danger. The Wehrmacht was in retreat, and the remaining fifty-five thousand Jews in Transnistria were gravely imperilled and, for the most part, abandoned. The Vatican was notified of the danger by Archbishop Roncalli, the apostolic delegate in Istanbul, who had received an urgent request for help from Isaac Herzog, the chief rabbi of Jerusalem. The Jewish Council of Rumania was immediately provided with a large sum of money for humanitarian relief in the province; and after the sum was expended, the pope sent a further remittance. In the meantime, the nuncio became engaged in several diplomatic exchanges with the government with a view to effecting the repatriation to Rumania of the Jews in Transnistria. Cassulo's efforts prospered when, after several notes had been sent to the prime minister, General Ion Antonescu, the latter finally agreed to have the Jews withdrawn to safety behind the front lines.

After Rumania surrendered to the Red Army on 24 August, Rabbi Safran spoke glowingly of the high moral authority of the papal nuncio, to which, he said, was owed the survival of a quarter of a million Jews. To Safran's expressions of gratitude the grand rabbi Herzog added his own; these were conveyed to the pope by Cassulo.

Bulgaria

Bulgaria was predominantly Eastern Orthodox, with a Muslim minority and a scattering of Catholics. Having combined with Germany in the attack on Yugoslavia, the government faced insistent German demands for the expulsion of its Jews. King Boris at first complied when Jews were taken from Bulgarian-controlled Thrace and Macedonia. The official figure of twelve thousand is thought to be much exaggerated. Many Jews evaded capture due to the intervention of foreign embassies in Sofia, influenced, in part, by Archbishop Roncalli, whose bailiwick included Turkey and Greece. Roncalli had formerly been accredited to Bulgaria, where he was very highly thought of. Now he personally interceded with King Boris to effect the release of several hundred Jews who were scheduled to be deported and prevailed upon the king to have all of Sofia's Jews evacuated to the safety of the countryside.[12]

Bulgaria proper had close to fifty thousand Jewish inhabitants. None were deported. Yielding to German pressure, the government at first authorised the order for their expulsion, even though King Boris and Queen Giovanna were both opposed to Nazi racial policy. But in an unprecedented move, the result of a countrywide revulsion, the order was revoked, and Jews who had already been detained were released. Effective opposition was mounted by intellectuals, by members of Parliament, by Orthodox churchmen led by their bishops, and by Catholic priests, who were under Vatican orders to assist Jews. The queen took a hand in the matter after Roncalli's successor in Bulgaria, Monsignor Giuseppe Mazzoli, showed her a petition from six hundred women whose husbands were in imminent danger of expulsion.

Of material significance in the frustration of German demands was the determined noncooperation—in many cases, active resistance—on the part of the Bulgarian people, who appear to have been uniquely lacking in anti-Semitic sentiment. Martin Gilbert, the historian of the Holocaust, instances the defiant attitude of Bulgarian farmers, who threatened to lie on the railway tracks in advance of the deportation trains. Disregarding German anger, and a personal reprimand from Ribbentrop, the king continued to defer the execution of the expulsion orders until

[12]Frain, *The Cross and the Third Reich*, 138.

the withdrawal of German forces from Bulgaria in 1944 spelled an end to the danger. Bulgaria's unpopular anti-Jewish laws were then repealed.

Greece

With the lessons of the First World War still fresh in mind, Hitler laid plans to occupy Greece and Yugoslavia in order to prevent a Balkan front. His plans were pre-empted by Mussolini, who, having invaded Albania in 1939, launched an attack into Greece in October of the following year. But the Greeks were unwilling to be conquered, and much to Mussolini's chagrin, his forces were driven back into Albania. The Italian dictator was delivered from his quandary when, after a coup in Yugoslavia replaced a pro-German government with a pro-Allied one, the Wehrmacht overran the Balkan peninsula in the spring of 1941.

Vatican interests in Greece were represented by Archbishop Roncalli, who at once began to organize humanitarian aid. Although not resident in the country, Roncalli made several official visits in 1941, when he stayed at the residence of the head of the Greek Orthodox church, Archbishop Damaskinos. Using Vatican funds, Roncalli established the Good Samaritan Clinic in Athens, where the sick and wounded could receive treatment. His most pressing task, however, was to find means to relieve the famine caused by the British blockade. The Greek people were starving. By September, with winter approaching, the dead were being buried in mass graves; and although Roncalli was able to procure flour from Hungary and medicines from Monaco, this represented no more than a trickle and did not go nearly far enough to alleviate the distress.[13] The German military commander in Greece agreed to allow food into the country if the British could be persuaded to lift the blockade. Archbishop Damaskinos appealed to the pope for help. It was then that Monsignor Montini—an under secretary at the Vatican, and, like Roncalli, a future pope—brought his considerable powers of persuasion to bear on the British minister, Osborne, with the result that the British were induced to lift the blockade. Soon after, grain ships began arriving in Greek ports, and the threat of starvation receded.

Greece had about seventy-six thousand Jewish citizens, the majority being concentrated in Salonika. After the Nazis subjugated the country, most of these, some forty-eight thousand, were rapidly herded together and transported to Auschwitz. A few hundred Sephardic Jews were spared this fate after Franco intervened and had them returned to Spain.[14] Jews in other parts of the country, where their numbers were more thinly spread, immediately went into hiding.

Anyone caught rendering assistance to Jews faced summary retribution, usually in the form of shooting. Nonetheless, the Jews found friends in Greece willing to accept the risks. After failing to thwart the deportation order, Archbishop Damaskinos directed Greek monasteries and convents to provide asylum. On the island of Zante, Archbishop Chrysostomos supervised rescue operations, assisted by the local mayor, Lukos Karrer, and Jews were guided to safe abodes awaiting them in hilltop villages. Jews in Athens and Salonika were greatly assisted by consular officials.

---

[13] Lawrence Elliott, *I Will Be Called John: A Biography of Pope John XXIII* (London: William Collins Sons, 1976), 162.

[14] Martin Gilbert, *The Holocaust: The Jewish Tragedy* (London: Collins, 1986), 595.

In Athens, they managed to obtain false identity papers provided by the Italian consulate and also by the chief of police.

Just as they had done in Vichy France, Jews thronged into the Italian zone of the country, where they were shielded from persecution by the military. And, as in France, the Italians stubbornly refused to give them up for deportation. Yet, in spite of these estimable efforts, the number of Greek Jews who evaded capture was small. There remained only about twelve thousand when Hitler ordered the withdrawal of German forces from Greece. Most of these had found a refuge in the remote regions in the south of the country.

Croatia

Since its creation in 1918, the religious and ethnic mix that was Yugoslavia proved to be a volatile concoction. By maintaining a monopoly over the administration and the army, by operating a harshly discriminatory educational policy, and by their repressive methods, the Orthodox Serbs had succeeded in keeping the Catholic Croats and Slovenes in a state of subjection.

When the Germans overwhelmed Yugoslavia in 1941, the Croats broke away and, with the endorsement of Hitler and Mussolini, proclaimed an independent Croatia. Although governed independently, the new state remained under Axis occupation. Italian and Wehrmacht troops had their respective zones, and it was agreed between the two Axis dictators that Croatia would become an Italian dependency. Dr. Ante Pavelic, who had founded the Ustashe, the Croatian Fascist Party, in 1921 and had been its leader ever since, was installed as head of the new regime.

The Holy See declined to receive a Croatian minister at the Vatican or to appoint a papal representative in Zagreb. When Pavelic journeyed to Rome for an audience at the Vatican, the pope made it plain that he was greeting the Croatian leader as a son of the Church and that the audience implied no recognition of Croatia. A circular was put out by the secretariat of state stressing the private nature of the meeting. This infuriated Pavelic, and, following bitter remonstrations from the Croatian head of state, the Holy See agreed to appoint Abbot Giuseppe Marcone to Zagreb, but as an apostolic visitor, to be accredited not to the government but to the Croatian hierarchy. At the same time, the Holy See welcomed Dr. Rusinovic from Zagreb as Croatian representative at the Vatican, although it was impressed upon him that his status in Rome was unofficial and that his assignment was restricted to Church matters. Significantly, the names of Marcone, Rusinovic, and Prince Lobkowicz, Rusinovic's successor at the Vatican, were not included in the official Vatican list of diplomats.[15]

The Croats, who, since the creation of Yugoslavia, had experienced years of persecution at the hands of the Serbs, and centuries of persecution before that, now became the persecutors. In a reign of terror lasting four years, the Ustashe indulged its tribal bloodlust, sparing neither Serb nor Jew, while Wehrmacht troops, experienced in the harsh realities of warfare, and many having witnessed pitiless anti-Jewish pogroms, looked on aghast. In a move calculated to eradicate forever Serbian ethnicity, Serbs were offered the stark choice of conversion to Catholicism or death. Thousands converted to avoid the latter fate. Even

---

[15] Harold H. Tittmann Jr., *Inside the Vatican of Pius XII: The Memoir of an American Diplomat during World War II* (New York: Image Books, 2004), 51. See also Blet, *Pius XII and the Second World War*, 108–9.

though the archbishop of Zagreb, Dr. Aloysius Stepinac, had condemned forced conversions and ordered his clergy to withhold absolution from murderers, by 1945 half a million people—Serbs and Jews as well as nonconforming minorities such as Communists and Gypsies—had perished at the hands of Ustashe fanatics.

It was a singular experience for Jews living in a pro-Nazi state to know that there were people more hated than they were. Nevertheless, a familiar sequence of events unfolded in the weeks following independence. Racial laws came into force almost immediately. Jews found themselves suddenly deprived of their property, debarred from the professions, and prohibited from marrying Aryans. Their expulsion from Zagreb followed soon after.

Archbishop Stepinac had welcomed the establishment of an independent Croatia. Every year of the war he had a Te Deum sung in commemoration of the event. As time passed, however, he became increasingly at odds with Pavelic over the regime's oppressive measures enacted against both Serbs and Jews, most of whom among the latter were baptised. He vehemently protested when, in April, Jews were compelled to wear the Star of David as a mark of abasement and separateness and would not allow it to be worn in church. Although unable to prevent Jews from being deported from Zagreb, Stepinac made numerous intercessions on their behalf, and in June he led a delegation to Prime Minister Pavelic to demand that they be accorded humane treatment.

The Italians, in their zone of influence, operated an uncompromising policy of opposition to the Ustashe and, with Vatican funding, were successful in arranging for Jews to flee the country. Thousands of fugitives from the Ustashe owed their lives to the Italians, who routinely intervened to avert massacres. From the summer of 1941, it became official policy, agreed at the highest level, to offer protection to Jews in those parts of the country under Italian jurisdiction.[16]

Later that year, Archbishop Stepinac convened a conference of the country's Catholic bishops, during which the practice of forced conversions was condemned and the rights of the Orthodox church were affirmed. Stepinac subsequently had a strongly worded letter sent to Pavelic, repeating the demand for humane treatment for Jews. As 1941 drew to a close, he delivered a hard-hitting sermon denouncing the violence of the regime.

At the turn of the year, an emissary of the Holy See, Father Tacchi Venturi, S.J., wrote to Cardinal Maglione, regretting that he was unable to prevent the deportation of Jewish children from Croatia. On a more auspicious note, Vatican efforts to assist the emigration of Jewish children to neutral Turkey were attended by success. Nevertheless, Abbot Marcone reported his frustration on being continually thwarted in his efforts to help, as protests to the authorities and requests for information were routinely ignored. It was the chief of police who, in private communication, revealed to him that to satisfy German demands, all Jews were to be shipped to Germany. Once there, he said, they would be quickly exterminated, a fate that had already befallen some two million of their fellow Jews. The police chief added that he had forestalled the evictions for as long as he dared. After an appeal for help from the chief rabbi of Zagreb, Salom Freiberger, the pope managed to wring concessions from Pavelic, and many Jews listed for deportation were reprieved. Nothing could be done about the policy of deportation itself, which remained firmly in place.

[16] Eva Fogelman, *Conscience and Courage: Rescuers of Jews during the Holocaust* (London: Victor Gollancz, 1996), 36.

A police order of March 1943 calling for the transfer of Jews to concentration camps in Poland was brought to the attention of the pope, who instructed Marcone to do everything in his power to prevent the order from being implemented. Archbishop Stepinac, meanwhile, lodged an official complaint with Pavelic. In a Sunday sermon dwelling on the evils of racism, Stepinac proclaimed: "No civil power or political system has the right to persecute a person on account of his racial origins."[17] Shortly after, the police order was revoked. But in a stealthy nighttime manoeuvre that occurred a few weeks later, the police swooped to carry off a large number of Jews. Those who had contracted marriages with Aryans in the past were spared, and a promise was given that they would always be protected.

The Holy See, through the dedicated efforts of its envoy in Zagreb, did everything humanly possible to mitigate the worst excesses of the Croatian genocide. Marcone remained in constant communication with Maglione at the Vatican and had frequent meetings with both Pavelic and Rabbi Freiberger. Archbishop Stepinac never desisted in his opposition to the Ustashe regime. In a stream of letters sent to Pavelic, the Croatian primate protested the cruel and unjust treatment of its victims and condemned the destruction of Orthodox churches. Official German reports testify to Stepinac's intercessions on behalf of both Serbs and Jews, which by May 1943 he had made on thirty-four occasions. His episcopal palace became a refuge for Jews on the run. He was regularly attacked in the Fascist press, and he so exasperated Pavelic that the Croatian premier applied to Rome three times to have him removed from office. Preaching towards the

[17] Anthony Rhodes, *The Vatican in the Age of the Dictators, 1922–1945* (London: Hodder and Stoughton, 1973), 332.

end of 1943, Archbishop Stepinac declared: "The Catholic Church cannot admit that a race or nation, simply because it is larger or stronger, can use violence against another which is smaller or weaker." More than thirty priests were arrested after they had read his sermon from their pulpits.

Croatia had about forty-five thousand ethnic Jews in 1941, of which some thirty thousand perished in the Holocaust. The task of mounting organised and effective rescue operations when the Ustashe was hell-bent on eliminating a large part of the population was, alas, impossible. On 11 June 1943, the secretary of a Jewish welfare commission wrote to Archbishop Roncalli in Istanbul, expressing the commission's gratitude to the Holy See for the assistance given to European Jews. Singled out for special praise was Archbishop Stepinac, who, the note said, "has done everything possible to aid and ease the unhappy fate of the Jews in Croatia".[18]

In May 1946, on the basis of fabricated evidence, the Communists put Archbishop Stepinac on trial for alleged collaboration with the Nazis and for the forcible conversion of Serbs. The trial was widely regarded as a travesty of justice. Marshal Tito prejudiced the court by pronouncing Stepinac guilty before the trial began. His conviction was a foregone conclusion, and he was sentenced to sixteen years' hard labour. Dr. Stepinac never completed his sentence but died in 1960 while under house arrest.

Hungary

Although Hungary had been reconstituted a kingdom in 1920, the throne had been left vacant. Admiral Nicholas

---

[18] Blet, *Pius XII and the Second World War*, 181.

Horthy, who had been instrumental in the overthrow of Béla Kun's Communist regime, was from that time the Protestant regent of this largely Catholic country.

In 1944, in Hungary there were close to a million Jews whose welfare until then had not been seriously threatened despite the enactment of racial laws. In fact, Hungary had become, in the words of the chief rabbi of New York, "the asylum of the Jews in Europe".[19] Tens of thousands poured over its borders from Poland, Slovakia, Rumania, Transylvania, and other parts of Eastern Europe. When Admiral Horthy met with Hitler at Klessheim Castle near Salzburg in April 1943, Hitler rebuked him for the negligence of his government's handling of the Jewish problem. Hitler urged the deportation of Hungarian Jews. Horthy flatly refused.

In March of the succeeding year, the two leaders met again at Klessheim Castle. Horthy was a man of a different mettle than Hitler was accustomed to dealing with, and the meeting was a stormy one. Finding the Hungarian regent uncooperative, Hitler flew into a rage. Humiliated, though not cowed, Horthy stalked out in anger. But he was friendless and ultimately powerless. Hitler finally got him to agree to hand over a hundred thousand Jewish workers for Germany. The Hungarian premier was also constrained to permit the military occupation of Hungary by German troops, which began early the following day.

The German occupation provoked a flurry of diplomatic activity directed to the protection of the Jews. Over the first few days, the nuncio, Archbishop Angelo Rotta, had urgent interviews with Prime Minister Sztojay and Deputy Foreign Minister Arnothy-Jungerth. Only days after a second meeting with Sztojay, Rotta managed to

[19] Kallay, *Hungarian Premier*, 328.

obtain some exemptions from the racial legislation as it affected foreign Jews, Jews in mixed marriages, and certain others. The intervention of the primate, Cardinal Seredi, on behalf of all Jews who had undergone baptism was, alas, unsuccessful. Seredi's discussions with Sztojay concerning the race laws generally and his protest over the transfer of Jews to internment camps in Hungary also came to nought. Still, the authorities were not acting with the speed and efficiency that Hitler expected. Hitler pressed the point in an angry exchange with Horthy, following which the government was forced to fall in with Hitler's designs. In a meeting with Arnothy-Jungerth, the nuncio told him that the pope was deeply saddened by these events.

More oral protests followed, before the deportation to Auschwitz began in early May. Archbishop Rotta immediately sent a formal note of protest to the prime minister. Hungary claims to be a Christian country, he told Sztojay, but deporting Jews who are baptised Christians contradicts that claim. What is more, he added, it is a violation of natural law to persecute any person on the grounds of his race.[20] A separate note was sent to the foreign minister, calling for the government to respect fundamental human rights. In a letter to the nuncio, Pius XII described the treatment of the Jews as being "unworthy of Hungary, the country of the Holy Virgin and of St. Stephen".[21]

Two weeks after receiving Rotta's official protest note, Sztojay sent his reply. He categorically denied that any mass transfer of Jews from Hungarian soil had taken place or that such a course of action had been contemplated. He conceded that some Jews had been removed, but only to satisfy labour requirements for Germany. Archbishop

Rotta's rejoinder a week later gave chapter and verse. Among the deported were children, the sick, men and women past the age of seventy and in some cases eighty. He demanded to know what kind of labour these people are fitted to perform. Rotta insisted that the fundamental rights of Jews as men be respected and that all Jews be treated in a humane way. The Hungarian people, said Rotta, "who have justly acquired the title of defender of the faith and of civilization, do not want to sully their reputation by following methods that the conscience of the Christian world could not sanction".[22]

In May, two escapees from Auschwitz submitted a report on the gassings taking place there and claimed that preparations were being made for the reception of Hungarian Jews. The report was brought to the attention of the pope, who at the time was preparing an appeal to Admiral Horthy. On 25 June, Pius XII issued a plea on behalf of all those who were enduring persecution on account of their nationality or race. He implored Horthy to intervene "in order that so many unfortunate people be spared further afflictions and sorrows".[23]

Horthy's reply was gracious. He thanked the pope for his timely intercession and promised that he was doing everything possible to alleviate the situation. At the request of the pope, Cardinal Spellman, the archbishop of New York, protested the inhuman treatment of Jews in a lengthy radio broadcast beamed to Hungary. "Spiritually, we are Semites. No man can love God and hate his brother", Spellman declared. At the same time, the archbishop of Canterbury, William Temple, denounced the deportation of Hungarian Jews. Both his and Cardinal

[22] Quoted in Blet, *Pius XII and the Second World War*, 193.
[23] Ibid., 194–95.

Spellman's protests were transmitted by the BBC. A few days after the pope's telegram to Horthy, appeals were submitted from the king of Sweden and the International Red Cross. Meanwhile, the cardinal secretary of state, Maglione, ordered the nuncio to press the Hungarian hierarchy to take action.

In consequence of the pope's intervention, Horthy convened the Crown Council and demanded an end to the expulsions. Three days later, he gave the order for their suspension. The World Jewish Congress was informed of these events by the apostolic delegate in London. By this time, more than four hundred thousand Jews had already been transferred to Auschwitz. Ribbentrop pressed Edmund Veesenmayer, the German ambassador in Budapest, to complain to the government for yielding to what he described as foreign pressures in its handling of the Jewish situation. A disgusted Hitler told Sztojay that Horthy was "too squeamish".[24]

The continuing silence of the Hungarian hierarchy was puzzling to the nuncio and to the pope. Although some of the bishops favoured a protest in the form of an episcopal letter, Cardinal Seredi had resisted the idea. When Rotta raised the matter with him in early June, Seredi pointed out that the episcopacy was hampered by government censorship and that, in any case, a pastoral letter would not allay the suffering of the Jews but would only bring harm to the Church. Threatening to publish a letter, said Seredi, would have more weight with the authorities than actually publishing one. Seredi may well have been right in his judgement. No one could accuse him of kowtowing to Hitler. In 1934, he had attacked Nazism in a pastoral

[24] Milan Hauner, *Hitler: A Chronology of His Life and Time* (London: Palgrave Macmillan, 2008), 194.

letter and had forbidden his priests to take any part in the movement. When the anti-Semitic legislation was passed in the Senate, Seredi spoke out in opposition, and he and all the bishops voted against it.

By the end of June, however, the pope had grown impatient, and he made known his wish "that the Hungarian episcopate should publicly take a stand ... on behalf of their compatriots who are unjustly hit by racial decrees".[25] Cardinal Seredi was notified in an official note from the nuncio, by which time a pastoral letter was already in preparation. It was read from the pulpits of several churches on 1 July but was not generally broadcast. The letter contained strong condemnations of the abuse of human rights and of the confinement of Jews to ghettos. It called for the deportation orders against all Jews to be cancelled.[26] Pressure was brought to bear to have the pastoral suppressed, and Seredi did agree to its suppression after the Hungarian minister of the interior assured him that baptised Jews would be exempted from deportation. These matters were overtaken by events when Admiral Horthy cut short the deportations on receipt of the pope's telegram.

Horthy's merciful intervention incensed Adolf Eichmann, the SS officer in charge of the Jewish Evacuation Department. On 14 July, Eichmann tried to remove 1,500 Jews from Kistarcza, a camp a few miles from Budapest. Having been informed of the plan by the Jewish Council, Horthy had the transport stopped at the border and the Jews returned to Kistarcza. But Eichmann was not to be outdone, and only days later, in overruling Horthy, he ordered the resumption of the transports. By this time,

[25] Lapide, *The Last Three Popes and the Jews*, 154.
[26] Cardinal Jozsef Mindszenty, *Memoirs* (London: Weidenfeld and Nicolson, 1974), 14.

telegrams were arriving daily on Horthy's desk, as leaders of neutral countries, including the king of Sweden, added their voices to those of the World Jewish Congress, the Red Cross, and the pope. All demanded humane treatment for Hungarian Jews and an end to the evictions. Archbishop Rotta telephoned Horthy several times a day and beseeched the German ambassador Veesenmayer to use his influence to block the transports.

After a lull in activity lasting several weeks, it came to the notice of Rotta that the Germans were on the point of removing the Jews of Budapest, who until then had been left alone, to internment camps in the country, preparatory to their transfer to Auschwitz. The nuncio promptly marshalled the leading delegates of the diplomatic missions of the four neutral countries, Sweden, Switzerland, Spain, and Portugal, when an official note was drawn up protesting unjust and inhuman acts "that dishonoured Hungary and its people". Bearing the signatures of all five envoys, it was delivered to Horthy on 21 August. A few days later, Horthy formed a new military government. Prime Minister Sztojay was dismissed from office and replaced by General Géza Lakatos. Under the new administration, the anti-Jewish measures were relaxed and the evictions discontinued. For a time, some semblance of normal life returned to Hungary.

On 15 October, as the Red Army drew near, and following secret negotiations, Horthy announced on the radio that a truce had been agreed with the Allies. A furious Hitler responded by ordering the Wehrmacht to take control of Budapest. Horthy was arrested and imprisoned in Germany, where he remained until liberated by the Allies. Ferenc Szálasi, the leader of the Hungarian Fascists, the Arrow Cross, an organisation described by former Prime Minister Nicholas Kallay as "a disreputable gang of leaders without faith or honour", was installed as the new head of state. Most government ministerial posts fell to German nominees.[27]

Cardinal Seredi lost no time in sounding out the new regime with a view to obtaining improved conditions for Jews but found his recommendations were not well received. The nuncio had rather better, if limited, success, after meeting with the new foreign minister, Gabor Kemeny; and when the Red Cross and the envoys of the neutral countries made similar representations, several hundred ailing Jews were allowed medical treatment. The nuncio also got Szalasi to promise that Jews would no longer be deported from the country, though the prime minister insisted they would be made to work for Hungary.

It was then that Eichmann turned up in Budapest determined to transfer 22,000 Jews to a concentration camp on the border with Austria. As no trains were available, Eichmann forced them to undergo the journey on foot. About 2,000 escaped, bearing safe-conduct passes signed by Rotta. Trucks displaying the papal insignia got through with essential food and medical supplies. Even so, most of those on the march died along the way.

The departure of Admiral Horthy and the arrival of Szalasi had put the lives of the 180,000 Jews still living in Budapest in even greater jeopardy. Jewish leaders wanted the pope to broadcast an appeal to Hungary on Vatican Radio. In declining their request, the pope was almost certainly influenced by events surrounding the Vatican Radio broadcasts to Poland a few years earlier. Instead, he telegraphed an appeal to Cardinal Seredi and the Hungarian bishops, beseeching them in the name of the Holy See

---

[27]Kallay, *Hungarian Premier*, 472. Kallay was replaced by Sztojay when the Germans invaded in 1944.

to intercede. Seredi responded by issuing a protest letter. Several bishops made individual appeals and also tried to stop the expulsion of Jews in the areas under their episcopal jurisdiction. In late autumn, Archbishop Rotta relayed to the foreign minister an official papal protest over the regime's heartless treatment of its Jews.

In spite of these exertions, and Szalasi's assurances to the contrary, it became clear by 17 November that the government was intent on deporting all Jews from Budapest. The nuncio promptly convened a meeting of the diplomatic corps, at the conclusion of which he and the envoys of the four neutral countries submitted a second official protest, expressing "their most profound distress".[28]

Meanwhile, thousands were fleeing before the marauding Red Army on its rampant march towards the capital. As the Wehrmacht prepared to make a last stand, Bishop Mindszenty of Veszprém warned the government of the threat to the country's cultural sites and to the remaining population if Hungary were to become a battleground. Although Mindszenty's memorandum bore the signatures of all the bishops of Western Hungary, he was arrested for his counsel and imprisoned; it was his second term of imprisonment since the German occupation.[29] On Christmas Day, Archbishop Rotta again assembled the leading members of the diplomatic corps, and a third, and final, note of protest, made this time in the interests of Jewish children, was delivered to Szalasi's government.

Diplomatic protests apart, the lives of thousands of Jews were saved due to the actions of emissaries of the neutral countries. The Swedish delegate Raoul Wallenberg is

[28] Ralph McInerny, *The Defamation of Pius XII* (South Bend, Ind.: St. Augustine's Press, 2001), 141.

[29] Mindszenty, *Memoirs*, 16–17.

credited with having saved at least twenty-five thousand lives, and possibly double that number, by distributing Swedish safe-conduct passes and by placing Jewish refugees under the protection of the Swedish crown. Carl Lutz of the Swiss legation, and Spanish envoy Angel Sanz-Briz, together with Sanz-Briz' assistant and eventual successor, Giorgio Perlasca, worked untiringly in the cause of rescuing Jews, as did Friedrich Born, the Red Cross delegate.[30] Chaim Barlas of the Jewish Rescue Agency in Turkey acknowledged the special role played by Archbishop Roncalli. Learning that the Nazis had recognised baptismal certificates given to Jewish children by nuns in Budapest, Roncalli declared himself prepared to make available as many certificates as were required. Thousands were signed by him and sent to Hungary.[31]

As doyen of the diplomatic corps, the nuncio Archbishop Rotta provided outstanding leadership throughout the nightmare months of 1944 to 1945, when he made almost daily visits to the head of state. He pleaded, successfully, for better treatment for the inmates of internment camps and was especially solicitous for the welfare of women and children. At one time, about two hundred Jews were hidden in his place of residence; and he encouraged others to hide Jews. Some twenty thousand passports were distributed by Rotta in 1944, together with hundreds of blank safe-conduct passes. To produce the thousands of papal letters of protection, a battalion of priests and nuns worked under his direction. Rotta also had buildings in

---

[30] See Lapide, *The Last Three Popes and the Jews*, 159–60; Fogelman, *Conscience and Courage*, 53, 198; and Guido Knopp, *Hitler's Holocaust* (Stroud, UK: Sutton, 2004), 257–58. Knopp is rightly lavish in his praise of Raoul Wallenberg, but he denies any credit to the papal nuncio, while insinuating that the Holy See remained indifferent to the plight of Hungarian Jews.

[31] Elliott, *I Will Be Called John*, 116.

Budapest that were housing Jews placed under the protection of the Vatican.

Countless numbers of Catholic priests, nuns, and laypeople involved themselves in rescue work of one kind or another; and many paid with their lives or suffered imprisonment as a result. In Budapest during the terrible autumn and winter of 1944, virtually every Catholic church and religious institution was giving shelter to Jews. A report of the commissioner for Jewish affairs complained that the clergy of all ranks were foremost in the attempts to save Jews. The report added that they justified their illegal activities by invoking the Gospel injunction to love one's neighbour.[32] The monumental work of rescue was, alas, attended by only limited success. About two hundred thousand Hungarian Jews, including more than a hundred thousand in Budapest, lived to greet the victorious Red Army in February 1945. Many thousands more were not so lucky.

---

[32] Mindszenty, *Memoirs*, 15.

7

Rome under the German Occupation

Within days of the Allied invasion of Sicily in July 1943, the Fascist Grand Council deposed Mussolini, who was then arrested and imprisoned in Central Italy. The fate of the country was left in the hands of King Victor Emmanuel III and his newly appointed head of state, Marshal Pietro Badoglio. After an interview with Badoglio, Field Marshal Albert Kesselring, the commander in chief of German forces in Italy, came away feeling confident that the Italians would continue to prosecute the war. Badoglio even issued a proclamation to that effect. When, however, he announced the Italian surrender on 8 September, after weeks of secret talks with the Allies, German troops swiftly took control of most of the country, forcing the king and Badoglio to flee to Allied-occupied southern Italy.

Hitler vowed to make Italy pay for her treachery. On 12 September, he had German parachutists rescue Mussolini from his place of detention in the Apennines. The former Duce was then installed in Salo in northern Italy as the head of a new Fascist republic. In reality, he was no more than Hitler's pawn, and the new republic a German puppet creation that was spurned by most Italians. All members of the Grand Council who had voted for Mussolini's deposition and who had not fled abroad or to southern Italy were apprehended and shot as traitors, among them the former foreign minister Count Ciano.

The scene in Rome was one of utter confusion. The Germans looted at every opportunity. Gangs of Fascists rampaged through the streets, seeking revenge for the overthrow of their leader, Mussolini. They, and the Germans, were sniped at by members of the Resistance. Assassinations, followed by the inevitable reprisals, were commonplace occurrences. While the pope appealed for calm, multitudes of British and American servicemen, released from captivity by the Italians, converged upon the capital. Added to their number were Jews fleeing Vichy France and political fugitives, mainly Communists. Church buildings and the private residences of priests and nuns and members of the Roman population provided shelter for many of these fugitives. Some Allied servicemen were domiciled in the barracks of the papal gendarmerie, after the pope, in possibly a minor breach of Vatican neutrality, granted them asylum. From within the Vatican, the British minister to the Holy See, Sir D'Arcy Osborne, and the American diplomat Harold H. Tittmann secretly organised welfare relief for the many Allied ex–prisoners of war and also greatly assisted hard-pressed Jews. Although the diplomats were flouting Vatican neutrality, Vatican officials obligingly turned a blind eye to their activities.[1]

Fears awakened by the threat of Allied bombing added to the general tumult in Rome. The pope was anxious to have Rome declared an open city. Badoglio's government had made such a declaration; but that was before the German takeover of the city, and the declaration remained a dead letter. The Allies were not unmindful of the apprehension felt for the safety of Rome's historic buildings; nor of the fact that the already endangered Roman population

---

[1] Harold H. Tittmann Jr., *Inside the Vatican of Pius XII: The Memoirs of an American Diplomat during World War II* (New York: Image Books, 2004), 188–90.

was every day swelled by the arrival of yet more refugees. But Rome was held by the Germans, and therefore a legitimate military objective.

American bombs, directed against the main railway depot and freight yards, resulted in many civilian casualties. Having first emptied the Vatican treasury, Pius XII hurried to the scene, accompanied by Monsignor Montini. After hours spent distributing alms and bringing solace to the survivors of the raid, the pope returned to the papal apartments at eight in the evening, his soutane covered in blood. On the evening of 5 November 1943, stray bombs fell in the Vatican gardens, causing some damage to buildings but not resulting in loss of life. The Germans were suspected; their target was thought to have been Vatican Radio, which sustained slight damage but remained operational. The incident must have gladdened the heart of the writer H. G. Wells. The anti-Catholic Wells had called for the bombing of Rome and had suggested that a two-thousand-pound bomb be dropped in the Vatican gardens.[2] Bombing raids continued to devastate the city and the surrounding area. The pope's summer residence at Castel Gandolfo, which housed some fifteen thousand refugees, was hit several times, most seriously on the morning of 10 February, when five hundred people lost their lives. The terror caused by bombing raids was brought to an end only after the Germans evacuated the city in June 1944.

When the Germans descended upon Rome, it was at first feared that they might overrun the Vatican. Although sentries were posted at the entrance to Saint Peter's Square, the claim made by the BBC that the pope was being held

[2] Cardinal John C. Heenan, *Not the Whole Truth: An Autobiography* (London: Hodder and Stoughton, 1973), 266–67, quoting Wells' article in the *Sunday Dispatch* of 30 August 1942.

hostage was wide of the mark. The German military generally behaved correctly and were careful not to contravene the Lateran Treaty. The behaviour of senior German officers stands in marked contrast to that of Italian Fascists, who, because the Holy See refused to recognize the new republic, exhibited a contemptuous disregard for Vatican City and the extraterritorial buildings. The Lombard College, the Oriental Institute, the Russicum, and buildings of Saint Paul's Basilica were all broken into and ransacked in the Fascists' quest to uncover Jews and members of the Resistance. Vatican food supplies were, however, confiscated by the German military, and all residents had their rations halved. Being an enclave of Rome, the Vatican was placed in a highly dependent, not to say precarious, position for the supply of utilities such as water and electricity. Although its postal services were curtailed and telephone trunk lines tapped, life in the Vatican was to no great extent inconvenienced. In an act of solidarity with the people, the pope refused all heating for his private apartments, although he did not insist that others follow his example.

The German grip on the country held a bleak outlook for Italian and foreign Jews, if experience was anything to go by. Yet, the danger seems not to have been readily appreciated. The rector of the Rabbinical College, Rabbi Zolli, wanted the Jewish community to quit Rome; and he recommended that the registers containing the names and addresses of Jewish residents be destroyed. The president of the Jewish community could not be persuaded, however, having been lulled into a false sense of security by German assurances. Then, recent history seemed to auger well for Italian Jews. Since 1938, they had faced discrimination in their professional and social lives but otherwise had not been harshly treated, and none had been killed. The racial laws were enforced with nothing like the severity with which they were enforced in Germany. The Holy See's intercession with the Italian government had been successful in obtaining many exemptions from racial legislation, especially for Jews who were baptised Catholics and for those married to Catholics. Mussolini had himself steadfastly refused all Himmler's demands for the deportation of Jews from Italy.

Italians went out of their way to protect their Jews. One of Mussolini's recent biographers has underlined the distinction that existed between "legal" Italy and "real" Italy.[3] Italian officials discovered numerous "special cases" that called for exemptions from the racial code, while the negligence of border officials made Italy a haven for those fleeing racial persecution in other countries. Jews came under Italian protection in France, Tunisia, Croatia, Greece, and Yugoslavia. Italian laxity in such matters was a provocation to such as Goebbels, who confided to his diary, "Everywhere, even among our allies, the Jews have friends to help them."[4]

The pope was debating the advisability of making an official recommendation to the German embassy on behalf of the Jews and of the civilian population. Weizsäcker, formerly of the German Foreign Office and recently appointed ambassador to the Holy See, could be expected to be sympathetic. He desired nothing more than an end to the war, and to that end, he believed he could play a more useful role at the Vatican. Thus, it was at his own request that he had been assigned to head the German delegation there.[5] His dislike of Hitler and his friendliness

[3] R. J. B. Bosworth, *Mussolini* (London: Arnold, 2002), 344.
[4] *The Goebbels Diaries: The Last Days*, ed. Hugh Trevor-Roper (London: Book Club Associates, 1978), entry for 13 December 1942.
[5] *The Memoirs of Ernst von Weizsäcker* (London: Victor Gollancz, 1951), 258.

towards the pope, who, Weizsäcker hoped, would act as mediator in a negotiated peace deal with the Allies, placed him under suspicion. Ludwig Wemmer, a chancellery official in Berlin, was sent to Rome by the mistrustful Martin Bormann to spy on him. Wiezsäcker's deputy, Albrecht von Kessel, shared his superior's sentiments, being an active conspirator in plots directed to the overthrow of Hitler. Both men warned the Jews to leave Rome.

Towards the end of September 1943, the head of the Gestapo in Rome, Lieutenant Colonel Herbert Kappler, threatened to send Jews to concentration camps in Poland unless they handed over fifty kilos of gold within thirty-six hours. The Jewish community managed to raise the bulk of the amount, but fifteen kilos remained to be found. Rabbi Zolli appealed to Pius XII, who guaranteed to make good the deficit. It is thought that this was done by melting down sacred vessels. In the event, the Vatican contribution was not required, as the balance was obtained from other sources—according to a special-affairs delegate of the Holy See, from "Catholic communities".[6]

It was most unfortunate that Rabbi Zolli's advice, which the president of the Jewish community had declined to act upon, should prove sound. In a dawn raid of 16 October, the SS descended upon Jewish homes to seize more than a thousand Jews. It was their fate to be transported by rail to Auschwitz, although a few managed to escape. The roundup was the first move in the planned expulsion of all eight thousand Roman Jews. No arrests were made of foreign Jews. Although the Allies had advance knowledge of the scheme, British Intelligence having intercepted and decoded the order sent from Berlin, both the British

[6]Pierr Blet, S.J., *Pius XII and the Second World War according to the Archives of the Vatican* (Herefordshire: Gracewing, 2003), 215.

and the Americans, for whatever reasons, maintained a diplomatic silence.[7]

Pius XII learned of the arrests early on the morning they took place, when the news was brought to him by his former student Princess Enza Pignatelli Aragona. Weizsäcker was immediately summoned to the Vatican, where Maglione protested the outrage. The German ambassador, who was taken by surprise by the speed and secrecy of the arrests, promised to do what he could, and he assured Maglione that he would faithfully represent the views of the Holy See when he came to write his official report. Due to Weizsäcker's intercession, about two hundred Jews were released.

That same day, the pope directed the rector of the German church in Rome, Monsignor Alois Hudal, who was noted for his pro-German leanings, to make an official approach to General Rainer Stahel, the military governor of Rome. Hudal was to say that if there were any further arrests, the pope would issue a public protest. Monsignor Hudal's letter to Stahel was forwarded to Reichsführer-SS Himmler. General Stahel was a courteous and compassionate Austrian, a member of Döllinger's Old Catholic sect, and was opposed to the roundups on moral grounds. To Hudal's warning Stahel joined an objection of his own—namely, that targeting the Jews would interfere with his plans to reinforce the German divisions south of Rome. Himmler promptly responded with an order calling a halt to the arrests, giving as his reason his "consideration for the special character of Rome".[8] After this, there were no further arrests. The Vatican simultaneously, through the

[7] Nicholas Farrell, *Mussolini* (London: Weidenfeld and Nicolson, 2003), 367, quoting the *Daily Telegraph* of 27 June 2000, on the recent release of documents of the U.S. Office of Strategic Studies.

[8] Blet, *Pius XII and the Second World War*, 261.

mediation of Father Tacchi Venturi, attempted to obtain information on the deportees, but without success. All efforts to get through with material assistance were equally unavailing. Not even Weizsäcker could help.

In the meantime, about five thousand Jews, most of what remained of Rome's Jewish population, were being sheltered in church buildings, whose doors had been opened to them on the orders of the pope. Many found a sanctuary in the Vatican itself and in the papal summer residence of Castel Gandolfo. The Gregorian University and the Pontifical Biblical Institute also housed Jews. Altogether, some 155 ecclesiastical institutions in Rome—monasteries, convents, and church and academic buildings—offered an asylum to refugee Jews. Political fugitives from Fascism were also protected. The number of the Palatine Guard increased tenfold overnight. At least four hundred of the new "guardsmen" were Jews. Others, including Rabbi Zolli, found a welcome in the homes of lay Catholics. Princess Pignatelli Aragona took them under her roof and found safe houses for many others.

Pius XII's critics have accused him of failing to issue a public protest when the initial thousand Jews were expelled from Rome. Yet, the pope remained convinced that such a protest would have made no material difference but would almost certainly have endangered lives. Jewish survivors agreed with him and did not want him to speak out lest a public protest place in danger those already in hiding.[9] Weizsäcker gave this as his opinion, as did Kessel in a statement before the Military Tribunal at Nuremberg.[10] The Jewish historian Pinchas Lapide credits

---

[9] Pinchas E. Lapide, *The Last Three Popes and the Jews* (London: Harper Press, 2009), 263.

[10] Blet, *Pius XII and the Second World War*, 212–13; Anthony Rhodes, *The Vatican in the Age of the Dictators, 1922–1945* (London: Hodder and Stoughton, 1973), 344.

Pius XII with having saved close to 90 percent of Roman Jewry through caution and circumspection. "Would papal clamour have saved more?" he wonders. Or would it not have endangered the lives of Jews still in hiding? The pope had to tread carefully. Although the Germans had thus far respected Vatican neutrality, the possibility remained that they might be provoked into invading the Vatican and the extraterritorial religious institutions in Rome. And these, as Weizsäcker well knew, were crammed with Jews.

Within days of the arrests, *L'Osservatore Romano* published an editorial tendering the pope's support for the oppressed, without limitation, "neither of nationality, nor religion, nor race". The pope's words were interpreted as an exhortation to Catholics to lend assistance to Jews, as indeed many of them were doing already. Yet, the editorial made Weizsäcker uneasy. So as not to arouse the wrath of Hitler, who could fly into a rage at the mere mention of the word *Jew*, Weizsäcker habitually softened the tenor of papal protests in his communiqués to Berlin. "Tactical lies" was how Kessel represented the contents of his superior's dispatches. In his official report following the arrests of 16 October, Weizsäcker contrived to give the impression that the fate of the Jews was a matter of little consequence to the Holy See, which desired only to be on friendly terms with Germany. As a consequence of this flawed report, a distorted version of the position taken by the pope and the Holy See has emerged in the works of those less prudent writers who have taken Weizsäcker's dispatches at face value. Pius XII's reputation has suffered unjustly as a result.

Weizsäcker had another reason for misrepresenting the views of the Holy See—to wit, his desire to protect the pope from kidnap and possible death. Rumours concerning a Nazi plot to kidnap the pope had been circulating in Rome for months, becoming more persistent after the fall of Mussolini. The Vatican had even made preparations lest a sudden evacuation became necessary.[11] President Roosevelt suggested that the Allies adopt the slogan "Save the pope"; and diplomats residing in the Vatican passed a resolution binding them to go with the pope to Germany if he were to be abducted.[12] The plan to storm the Vatican and seize the pope originated with Hitler. The idea alarmed German officials in Italy. Rudolph Hahn, a German diplomat, and Karl Wolff, the head of the SS in occupied Italy, eventually dissuaded Hitler from activating the plan, though he never abandoned the idea completely.[13]

Resistance, in Rome and in Italy generally, involved Italians from all sectors of the community and included members of Catholic Action and former members of Popolare. Rescue operations and the provision of humanitarian relief engaged the most exalted dignitaries of the Church, including the pope himself. The pope was kept in contact with the underground through Monsignor Barbieri of the Lombardo Seminary, where many Jews found sanctuary and thus caused it to be invaded by the Fascists.

Archbishop Montini directed the Vatican rescue operations from inside the Vatican, with the roving assistance of an indefatigable Irishman, Monsignor O'Flaherty. The latter's clandestine exploits earned him the nickname the Vatican Pimpernel and a Hollywood film tribute, when he was portrayed by actor Gregory Peck. O'Flaherty collected

---

[11] David Alvarez and Robert A. Graham, S.J., *Nothing Sacred: Nazi Espionage against the Vatican, 1939–1945* (London: Frank Cass, 1977), 84.

[12] Tittmann, *Inside the Vatican of Pius XII*, 186–87.

[13] Gerard Noel, *Pius XII: The Hound of Hitler* (London: Continuum, 2008), 135. An extensive treatment of the subject can be found in Dan Kurzman, *A Special Mission: Hitler's Secret Plot to Seize the Vatican and Kidnap Pope Pius XII* (Cambridge, Mass.: Da Capo Press, 2007).

details of prisoners of war interned in the camps of northern Italy, whose relatives were kept informed of their whereabouts through Vatican Radio. All the safe places in Rome were known to him. He and his associates have been credited with saving more than six thousand Jews and political refugees from the clutches of the Gestapo.

Father Pancrace Pfeiffer, a German priest and the superior general of the Salvatorian Order, was the pope's liaison with the German military. Several hundred hostages, including some under sentence of death, owed their release to the efficacious intervention of Father Pfeiffer. Even Kappler, the head of the Gestapo, was induced to grant him favours. The ubiquitous Father Marie-Benoît, previously active in Vichy France, from his base of operations in the Capuchin College and through his contacts in various foreign embassies, was able to supply large numbers of Jews with false identity papers. One of Father Marie-Benoît's helpers was Mario DiMarco, a senior police officer. Apprehended by the Gestapo and severely tortured, he nevertheless refused to divulge the organisation's secrets.

The Catholic Refugee Committee provided thousands of Jews with money and passports to expedite their emigration to friendly countries. The work was dispersed through the Saint Raphael Association, which the Holy Father entrusted to the Pallottine Fathers. The association fulfilled a similar mission in Germany. Jews fleeing Europe for destinations in Britain, the United States, and South America took with them signed baptismal certificates issued by the Vatican. The ruse enabled them to circumvent the quotas on Jewish immigration set by the host countries. Over three years, 1943 to 1946, at least four million dollars were allocated to this great humanitarian work, much of it donated by the Catholic Refugee

Committee of America and put at the disposal of the pope. The pope expended his personal fortune in addition, and American Jewish organisations also donated funds.

The papal injunction to save Jewish lives by every possible means went out to other parts of Italy. Jews hidden in monasteries around Assisi on the orders of the local bishop were passed off as monks and taught to sing plainchant. Three hundred found sanctuary over a period of two years. Cardinal Boetto of Genoa saved at least eight hundred lives. In Fiume, Monsignor Palatucci, bishop of Compagna, saved close to a thousand with the assistance of two of his close relatives. The task of organizing rescue in Assisi fell to Father Rufino Niccacci, who was aided by priests, nuns, and members of the Catholic laity. Guided by Father Rufino himself, Jews disguised as monks and nuns made their escape across Allied lines. Others, bearing forged passports, were successful in crossing the border into neutral Switzerland. Many political refugees from Fascism also received help. Assisi was eventually declared an open city, compelling the SS to withdraw from the area. According to Pinchas Lapide, the order of authorisation was forged by one of Father Rufino's accomplices.

More than seven thousand Jews were seized throughout northern Italy, and most of these died in Auschwitz. More than forty thousand Jews throughout Italy, in addition to many destitute ex–prisoners of war, owed their lives to the courageous intervention of ordinary Italians, religious and lay. Farmers, peasants, parish priests, and village policemen risked their own lives in the hazardous business of rescue.

By the summer of 1944, Rome was bursting with half a million refugees, who, together with the indigenous population, were threatened with starvation. Faced with the enormous task of feeding them, the pope instituted a worldwide campaign to raise the necessary funds. Food was procured from Umbria, Tuscany, and the Marches and conveyed to Rome by a fleet of lorries bearing the papal colours. Soup kitchens were opened within Vatican City, where fifty thousand meals were served daily. Throughout Italy, five refugee camps, set up by the Vatican, provided shelter, food, clothing, and essential medical supplies. The work was directed by the pope personally.

On 23 May 1944, Kesselring abandoned the German line of defence, the Gustav Line. Having met with stubborn resistance throughout the long Italian campaign, the Allies were now almost at the gates of Rome. Fearful lest the Eternal City should suffer the same fate as Monte Cassino and be reduced to rubble, the pope appealed to Weizsäcker and to Kesselring not to make Rome a battleground. In the end, the Germans were persuaded to make a peaceful retreat, having first destroyed the railway yards and the ammunition and petrol dumps.

Rome was liberated by the Allies in June 1944, when more than 150,000 Allied servicemen were received in audience by the Holy Father. Weizsäcker was not alone in his belief that the centre of Christian civilisation had been preserved mainly intact due, in large part, to the ceaseless diplomacy of the Holy Father. Three times in one day, the pope had to come to the balcony of the papal apartments to acknowledge the acclaim of tens of thousands of Roman citizens who filled Saint Peter's Square in spontaneous demonstrations of gratitude.

Chief Rabbi Israel Zolli called on Pius XII to thank him for all that the Vatican had done for his people during the Nazi occupation. The American Jewish Welfare Board communicated its thanks: "We are deeply moved by the remarkable display of Christian love, the protection afforded to Italian Jews by the Catholic Church and the Vatican during the German occupation of Italy."[14] The numerous other expressions of gratitude from Jewish authorities are recounted over five pages of Pinchas Lapide's book *The Last Three Popes and the Jews*.[15]

---

[14] Quoted in Rhodes, *The Vatican in the Age of the Dictators*, 341.
[15] Lapide, *The Last Three Popes and the Jews*, 129–33.

8

Varieties of German Opposition to Hitler

The Church in Wartime Germany

Only days after the papal election of 1939, Count Ciano was received in audience by Pius XII. Ciano recalls that he found the pope "exactly as when he was Cardinal Pacelli, benevolent, courteous and human".[1] But the pope could not conceal from Ciano his anxiety over continued German attacks upon the Church. Localised raids carried out against the confessional schools and monastic institutions persisted unchecked, despite the pope's efforts at the outset of his reign to effect a détente with the Hitler regime. The spoliation of Church property reached a peak in the summer, provoking a lengthy note of protest from the Holy See. The publication in October of the pope's first encyclical letter, *Summi Pontificatus*, and the manner of its reception in Germany, may have torpedoed any remaining hopes that the situation might be diffused.

The official visit to the Vatican by the German foreign minister in the spring of 1940 ended in failure, as Ribbentrop obstinately refused to listen to Maglione's complaints. Diplomatic relations between the Holy See and the Reich remained at a low ebb throughout the remainder of

---

[1] *Ciano's Diary, 1939–1943*, ed. Malcolm Muggeridge (London: William Heinemann, 1947), entry for 18 March 1939.

1940. On the last day of the year, the totalitarian nature of National Socialism was assailed in a sermon by Bishop Gröber of Freiburg, which did little to help matters.

Resistance at grassroots level broke out the following year, when Christians in Munich and Upper Bavaria rose in revolt after the *gauleiter* (district leader) Adolf Wagner attempted to remove crucifixes from schools. Angry protesters invaded school premises and tore Hitler's portrait from the walls. Hitler later countermanded Wagner's decree. A controversial move to outlaw baptisms in hospitals and hospital visits by clergymen was defeated when Protestant and Catholic mothers united to oppose it. The measure was soon quashed. In June, the Fulda bishops' pastoral letter was read out in Catholic churches and was more than usually scathing in its condemnation of Nazi abuses. In particular, it deplored the unlawful sequestration of monastic buildings by the Gestapo. Heydrich perceived the pastoral as constituting a direct attack upon the state. He complained to Ribbentrop: "Here we see what a bitter and irreconcilable enemy we have in the Catholic Church."[2]

When the war began, the bishops demonstrated their patriotism in a pastoral letter urging Catholic soldiers to do their duty for the Fatherland. When certain religious houses in Germany and the Ostmark (formerly Austria) were requisitioned as hospitals for the duration of the war, their occupants willingly complied with the requirement. But as time passed, it increasingly perturbed the hierarchy that religious houses were being appropriated needlessly and that the war was being made to serve as a convenient excuse for the confiscation of church property. In many

---

[2] See Anthony Rhodes, *The Vatican in the Age of the Dictators, 1922–1945* (London: Hodder and Stoughton, 1973), 297.

cases, moreover, religious personnel had been unceremoniously ejected from their homes by the Gestapo, which then forced them into exile after seizing their belongings. The nuncio, Orsenigo, protested the abuse, and in July 1941, the Holy Office complained to Foreign Secretary Weizsäcker.

The eviction and subsequent banishment of the Jesuits from two of their houses in Munich, and of the Sisters of the Immaculate Conception from their convent, brought the matter to a head, provoking one of the most courageous acts of defiance of the war years. The outrage aroused the wrath of the diocesan bishop, the indomitable Clemens August von Galen. From the pulpit of St. Lambert's Church on Sunday, 13 July 1941, Bishop Galen launched into an unprecedented attack upon "the enemy within our midst".[3]

In calling the Gestapo to account, Galen charged it, in general, with the curtailment of personal liberty, and the unlawful imprisonment of German citizens. Then, in impassioned tones, he protested the indignity that had occasioned the sermon, the Gestapo's "rape of the religious houses". It was an outrage, he said, that their occupants should be "thrown into the streets like dissolute slaves and hunted from the country as so much riffraff". Galen warned the authorities of the arbitrary nature of justice, and the threat to the legal system, when it was left in the hands of the Gestapo:

No German citizen has any defence against the power of the Gestapo.... [N]ot one of us is certain that he will not

[3] The extracts that follow, from this and from the two other of Bishop Galen's most celebrated sermons, hardly convey the full power of his preaching. The sermons may be read in their fullness in the appendix to Reverend Heinrich Portmann's biography of Bishop Galen, from which I quote. See Heinrich Portmann, *Cardinal von Galen* (London: Jarrolds, 1957).

any day be dragged from his house and carried off to the cells of some concentration camp.... When the Gestapo inflicts its punishments, jurisdiction on the part of the administration goes by the board.

Rounding on the government for permitting such a misuse of power, Bishop Galen declaimed:

Any state which ... allows or causes the punishment of blameless men undermines its own authority and the respect for its dignity in the conscience of its citizens.

Further sequestrations of church property called forth a second thunderbolt from Bishop Galen a week later. In an inspired use of metaphor, he likened the Gestapo to a hammer striking an anvil and the Gestapo's victims to the anvil that receives the hammer blows. However, the anvil too can be a weapon:

Whatever is beaten out on the anvil receives its shape from the anvil as well as the hammer. The anvil cannot and need not strike back.... If it is tough enough it invariably outlives the hammer.

Christians, and parents especially, were urged to become hard and unyielding like the anvil, so to make themselves into a weapon of God's will.

Bishop Galen did not let matters rest there but dispatched telegrams to the Reich chancellery and to several government ministers, including Goering, demanding justice for victims of the Gestapo. Two weeks after the hammer-and-anvil sermon, Hitler called a temporary halt to the seizure of monastic dwellings and, though doubtless infuriated by Galen's temerity, ordered that no action be taken against him in the interests of national unity.

Hitler took care never to attack the Church openly. If Speer is to be believed, the führer thought a permanent arrangement with the Church was achievable and that the Church eventually would learn to adapt to the political goals of National Socialism.[4] It was Hitler's conviction that powerful institutions such as the Catholic Church could and should be made use of, not abolished, a lesson he learned in his Vienna days from his hero Karl Lueger.[5] It seems that the seizure of certain church property had been carried out indiscriminately and in defiance of Goebbel's explicit instructions to the contrary. The propaganda minister complained in his diary of "rowdies and beer-hall fighters" making trouble for him in Berlin. His complaint came in the wake of a highly critical pastoral letter by Bishop Preysing of Berlin. The Church question, wrote Goebbels, was not to be discussed during the war, "no matter how recalcitrant the parsons may prove to be".[6] Goebbels later became incensed after the Church struggle found an echo in the American press. He accused the Catholic clergy of collaborating with the enemy and expressed regret that present circumstances prevented him from calling them to account. He vowed to take revenge at a later date.[7]

Bishop Galen's attacks upon the Gestapo added to his already well-deserved reputation as a fearless opponent of the Nazi regime, although it is for his sermon denouncing the Nazi euthanasia programme that he is best remembered. Given Hitler's unequivocal pronouncements on

[4] Albert, Speer, *Inside the Third Reich* (London: Weidenfeld and Nicolson, 1970), 95.

[5] Konrad Heiden, *The Fuehrer* (London: Robinson Publishing, 1999), 57.

[6] *The Goebbels Diaries: The Last Days*, ed. Hugh Trevor-Roper (London: Book Club Associates, 1978), entry for 11 March 1942.

[7] Ibid., entry for 16 May 1943.

the subject of eugenics,[8] it seemed but a logical extension of the compulsory sterilisation procedure, put in place in 1934, to the elimination of all the mentally and physically unfit. Propaganda was devised to soften public attitudes and make euthanasia appear the merciful option. The mentally ill and adults and children suffering from congenital diseases were represented as being a financial burden on the nation. Thus had Dr. Gerhard Wagner argued at the Nuremberg Rally of 1934.

Church-run institutions in Germany had an outstanding record in caring for the mentally ill. When attempts were made to transfer their patients to state asylums, naturally they were resisted. Conway has drawn attention to the difficulty facing religious authorities if they did not comply with the government's demands. In such cases, he says, the Church's institutions might well have been forcibly appropriated, as, indeed, happened to at least one Church-run asylum that refused to cooperate.[9] Once taken over, the fate of the inmates would then be utterly beyond the control of the Church authorities.

On the day Nazi Germany invaded Poland, Hitler authorised the killing of all persons suffering from incurable diseases. By the summer of 1940, the transference of feebleminded and chronically disabled patients from nursing homes to euthanasia centres was being implemented in most parts of the Reich. At first these unfortunate people were shot, but gassing soon became the preferred means of elimination. Coaches taking the inmates of asylums to the

[8] Hamilton T. Burden, *The Nuremberg Party Rallies, 1923–1939* (London: Pall Mall Press, 1967), 54; see also J. Noakes and G. Pridham, *Nazism 1919–1945*, vol. 3, *Foreign Policy, War and Racial Extermination* (Exeter: University of Exeter Press, 1995), 1002.

[9] J. S. Conway, *The Nazi Persecution of the Churches, 1933–1945* (London: Weidenfeld and Nicolson, 1968), 26.

killing centres occasionally met with hostile demonstrations from members of the public. Hitler was caught up in one while delayed at a railway station at the same time that a transportation of mentally handicapped children took place. Protest letters began piling up in the Reich chancellery and the Justice Ministry, some, as Ian Kershaw has noted, "from dyed-in-the-wool National Socialists".[10]

Throughout 1940 to 1941, Protestant and Catholic voices were repeatedly raised in defiance of the government's euthanasia policy. In July 1940, Evangelical Bishop Theophil Wurm and Pastor Paul Braune each sent lengthy memoranda to the Reich chancellor's office deploring the transference and wholesale murder of inmates of sanatoria and nursing homes. Not stopping at that, Braune and Pastor von Bodelschwingh sought out government ministers to press home their complaints. After his arrest in August, Braune spent several weeks in prison. Ernst Wilm, another pastor who voiced opposition, was sent to Dachau, where he remained for the duration of the war.

On 1 August, Bishop Gröber protested the killing of the insane to the Reich minister of justice, Dr. Franz Gürtner, and offered to meet the expenses of mentally ill patients himself. A few days later, Cardinal Bertram addressed a letter to Hans Lammers, head of the Reich chancellery, expressing his dismay. Most Catholic bishops made individual protests; and it was brought to the attention of the Catholic faithful that the state was killing people on a large scale as a matter of official policy.

In November, Cardinal Faulhaber wrote to Gürtner, citing article 16 of the concordat as the authority for his right to protest euthanasia. The following month, the

[10] Ian Kershaw, *Hitler*, vol. 2, *1936–1945: Nemesis* (London: Allen Lane, 2000), 426; Noakes and Pridham, *Nazism*, vol. 3, 1040.

Holy Office declared it not permissible to kill an innocent human being because of mental or physical disability; and it rejected the argument that the state may kill its citizens when it deemed them to be a burden on society. The practice was denounced as being contrary to both divine and natural law, a point that was restated four days later in *L'Osservatore Romano*. The following month, Bishop Preysing weighed in with a sermon in which he declared the very idea of euthanasia to be unacceptable.

Until August 1941, the protests had been of a general nature or had been made privately or through official channels. The event that really brought the issue into the public domain, and gave it worldwide attention, came after Nazi officials began transferring mental patients from Bishop Galen's diocese of Münster. Galen had earlier issued a condemnation from the pulpit, but this was merely a preamble to his protest of 3 August, when, "with unmatched and unforgettable incisiveness", he "castigated the practice of euthanasia".[11] In the church of Saint Lambert where, three weeks earlier, he had preached the first of his two sermons against the Gestapo, Bishop Galen pictured for his congregation what was at that moment taking place throughout Germany. Incurably ill patients were being forcibly removed from nursing homes, never to be seen again. Their loved ones were later informed of the patients' deaths and invited to claim the ashes. The "ghastly doctrine" that it is lawful to take away life that is unworthy of being lived had led, Galen claimed, to the compilation of death lists of "unproductive citizens", and he attacked the notion that people have the right to exist only because they are productive:

---

[11] Ernst Wolf, "Political and Moral Motives behind the Resistance", in Hermann Graml et al., *The German Resistance to Hitler* (London: Batsford, 1970), 225.

If the principle is established that unproductive human beings may be killed, then God help all those invalids who, in order to produce wealth, have given their all and sacrificed their strength of body. If all unproductive people may thus be violently eliminated, then woe betide our brave soldiers who return home wounded, maimed or sick.

The last point could not fail to hit the mark, as, at that very moment, thousands of German parents had sons fighting on the front line. Once the principle is established that it is lawful to kill unproductive persons, then, said Galen, no one can be sure of his life. "Who can have confidence in any doctor?" he wondered.

Without mentioning names, the bishop related a case in his own diocese of a mentally ill peasant, the father of a serving soldier, who had been cared for in a clinic near Munich but had since disappeared. "And so the son who is now risking his life at the front for his German compatriots will never again see his father." For such unspeakable crimes, said Galen, it is possible to obtain God's forgiveness only by living according to God's laws and by prayer and penance.

But those who persist in inciting the anger of God, who revile our faith, who hate His commandments ... who condemn to death our innocent brothers and sisters, our fellow human beings, we shun absolutely so as to remain undefiled by their blasphemous way of life.

It is almost impossible to exaggerate the impact of Bishop Galen's "stinging sermons", as a contemporary Protestant report styled them. Throughout Germany, in the occupied territories of the New Reich and among soldiers at the front, Galen's sermons were pondered over and made the subject of clandestine discussions, as copies were secretly made and passed around. The British government gained considerable propaganda value from Galen's euthanasia sermon and, knowing that it would be suppressed by the authorities, had the RAF drop copies of it over Germany. The sermon made headlines in the British press and was broadcast by the BBC. The pope expressed his appreciation by reading aloud all three sermons to his closest confidants.

For his courageous stand against Nazism, Bishop Galen became renowned as the Lion of Münster. After his euthanasia sermon, he was arrested but was immediately released following a public outcry. A vast crowd gathered outside the cathedral in Münster to celebrate his release. Others joined their protests to his, including Bishop Franz Bornewasser and Godehard Machens, and the Catholic bishops of Berlin and Limburg. Father Bernhard Lichtenberg, the director of Bishop Preysing's Office of Special Relief, challenged Dr. Conti of the Department of Health over the unlawful killing of the disabled, quoting the Reich penal code. He was arrested for his trouble and later imprisoned.

By undermining its authority, Bishop Galen imperilled the very fabric of the National Socialist state. His attack on the euthanasia programme particularly is recalled as the single most effective public protest of the Nazi era. By the time Hitler called a halt to it on 24 August, between fifty thousand and sixty thousand patients had been gassed.[12] Some of the party elite, including Himmler and Bormann, called for Galen to be hanged. Goebbels, however, cautioned against it. Such a measure, he said, might result in

[12] This is the figure according to Portmann, Bishop Galen's biographer. Portmann, *Cardinal von Galen*, 108. Guenter Lewy gives the higher figure of about seventy thousand. Guenter Lewy, *The Catholic Church and Nazi Germany* (London: Weidenfeld and Nicolson, 1964), 264.

"writing off Münster and the whole of Westphalia for the duration of the war".[13] Although Hitler fumed against Galen, he saw the sense in Goebbel's advice and resolved to deal with the troublesome bishop at a later date. As Goebbels said, revenge should be taken coldly. Hitler meanwhile took a measure of revenge by imprisoning twenty-nine of Bishop Galen's diocesan clergy.

Church-state relations remained intractable, with accusation and counteraccusation being fired off in 1942. Early in the year, Goering dispatched angry letters to Bishop Galen and Bishop Berning, charging them with holding treasonable attitudes, and reminded them of their oath of loyalty to the state. Cardinal Faulhaber hit back by accusing the Nazis of declaring war on Christianity. A Gestapo report of August noted that Catholics were displaying a passive resistance to the regime by their attachment to the Mass and religious devotions such as processions. Passion Sunday was the occasion for the German bishops' pastoral letter, which contained a strongly worded protest about Nazi atrocities. The *New York Times* trumpeted: "A courage no less exalted than that of the Christian martyrs in pagan Rome inspires the Passion Sunday letter of the German bishops."

Throughout the war, the Catholic bishops remained undecided on how best to withstand the Nazi regime, in particular with reference to its oppression of the Jews. As president of the Fulda Bishops' Conference and the most senior Catholic prelate, Cardinal Bertram wielded the greatest influence. But some bishops, notably Cardinal Faulhaber and Bishops Galen and Preysing, eschewing Bertram's policy of quiet diplomacy, adopted a more

[13] See Bishop Galen's entry in Robert S. Wistrich, *Who's Who in Nazi Germany* (London: Routledge, 2002).

confrontational stance. Preysing's public opposition to
Nazism went back many years. When he was consecrated
bishop of Berlin in 1935, Nazi officials boycotted the cer-
emony, as even then Preysing was regarded as an enemy
of the party. A civil lawyer by training, he was outspoken
in defence of human rights, and his sermons were scathing
in their attitude to racialism. Like Faulhaber, he actively
assisted fugitive Jews by hiding them in his episcopal residence before arranging their escape. For his devotion to
the cause of rescuing Jews he was praised by the pope,
who was his personal friend.

Preysing sponsored the Office of Special Relief for the
Berlin Diocese, for which the task of helping Jews escape
from Germany was given priority. In October 1941, the director, Canon Bernhard Lichtenberg, was imprisoned for
offering public prayers for Jews and later died en route to
a concentration camp. To succeed him, Bishop Preysing
appointed the remarkable Margarete Sommer as executive
director of the organisation. Sommer quickly became the
principal adviser on Jewish affairs to the German hierarchy. No one in Germany was better informed than she.
For a time, she was associated with Gertrud Luckner of
Freiburg, until the latter's transfer to a women's concentration camp for her rescue activities. As the Jewish persecution intensified, Sommer acquired the support of parish
groups in hiding Jews and initiated contacts with other
resistance movements. Both Sommer and Preysing urged
the bishops to protest atrocities committed against Jews.

From 1943, Preysing wrote several times to the pope
urging him to speak out against the extermination of the
Jews. Anxious to avoid reprisals, which he felt sure would
follow in the wake of a papal denouncement, the pope
preferred that the German bishops should address the matter themselves, taking into account the retaliatory measures

that could follow upon episcopal protests, as he explained to Preysing. The hierarchy did indeed issue a succession of pastoral letters deploring racialism and exhorting the faithful to show respect for Jews. Preysing, however, requested stronger, more specific statements. When, in November 1941, he and Galen had wanted the Fulda Bishops' Conference to protest the deportation of Jews, Cardinal Bertram argued that such an action could have grave consequences for the Church.[14] Bertram felt vindicated in his policy by the experience of the Dutch bishops' protest and the consequent reprisals taken against Holland's Catholic Jews, all of whom wound up in Auschwitz.

In his admirable book *Catholic Theologians in Nazi Germany*, Robert A Krieg has intimated that the disagreement between Bertram and bishops such as Preysing, who favoured more direct action, involved more than political strategy and was, at bottom, theological. Bertram represented a majority of the bishops, who viewed the Church's mission as being primarily concerned with saving souls. So long as the churches remained open, Bertram was content to trust in diplomacy rather than risk antagonizing Hitler. A different understanding of mission was offered by Preysing, one that stressed the Church's commitment to the protection of human rights arising from the natural and moral law. Who is to say that Preysing was right and Bertram wrong? Each ecclesiology, says Krieg, had its merits and limitations during the Third Reich.

Bishop Preysing was able to summon the support of the like-minded Archbishop Frings of Cologne, the successor, since 1941, of Cardinal Schulte. The sermons of the outspoken Frings were fearless in their condemnation of

---

[14]Robert A. Krieg, *Catholic Theologians in Nazi Germany* (New York: Continuum, 2004), 157.

the murder of Jews. In 1943, Preysing drafted a strong statement denouncing Nazi policy, taking inspiration from the Ten Commandments. Archbishop Frings got Cardinal Bertram and the other bishops to endorse it. It was called *Draft for a Petition Favouring the Jews* but became more popularly known as the Decalogue Letter. The document condemned the deportation and killing of Jews and protested the violation of their natural rights and the inhuman conditions of their existence.[15] Not all historians have expressed themselves satisfied with the condemnations contained in the Decalogue Letter. Helmreich, for instance, who is otherwise appreciative of Catholic efforts to withstand Hitler, notes that the letter gives no indication of the magnitude of the Nazi extermination policy.[16] A similar objection had earlier been made against the publications of the White Rose resistance group.[17] As with all protests, however, the contents of the letter had to be weighed against the possible repercussions. Two weeks earlier, the Catholic bishops had raised their voices in protest against a proposal to compel children of mixed Aryan-Jewish marriages to wear the Star of David. As a result of protesting this less weighty matter, Catholic hospitals, convents, and other resources throughout Germany were expropriated, and Faulhaber, Galen, and Preysing were placed under house arrest.[18]

---

[15] Ibid. Dan Kurzman quotes the document in his book *A Special Mission: Hitler's Secret Plot to Seize the Vatican and Kidnap Pope Pius XII* (Cambridge, Mass.: Da Capo Press, 2007), 153.

[16] Ernst Christian Helmreich, *The German Churches under Hitler* (Detroit: Wayne State University Press, 1979), 364.

[17] Annette E. Dumbach and Jud Newborn, *Shattering the German Night: The Story of the White Rose* (Boston: Little, Brown, 1986), 120.

[18] Monsignor Stephen M. DiGiovanni, H.E.D., "Pius XII and the Jews: The War Years as Reported in the *New York Times*", no. 49, citing the *New York Times* of 6 July 1943, in *Rutgers Journal of Law and Religion*, accessed 31 August 2015, http://lawandreligion.com/sites/lawandreligion.com/files/DiGiovanni.pdf.

Dissenting Youth and the Resistance of the White Rose

The totality of German youth did not succumb to the cult of Hitler, as is commonly supposed, but in significant areas young people manifested a rebelliousness that caused the authorities no small amount of trouble. Nonconformity was anathema to the new order, which required compliant young Nazis, not independent spirits. Scornful of the Hitler Youth, many young people found fulfilment in membership in loosely organised gangs, such as the Edelweiss Pirates and the Swing Youth, both of which were outlawed because of their rejection of the Hitler Youth but not least because of the alternative lifestyles they promoted.

Originating among Catholic youth in Bavaria, and named for the white Alpine flower they took as their emblem, the Edelweiss Pirates were locally based groups of mostly working-class boys and girls whose common bond was a love of the outdoor life. At weekends, dressed in their distinctive chequered shirts, the Pirates ventured into the neighbouring countryside, where they hiked, camped, sang songs, and, when the occasion presented itself, descended upon Hitler Youth patrols, with whom the Pirates were always willing to do battle.

In 1940, the Gestapo clamped down on groups in Düsseldorf, Duisburg, Cologne, Essen, and Wuppertal. Six hundred members of the Cologne Pirates were arrested in one day, and more than a hundred of these were sent to reform schools as punishment. On another occasion, the ringleaders in Cologne were publicly hanged as an example to the rest. Yet, although the Pirates exhibited a disdain for Nazism, only a few took any active part in the Resistance. And because Hitler perforce had to rely on German youth for future wartime service, he was loath to declare all-out war against the Pirates and other recalcitrant youth movements, as he did against the Jews. Thus, despite Himmler's call for their extermination, the Edelweiss Pirates continued to plague the authorities for the duration of the war.   ·

Whereas the Edelweiss Pirates came from working-class backgrounds, most of the young people of the Swing Youth belonged to the affluent lower middle class and were usually city dwellers. Though they eschewed the conventions of National Socialism, the Swing Youth were apolitical. In their mode of dress—followers went attired in fashionable Western-style clothes—and in the way of life they espoused, the Swing Youth owed much to British and American culture. Their songs were sung in English, which, not infrequently, was also the spoken language of their choice. The most distinguishing trait of the Swing Youth, however, was their devotion to American jazz, especially swing, which was listened to and danced to in nightclubs and in the homes of group members. To Nazis, who abominated jazz as the music of an inferior race, the Swing Youth appeared decadent and un-German. Hundreds of members were arrested in Hamburg in 1940; and two years later, Himmler demanded that the remaining ringleaders be sent to concentration camps.

In contrast to the free-spirited inducements of the Swing Youth and the Edelweiss Pirates, the Hitler Youth could offer only physical exercises, endless drill, and indoctrination by rote learning. Not surprisingly for some, initial enthusiasm for the movement soon evaporated. In fact, the Hitler Youth was beset by numerous problems intrinsic to the organisation itself. Compulsory membership after 1939 resulted in the conscription of the resentful and the apathetic. There was a need constantly to replace those at the top, as leaders either outgrew the movement or, following the outbreak of war, departed for military service.

Replacements were not always adequate to the task. Then, because membership was compulsory for all German youth, the organisation cut across class divisions. Like its parent organisation, National Socialism, the Hitler Youth was meant to be classless. Efforts to break down class proved futile, and class-based patterns of friendship persisted.[19] Hampered by the movement's anti-intellectualism, and the lack of a coherent belief system, Hitler Youth leaders proved no match for young Christians who were well instructed in the principles of their religious faith. The Catholic Church trained young people to combat Hitler Youth leaders so as to subvert the organisation from within. Dissension in the ranks was common. The Munich martyr Hans Scholl, who had demonstrated an initial enthusiasm for the Hitler Youth, was disciplined after expressing unwelcome sentiments and singing unacceptable songs. Despite strenuous efforts to capture the minds of German youth, the National Socialists often met with frustration. The Catholic Church, by contrast, was largely successful in retaining the loyalty of her young people.[20]

If there was an exception, it was to be found in the universities, the one department of German life where Nazi propaganda achieved notable success. Student loyalty to Hitler was generally unquestioning, and, notwithstanding the high level of political crime among the young, few of those who offered resistance to the regime were university

---

[19] Frank McDonough, *Sophie Scholl* (Stroud, UK: History Press, 2009), 28. See also Detlev J.L. Peukert, "Young People: For or Against the Nazis?" *History Today* 35, no. 10 (October 1985): 22. The whole article can be read with profit.

[20] Daniel Horn, "The Struggle for Catholic Youth in Hitler's Germany: An Assessment", *Catholic Historical Review* 64, no. 4 (October 1979): 581–82. Like Peukert's article above, Horn sets forth a corrective to the view that attributes unqualified success to the Hitler Youth.

students. Standing in honourable contrast to the majority was the example of the Munich students of the White Rose.

The prime mover in the White Rose organisation was a twenty-four-year-old medical student from Ulm, Hans Scholl. Hans had disappointed his middle-class father when he became a zealous participant in the Hitler Youth. But being of an independent mind, he found the total conformity to Nazism required of Hitler Youth members stultifying, and his initial fervour soon turned to disenchantment. Further, he became increasingly unsettled by the train of events in his native country, where "bondage, hatred and falsehood had become the normal mode of existence".[21] Later, Hans' love of music and outdoor recreations found expression in his association with a group of young people in ways not unlike those of the Edelweiss Pirates.

Hans was persuaded of the need for active resistance after duplicated excerpts from Bishop Galen's sermons found their way into his letterbox. "Finally a man has had the courage to speak out!" he exclaimed on reading them, and he immediately resolved to obtain a duplicating machine. Youth resistance usually took the form of daubing buildings with anti-Hitler graffiti or circulating flyers bearing information culled from BBC and Vatican Radio broadcasts. Those caught in the act faced long prison terms, and death sentences awaited the ringleaders; and the Gestapo had notable success in ferreting them out.

Hans conceived the more daring plan of producing a newsletter, written by him and other like-minded students, that would furnish an ongoing critique of the Hitler regime. Around him at the University of Munich he gathered a few close friends: Alexander Schmorell and

---

[21] Inge Scholl, *Students against Tyranny: The Resistance of the White Rose, Munich, 1942–1943* (Middletown, Conn.: Wesleyan University Press, 1970), 17.

Christoph Probst, who, like him, were medical students, later to be joined by Hans' younger sister, Sophie, and Willi Graf, a Catholic medical student from the Saar region. Intensely patriotic and anti-Hitler, the group was also united by a shared interest in the study of literature, philosophy, and theology. The Catholic thinker Theodor Haecker advised them. They evinced a familiarity with Augustine, Aquinas, and Newman, in addition to modern French and German thinkers. Sophie, particularly, drew inspiration from the writings of Saint Augustine, a copy of which she kept with her at all times. They called their organisation the White Rose, an arbitrary choice of name believed to have been borrowed from the title of a novel that Hans had been reading.

The first four White Rose leaflets were written by Hans Scholl and Alexander Schmorell and appeared in the summer of 1942. The tone of the leaflets was set by the opening words of the first one:

> Nothing is so unworthy of a civilized nation as allowing itself to be "governed" without opposition by an irresponsible clique that has yielded to base instinct. It is certain that today every honest German is ashamed of his government.[22]

The German people are indicted for being spineless and will-less and are urged to passive resistance to "forestall the spread of this atheistic war machine". The call to unite in offering passive resistance echoes throughout the series of leaflets, joined in the third by a call to engage in sabotage. The regime's persecution of the Jews—"the most frightful crime against human dignity ... unparalleled in the whole

---

[22] In total, there were six White Rose leaflets. They are to be found in Inge Scholl's book, together with numerous other documents, including transcripts of the indictment and sentencing of the principal group members.

of history"—is assailed in the second leaflet, and the series culminates in a vilification of Hitler, who is represented as the Antichrist.

Late in 1942, the little group attracted the interest of Sophie's tutor at the university, the Catholic philosopher Kurt Huber. He had read one of the leaflets and been profoundly impressed by it. A popular and inspiring lecturer, he now became mentor to the group. Meanwhile, Hans and several of his comrades were posted to Russia as medical orderlies, Hitler having launched Operation Barbarossa, his anti-Bolshevik crusade, the year before. While journeying to the Russian front, Hans witnessed the bestial treatment meted out to captive Jews and was revolted by it. Returning to Germany in late autumn, he arranged for the production of a new series of leaflets, to be called Leaflets of the Resistance. In the event, only two were produced, appearing early in 1943. Strongly influenced by Huber, who revised Hans' draft of the first and himself wrote the second, together they laid bare the scale of Nazi infamy and Hitler's disastrous conduct of the war. In the leaflets, a new future is envisaged, based on democratic freedoms, in which a new, federal Germany, free of Nazi criminality, would take its rightful place among the European nations.

The White Rose leaflets were posted to selected recipients and were usually accompanied by the request that copies be made and passed on. At intervals, they were packed into suitcases and taken by rail to other parts of Germany. Sympathizers distributed copies in Frankfurt, Ulm, Stuttgart, Bonn, Freiburg, Saarbrücken, Mannheim, Karlsruhe, Salzburg, Linz, and Vienna in the Ostmark. Willi Graf took leaflets to Berlin and distributed them there. Traute Lafrenz, another sympathizer, carried them to her hometown of Hamburg. White Rose leaflets found their way to

Norway, where they were translated into Norwegian, and to Sweden, and from Sweden to England.[23] The exiled writer Thomas Mann is said to have wept with pleasure on reading them. Soon branches of the White Rose resistance sprang up in Hamburg, Stuttgart, and the Rhineland. By early 1943, the scale of operations had increased markedly. According to a Gestapo estimate, there were between eight and ten thousand copies of the fifth leaflet in circulation.[24] Huber had prefaced it with the words "A Call to All Germans".

Despite the exercise of caution—the Scholls always posted leaflets to themselves—the clandestine operations of the group could not for long be kept secret from the authorities. While Hans and Professor Huber were at work on the last publication, Hans received a tip-off that the Gestapo was on to him and that he might expect to be arrested quite soon. Very possibly it was this information that decided Hans on the course of action he and Sophie were now about to undertake. Early on the morning of 18 February, brother and sister loaded a suitcase and briefcase with leaflets and, before lectures began, scattered them in the corridors and entrance hall of the university.

They were arrested that day, after a caretaker at the university informed on them to the Gestapo. The following day, Christoph Probst was taken. Under interrogation, brother and sister confessed their guilt but steadfastly refused to name their collaborators. Instead, they claimed full responsibility themselves. They were particularly concerned to deflect the blame for their actions away from Christoph, who was married with a young family. Summoned before

---

[23] Ger van Roon, *German Resistance to Hitler: Count von Moltke and the Kreisau Circle* (London: Van Nostrand Reinhold, 1971), 164.

[24] Dumbach and Newborn, *Shattering the German Night*, 165.

the notorious Roland Freisler, president of the People's Court, the three students were charged with conspiracy to commit high treason. After a trial lasting three and a half hours, they were found guilty and sentenced to death by beheading. The sentences were carried out in the court-yard of Stadelheim Prison on the evening of 22 February. Sophie went to her death trailing a broken leg, a result of a brutal seventeen-hour interrogation. Christoph Probst had for some time cherished a hope of becoming a Catholic. His request to see a priest was granted, and he was received into the Church hours before his execution. The exemplary bravery shown by the three young people throughout their interrogation and trial left a deep impression on their prison guards. Writing of all White Rose students, Inge Scholl, Hans and Sophie's younger sister, revealed the secret of their inner strength: "Christ became for them ... the elder brother who was always there, closer even than death. He was their path which allowed of no return, the truth which gave answer to so many questions, and life itself."[25]

That same night, Willi Graf was apprehended and, shortly after, Professor Huber and Alexander Schmorell, who was betrayed to the Gestapo by a former girlfriend. Fourteen members of the White Rose were accordingly arraigned before Freisler on 19 April. Graf, Schmorell, and Huber were each condemned to death. One member was acquitted, and the rest received prison sentences of varying duration. In a courageous address before Freisler and the People's Court, Huber spoke eloquently of the moral bankruptcy of the Nazi regime. He and Schmorell were guillotined on 13 July; Graf followed them to the scaffold on 12 October. Determined to stamp out every vestige

[25] Scholl, *Students against Tyranny*, 42.

of White Rose resistance, the Gestapo subsequently made arrests in Hamburg, Stuttgart, and the Rhineland. In all, about a hundred activists were rounded up. Seven members of the Hamburg branch were executed. Sentences ranged from prison terms to execution and, in at least two cases, enforced suicide.

The last White Rose leaflet had been addressed specifically to students. It concluded with this stirring, if somewhat quixotic, declaration: "Our people stand ready to rebel against the National Socialist enslavement of Europe in a fervent new breakthrough of freedom and honour." If Hans and Sophie Scholl had expected their fate to unleash an unstoppable tide of student revolt, however, what followed revealed their hopes to have been sadly misplaced. A few days after their deaths, a rally was held in Munich University, and hundreds of students demonstrated their loyalty to Hitler and loudly applauded Jacob Schmid, the university caretaker turned Gestapo informer.

An Alternative Germany

From the time of Hitler's acquisition of power, a minority of Germans of every class and political persuasion sought secret ways of opposing him. There were certain obvious ways of showing defiance. Most members of the Resistance lent assistance to Jews; some circulated anti-Nazi propaganda through underground newspapers. A resistance group formed by the Social Democrat Walter Schmedemann in Eilbeck, Hamburg, in addition to producing its own newspaper, provided a courier service and was particularly effective in obtaining news of concentration-camp inmates. Social Democrats in Augsburg, Berlin, and the Ruhr forged links with exiled Social Democrats in neutral countries and found willing sympathizers in Austria, Italy, and Hungary.

While these activities were directed to more immediate ends, others in the Resistance, convinced of the eventual collapse of National Socialism, or hopeful of its overthrow, were busily devising plans for a future Germany. In this regard, the university city of Freiburg became a breeding ground where secret discussions took place involving university teachers, predominantly economists and theologians associated with the Confessional church, as well as outsiders. A group formed in 1938 that counted the historian Gerhard Ritter among its members produced the Freiburg Memorandum, a reflection from a Christian viewpoint on the existing social and political order.

Berlin was the venue for secret discussions among a group of conservative intellectuals known collectively as the Wednesday Club. They were mostly older men and included monarchists in their number. General Ludwig Beck, the former chief of staff of the armed forces, assumed the leadership of the club in 1942. It had a distinguished membership, including Ulrich von Hassell, the former German ambassador to Rome, and Johannes Popitz, the Prussian minister of finance. Hassell and Popitz, among others, drew up draft proposals for a reconstituted Germany. Popitz was never a member of the Nazi Party and had wanted to resign his office after Crystal Night but was not allowed to. Hassell was a monarchist who had been dismissed from the diplomatic corps in 1938 for his anti-Nazism. After the war, his diaries were unearthed from the family garden, where he had buried them; much light has been thrown on the German Resistance as a result of their discovery.

In laying the ground plan for a new Germany, much of the attention focussed on a man whose followers had no party political affiliation, the former mayor of Leipzig Carl Goerdeler. A conservative and a devout Protestant, Goerdeler had resigned his government post in 1935 over Hitler's rearmament policy. Rejecting also the anti-Semitism of the Nazis, two years later he resigned as mayor of Leipzig in protest over the removal of Felix Mendelssohn's bust from the entrance to the City Hall. Goerdeler's frequent trips abroad as overseas representative of the Stuttgart firm of Bosch brought him important contacts in the West. He met Churchill in London in 1938, in furtherance of his scheme to form an alignment with Britain and the United States against Hitler. In addition to his extensive business connections, Goerdeler kept in close touch with prominent members of the Wehrmacht who were sympathetic to his aims, in the conviction that only the military could overthrow Hitler.

Links between various groups in the civilian resistance, and between the civilian and the military resistance, produced a certain amount of cross-fertilisation of ideas. Goerdeler collaborated on the Freiburg Memorandum and was closely associated with General Beck, the former army chief of staff who had resigned his post in 1938 rather than continue to serve under Hitler. Together with Beck, Goerdeler drew up his own programme for post-Hitler reconstruction known as the Goal.[26] Appalled by the suffering of the Jews, he issued a "Government Declaration" that, in the event of Hitler's removal, would bring their persecution to an immediate end.[27] Many in the resistance who looked ahead to the new Germany saw in Goerdeler a future chancellor. Nevertheless, he aroused a degree of

[26] David Welch, *The Hitler Conspiracies: Secrets and Lies behind the Rise and Fall of the Nazi Party* (Shepperton, UK: Ian Allan, 2001), 80–81.

[27] Guido Knopp, *Hitler's Holocaust* (Stroud, UK: Sutton, 2004), 264–65.

mistrust. Both Popitz and Hassell had doubts about his leadership.[28] Some thought him not merely conservative but reactionary, the representative of a type of older generation of German politician indissolubly wedded to the past. Moreover, Goerdeler's vision of a greater Germany that included some of Hitler's territorial gains, such as Austria and the Sudetenland, did little to commend him to either Britain or the United States. In the end, it was his habitual lack of discretion that brought about his downfall.

One of Goerdeler's contacts in the civilian Resistance was the legal adviser to the German Counterintelligence Department, Helmuth Count von Moltke. In the thirties Moltke became the inspirational leader of a group of resisters, mostly aristocrats like himself who met at his family estate at Kreisau in Silesia to discuss the New Order that would emerge after Nazism. Their function was not directed to the overthrow of the regime, and it was only gradually that individual group members came to the realisation that that would become necessary. Like Goerdeler, Moltke had extensive connections and travelled widely. It was he who alerted the Danes to the imminent roundup of their Jews, giving the date and even the precise time,[29] and who caused one of the Munich students' leaflets to be translated into Norwegian. Moltke visited France, where he spread word of the White Rose, and on several occasions visited Belgium to confer with General Falkenhausen, the military governor of occupied Belgium and northern France, who looked favourably on the Kreisau group.[30] Moltke had tried, unsuccessfully, to interest U.S.

[28] Ulrich von Hassell, *Diaries: The Story of the Forces against Hitler Inside Germany* (London: Frontline Books, 2011), entries for 22 January, 14 February, and 27 December 1943.

[29] Van Roon, *German Resistance to Hitler*, 211–12.

[30] Ibid., 209.

embassy officials in Berlin in the German opposition to Hitler. Beginning in the summer of 1941, he had regular discussions with Bishop Preysing, whom he had first met three years earlier. Moltke was also in communication with Bertram, Faulhaber, and Gröber at this time, but his dialogue with Preysing was more productive. They aired, among other things, the plight of the Jews and the content of pastoral letters. Preysing's 1942 pastoral letter on the law was written at Moltke's request,[31] and Moltke is also believed to have influenced the Fulda bishops' Decalogue Letter of the following August.[32]

The Kreisau Circle, as Moltke's group became known, had a nucleus of about twenty active members, with at least twice that number of committed supporters on the fringe of the movement. After Moltke widened the circle of participants to include Social Democrats, labour leaders, and Jesuits, the Kreisau Circle became one of the most significant resistance movements in wartime Germany, with feelers in numerous other countries, both neutral and Axis occupied. Between May 1942 and June 1943, a series of three important conferences took place at Kreisau, when the details of a programme of national reconstruction were worked out, based on Christian principles and the restoration of individual rights and freedoms.

The first conference was held over Pentecost 1942, when the topic under consideration was the relationship between church and state. Present were Moltke and his close associate Peter Count Yorck von Wartenburg, a senior civil servant with contacts in the military, together with their wives and several other members of the Circle. Of these, most had experience in other departments

[31] Ibid., 137–38.
[32] Ibid., 139.

of resistance. Harald Poelchau was a chaplain in Berlin's Tegel Prison who, aided by his wife, sheltered Jews and assisted their escape. The historian Adolf Reichwein, who had lost his teaching post when the Nazis came to power in 1933, was the group's adviser on education and the connecting link between the Kreisau Circle and the Social Democrats in the resistance. Theodor Steltzer contributed to the debate on church-state relations, giving a Protestant viewpoint. Steltzer had been introduced to the Circle by Otto von der Gablentz. Although Gablentz was not present at the conference, he had been in prior communication with Moltke, when they had exchanged views on the theory of the state and its connection with theology.[33] All of the above were Protestants. A religious balance to the conference was provided by the inclusion of Catholics Hans Lukaschek, a lawyer active in the cause of oppressed Jews, and Hans Peters, a scholar and former Centre Party deputy who had once taught Moltke. Completing the complement was the Jesuit provincial of the Upper German Province in Munich, Father Augustin Röesch. A diligent worker in the resistance, Father Röesch had long been the object of Gestapo surveillance.

Labour leaders Carlo Mierendorff, Julius Leber, Theodor Haubach, and Wilhelm Leuschner joined the Circle after the first Kreisau Conference. The first three had spent years in concentration camps for their opposition to Hitler. Before their arrest in 1933, Mierendorff and Leber had been Socialist members of the Reichstag, and Leuschner was a former deputy president of the Trade Union Association. On his release from Oranienburg camp, Leber became associated with Goerdeler and with Claus von Stauffenberg of the Military Resistance. They were

[33] Ibid., 300–5.

brought together by Josef Wirmer, a Catholic former Centre Party politician and lawyer who had lost his job for representing Jews.

As further discussions took place, usually in Berlin but occasionally in Munich, Father Röesch brought more Jesuits into the Circle: his secretary, Father Lothar König, Father Hans von Galli for his expertise in agriculture, and the brilliant young political philosopher Father Alfred Delp. König and Delp had both been activists in Catholic Youth and, like Röesch, could number among their acquaintances many within the resistance movement. An exceptional organizer, König acted as a go-between linking the Kreisau Circle and the Catholic bishops. Röesch had suggested Delp when Moltke requested a Catholic expert to advise on matters of political economy. An original thinker, Delp played a crucial part in the deliberations of the group, although it would be a mistake to underestimate the contribution of the others, and the group as a whole manifested a surprising degree of unanimity.

The Protestant theologian Eugen Gerstenmaier joined the Circle before the second Kreisau Conference convened in October. Gerstenmaier was closely associated with Bishop Wurm, who was associated with Goerdeler, and Gerstenmaier kept Wurm apprised of events. The Catholic bishops were briefed by the Jesuits, particularly König, and by the laymen Peters, Lukaschek, and Paulus von Husen, a lawyer closely connected to Bishops Galen and Wienken. Cardinals Bertram and Faulhaber lent their support to the movement, and several of the Catholic bishops became involved in the preparatory discussions. Delp and Gerstenmaier had the leading roles in the deliberations of the second conference, which took place from 16 to 18 October 1942, when the subject of debate was the state and the economy.

One of the advantages in having Father Delp join the group derived from the number of his contacts in the Resistance. Through Delp, the Kreisau Circle was put in touch with Bernhard Letterhaus and Nicholas Gross, who were leaders of the network of Catholic trade union and working men's associations. On several occasions throughout this period, Delp met with members of the group at Letterhaus' Cologne home. Delp also brought members of the Kreisau Circle into contact with the Sperr Circle, a Bavarian movement led by Franz Sperr, a former army officer with numerous useful connections in the military and among ex-Weimar politicians. The first of several meetings occurred at Father Delp's rectory of Saint George in Munich-Bogenhausen, and the association between the two groups remained a lasting one.

The same could not be said of the Kreisau Circle's relationship with Goerdeler's group. Following the second conference, leading Kreisau members met with Goerdeler and Beck at Wartenburg's house on the evening of 8 January 1943. The proceedings of the meeting were later described by Gerstenmaier in a letter to Wolf Hassell, Ulrich von Hassell's son.[34] The meeting was chaired by Beck and the agenda prepared by Hassell, Popitz, and Gerstenmaier. The meeting had been arranged by Count von der Schulenburg, a mutual associate with connections to the Kreisau Circle.[35] Kreisaurians Moltke and Adam von Trott zu Solz were also in attendance. None of the Jesuits were present, although Father Delp had taken part in a preparatory meeting in Berlin.

Social and foreign-policy issues were debated. Gerstenmaier complained later of the meeting's "poor cooperative

[34]Hassell, *Diaries*, 309, footnote.
[35]Peter Hoffman, *The History of the German Resistance, 1933–1945* (London: MacDonald and James, 1977), 360.

approach". Goerdeler displayed a reluctance to thrash out their differences, which did little to allay the suspicion that Kreisau members already held against him. Moreover, Goerdeler's habit of making copious notes was viewed with alarm by the Kreisaurians, who had themselves always been circumspect in their deliberations, and it caused Delp to advise against working with him.

Issues of foreign policy and the punishment of criminals, including war criminals, formed the basis of discussion at the third Kreisau Conference, which was held from 12 to 14 June 1943. At its conclusion, all matters agreed to over the three conferences were encapsulated in the document *Basic Principles of Reconstruction*. It was authored by Moltke and Wartenburg, and others assisted in revising it. The preamble to the document opens with the words: "The government of the German Reich sees in Christianity the foundation for the moral and religious renewal of our nation, for the conquest of hatred and deception and for the reconstruction of the European community of nations."[36] Mierendorff had requested a symbol for the Circle, and the proposal of the Socialist ring linked with the Christian cross received general approval.

The German opposition was keen to enroll support from abroad, and during the war, contacts were made in Allied and neutral countries as well as in countries in occupied Western Europe and in the Greater Reich. The Kreisau Circle enjoyed particular success in this regard, gaining friends in Norway, through Steltzer, and in Denmark and Holland, through Moltke, who also established connections in Austria and Poland. Moltke, Wurtenburg, and Trott zu Solz were all well connected to British and American political circles. At the time of the first Kreisau Conference in 1942,

[36] Quoted in van Roon, *German Resistance to Hilter*, 347.

Trott travelled to Geneva, where he handed Dr. Visser 't Hooft, secretary-general of the Ecumenical Council of Churches, a memorandum compiled by Gerstenmaier, Dr. Hans Schönfeld, and Trott himself.[37] The memorandum found its way to Sir Stafford Cripps, the Lord Privy Seal, who read it and then passed it on to Churchill. Although both men professed an interest, the matter was taken no further.[38] Hopes of attracting British and American support were never feasible. Even less so were they after the Casablanca Conference of January 1943, when Roosevelt and Churchill agreed that nothing less than the unconditional surrender of Germany would content them. Roosevelt in particular was immovable on this point.

It was probably a result of Allied coolness, combined with inertia on the part of the German military authorities, that gave increased prominence in Kreisau discussions to the controversial proposal for Hitler's assassination. Gerstenmaier, Trott, and Hans Bernd von Haeften were the most prominent advocates. Gablentz, Steltzer, and Röesch were unequivocally opposed to the idea. But some Kreisau members remained undecided or else, like Wurtenburg vacillated, at times expressing themselves in favour and later changing their minds. Moltke never countenanced it. For him, the removal by assassination of a lawful head of state, even if that head of state were Hitler, was nothing less than murder. In his book *The Christian Church in the Cold War*, Owen Chadwick poses the question: "Could a Christian plot to murder a tyrant?" For more than three centuries, the moral tradition of Christian Europe had held tyrannicide to be a wicked act. But, says Chadwick, all that changed with the Nazi occupation of Europe.

[37] Hoffman, *The History of the German Resistance*, 216.
[38] Ibid., 218.

Although the Kreisau Circle maintained links with other forms of opposition, it resisted all overtures from the Communists, who, it was well known, included many informers among their number.[39] Communist resistance focussed mainly on sabotage and the publication of anti-Nazi propaganda. The most successful group, the Rote Kapelle (Red Orchestra), supplied German military information to Moscow, until the Gestapo broke it up and executed its leaders in 1942. On 22 June 1944, the Social Democrats Reichwein and Leber, acting on their own behalf and on behalf of Stauffenberg of the Military Resistance, held talks with Communists, one of whom was a Gestapo agent. They were subsequently arrested, tortured, and later executed. After this, certain waverers in the Kreisau Circle gave reluctant support to the plot to assassinate Hitler. In January 1944, a few months before the arrest of Reichwein and Leber, Moltke had been seized by the Gestapo and interned for warning a friend that he was about to be arrested. Following these events, the Kreisau Circle virtually came to an end, although individual members remained active in other ways of resistance.

The Military Resistance

It is clear that by the end of the 1930s many among the officer class were dissatisfied with Hitler's rule. His expansionist policy alienated several of the more senior army officers, although none of them followed Beck's example and resigned their posts. Officers of the old school, moreover, were repelled by the anti-Jewish measures and the flagrant inhumanity of the SS.

[39] Van Roon, *German Resistance to Hilter*, 164.

During the Czechoslovakian crisis of 1938, General Beck initiated a plan to remove Hitler from power and take over the reins of government. Several generals, including Halder, Beck's successor as chief of the Army General Staff, and the Berlin Chief of Police von Helldorf and his deputy indicated their readiness to take part in the coup. Hans Oster, the chief of staff to Admiral Canaris in the Abwehr, who had been introduced to Beck by Canaris, and Oster's assistant Hans von Dohnanyi, an Austrian lawyer with links to Goerdeler, Moltke, and the Kreisau Circle, were also implicated in the plot. Oster, on behalf of Beck, contacted the British Foreign Office, since the conspirators depended on British support for the success of the coup. Beck also kept the pope posted through the anti-Nazi vice consul in Geneva, Hans Bernd Gisevius, who acted as liaison between Beck and Father Leiber in the Vatican. But the British were sceptical, while Roosevelt never wavered in his opposition to Western intervention.[40] The situation changed completely when, on 30 September, Hitler and Chamberlain concluded the Munich Agreement, relinquishing the Sudetenland to Germany. The agreement strengthened Hitler's position, and the conspiracy, which had relied for its success on the British taking a firm line with Hitler, fell apart. German military successes at the early part of the war made the likelihood of a successful coup even more remote.

Still, the Abwehr remained a hotbed of intrigue, with Oster its principal and most dedicated activist, seeking out and maintaining connection with anyone and everyone whom he suspected of harbouring reservations about

---

[40]Gerhard Ritter, "The German Opposition to Hitler", *Contemporary Review* 177 (January–June 1950): 341. Professor Ritter was involved in the German opposition and contributed to the Freiburg Memorandum. His article was based on Carl Goerdeler's papers, which Ritter retained in his possession.

the regime. The son of a Protestant minister, Oster had opposed Nazism from the outset and from at least 1942 had conspired to overthrow Hitler. He gave warnings of the projected invasion of Norway, Denmark, and the Low Countries, although his warnings went unheeded by the British. Oster created a network of support within the military intelligence service; his superior, Admiral Canaris, knew of his activities and protected him. Canaris himself took a backseat in the Abwehr resistance—Hassell was at least one who thought his leadership weak—but he nevertheless, like Oster, took grave risks.[41]

In 1942, Oster sent Dietrich Bonhoeffer to Sweden to meet with Bishop Bell of Chichester in a doomed attempt to enlist Allied support for peace talks. Bonhoeffer was a pastor in the Confessional church who had studied in America and served for a time in an English parish. The brother-in-law of Dohnanyi, he was connected to Goerdeler and the Kreisau Circle and was active in the work of rescuing Jews. Oster used his position in the Abwehr to rescue Jews and was dismissed from his office in April 1943 partly for this reason. In the same month, Bonhoeffer and Dohnanyi were arrested by the Gestapo on charges relating to conspiracy and to currency irregularities. Although Dohnanyi was released for lack of evidence, Bonhoeffer spent the next eighteen months in prison. Oster also was suspect, a fact that contributed to his sacking. The following June, Canaris was removed from office on Hitler's orders, effectively bringing to an end the resistance in the Abwehr. All intelligence and counterintelligence operations were henceforth taken over by Himmler.[42]

[41] Hassell, *Diaries*, entry for 15 May 1943.
[42] Guido Knopp, *The SS: A Warning from History* (Stroud, UK: History Press, 2002), 103.

It was evident that success in any conspiracy to remove Hitler would depend upon the active cooperation of the military. Hassell tried but failed to persuade generals such as Halder and Rommel to stage a military coup. Hassell was Goerdeler's choice for the post of foreign minister in the projected government that would follow the ousting of Hitler. He travelled widely on behalf of Goerdeler and Beck, but Hassell's vision of a future Germany, like Goerdeler's, included the retention of much of Hitler's territorial acquisitions; thus, he failed to arouse the interest of the British. From early 1942, the Gestapo had him under observation, and he was warned of the precariousness of his position by Weizsäcker, who was at that time serving in the Foreign Office.

By 1943, the focus of the military resistance had passed from General Beck, who remained the figurehead of the movement, to younger, more dynamic officers such as Henning von Tresckow and Claus von Stauffenberg. Tresckow was at first in sympathy with the National Socialists, but like many officers he changed his allegiance. A distinguished soldier, he was promoted to the rank of major general while barely forty, and, like Hassell, he made unsuccessful approaches to win over the generals to the idea of a putsch. Following the launch of Operation Barbarossa, Tresckow became the lynchpin of resistance among officers on the Eastern Front. In March 1943, together with his aide, Fabian von Schlabrendorff, Tresckow managed to smuggle a bomb onto the aircraft bringing Hitler back from the Russian front. But Hitler led a charmed life, having survived several assassination attempts. The bomb failed to go off. Later that year, Tresckow joined forces with Stauffenberg, who now emerged as the leading light in the military resistance, partly because of his proximity to Hitler.

Claus Schenk Count von Stauffenberg was a loyal officer and a devout Catholic who chose initially to support

Hitler for fear of the bolshevisation of Germany, but who turned anti-Nazi in the 1930s following the fearful glut of Crystal Night. In politics, he inclined to the left, aligning himself with Socialists such as Julius Leber, who was Stauffenberg's choice as a future chancellor. Like many officers, Stauffenberg was dismayed by Hitler's incompetence in military matters and by the prospect of defeat at the hands of the Russians. Associated with the Kreisau Circle—he was a cousin of Yorck von Wartenburg—like certain others in the Circle, he was eventually converted to the idea that Hitler had to be eliminated. In Stauffenberg's case, the necessity was borne in on him after witnessing SS atrocities committed against civilians on the Eastern Front. The persecution of the Jews he considered a scandal that dishonoured the German people.

In April 1943, Stauffenberg was seriously wounded in Tunisia when he stepped on a landmine, resulting in the loss of an eye and a hand and other, only marginally less serious injuries. On his recovery, he was transferred to Berlin to become chief of staff to General Friedrich Olbricht, who also conspired against Hitler. While in Berlin, Stauffenberg made elaborate preparations for the military takeover of the city. A promotion to the rank of lieutenant colonel in June 1944 was followed by an appointment as chief of staff to General Friedrich Fromm of the Home Army. Stauffenberg's new posting gave him access to Hitler's headquarters, an advantage his friend Tresckow had several times tried to angle for himself without success. Working in collaboration, Tresckow and Stauffenberg devised a plan for a coup that depended for its success on the assassination of Hitler.

On 20 July 1944, Stauffenberg attended a meeting at Hitler's headquarters in Rastenburg, East Prussia, carrying a briefcase containing a bomb. At a prearranged moment, he was called to the telephone and left the room, leaving the briefcase under the conference table near Hitler. But during the conference, someone moved it further from the führer. When the bomb went off, several officers were killed in the blast; Hitler, however, sustained only minor injuries.

Hearing the explosion and believing Hitler to be dead, Stauffenberg left for Berlin. He was met by a scene of confusion. When the bomb went off, Albert Speer was addressing a meeting at the Propaganda Ministry in Berlin. Goebbels also was present. In his memoirs, Speer recalls how easy it would have been for a determined band of rebels to seize the opportunity of capturing the Propaganda Ministry. "Practically all of political Berlin was assembled there", he observed. But not knowing whether Hitler was alive or dead, Olbricht and the conspirators wavered and, instead of taking command of Berlin as planned, found themselves outmanoeuvred by Goebbels and Major Remer, the commander of the Guard Battalion. Moreover, the plan to cut the telecommunication link with Berlin misfired, and Hitler was able to communicate with Goebbels and Remer by phone. Goebbels seized another opportunity in putting out a radio broadcast that evening, informing the German people that the führer was alive and well.

Stauffenberg was captured after a shoot-out with the Guard Battalion, in which he was wounded. He and Olbricht were conducted to the courtyard of the War Ministry on the orders of Fromm, where they were put against a wall and shot. Field Marshal Erwin von Witzleben, who was to have been commander in chief of the army if the plot had succeeded, was granted a trial but on his conviction was executed by slow strangulation. The hunt for the conspirators was now on, and thousands of arrests were made, many of them involving people who had had nothing to do with any plot to topple Hitler. Fromm, who had hoped to save his own skin by executing

Stauffenberg, was apprehended and later shot. According to Speer, Hitler had the names of all those he could think of who had opposed him in the past added to the list. Bishop Galen, though innocent of any part in the bomb plot, was transferred to Sachsenhausen concentration camp but was released the following year. Many of the arrested were shot or decapitated or died slowly at the end of a wire noose. The hangings were filmed and later screened for Hitler's delectation.

General Beck had been in failing health for some time and had been operated on for cancer. He anticipated his arrest by taking his own life. Henning von Tresckow also chose suicide. Knowing that he would be arrested, and fearing that under torture he would reveal the names of fellow conspirators, he killed himself with a hand grenade. Carl Goerdeler had gone into hiding days before the July plot, after the Gestapo had issued a warrant for his arrest. He was soon tracked down, when he was found to be in possession of incriminating documents, including a list of the names of the cabinet of a provisional government headed by himself as chancellor. After a lengthy interrogation, he appeared before the People's Court over 7 to 8 August, when proceedings were also instituted against Hassell, Leuschner, and Wirmer. Mussolini petitioned Hitler to spare the life of Hassell, who had been a popular ambassador to Rome, but to no avail. He and Wirmer were executed within hours of their conviction, and Leuschner later that month. Goerdeler languished in prison for several months after his execution was deferred. Before he died, Hassell wrote to his wife: "At this moment I am filled with the deepest gratitude towards God and towards you.... May God grant that your soul and mine may one day be reunited."[43]

---

[43] Hassell, *Diaries*, appendix, 241.

Josef Müller's mission to the Vatican at the beginning of the war now backfired on the Abwehr conspirators. The Gestapo agent's report on the episode, which at the time had been suppressed by Canaris, was now uncovered by the Gestapo while conducting their investigations into the July bomb plot. Its discovery, and the discovery of other damning evidence, sealed the fate of Oster, Canaris, and their confederates in the Abwehr. Oster was seized on 21 July and hanged at Flossenbürg in April of the following year, together with Canaris and Bonhoeffer. Bonhoeffer's brother, Klaus, an inveterate opponent of Hitler, was executed in Berlin three weeks later. Hans von Dohnanyi was transferred to Sachsenhausen concentration camp, where a few months later he was brutally murdered. The Catholic lawyer Müller was detained with the others and, after a cruel interrogation, spent the remainder of the war in various concentration camps until he was liberated from Dachau by the Americans. It was falsely rumoured that his marriage had been conducted by the pope, a circumstance that may have saved him from the noose.[44]

No action was taken against Gablentz, Peters, Horst von Einsiedel, Carl Dietrich von Trotha, or Poelchau of the Kreisau Circle, but the Jesuits Röesch and König were forced to go underground. Father Röesch was later betrayed to the Gestapo but survived the war, as did Father König. The remaining members of the inner circle were hunted down and, after interrogation by the Gestapo, were brought to trial before Freisler of the People's Court.[45]

Wartenburg and Trott were the principal defendants in the August trials. Undaunted by Freisler's hectoring

---

[44]James Taylor and Warren Shaw, *The Penguin Dictionary of the Third Reich* (London: Penguin Books, 1997), s.v. Müller, Josef.

[45]For a full account of the trials of the Kreisau Circle, see van Roon, *German Resistance to Hitler*, 276–80.

manner, Wartenburg explained that he never was and never could be a Nazi because Nazism was totalitarian and godless. Earlier he had penned these words to his mother: "At the end of a life which was more than blessed with love and friendship, I feel only gratitude towards God and humility in bowing to his will."[46] Yorck von Wartenburg was hanged on 8 August, within hours of his conviction. Adam Trott zu Solz, diplomat and Rhodes scholar, was hanged three weeks later.

The second trial didn't commence until October, when the Social Democrats Leber and Reichwein, both having been betrayed to the authorities before the bomb plot, were among the accused. Carlo Mierendorff was a notable absentee, having perished in an air raid the year before. Adolf Reichwein was found guilty and hanged that day. Hoping that Leber would furnish them with useful information, the Gestapo kept him incarcerated until 5 January of the succeeding year, when he was hanged at Plötzensee Prison.

The major trial took place on 9 and 10 January 1945 and involved Moltke, Delp, Gerstenmaier, Haubach, and Steltzer of the Kreisau Circle, together with the Catholic trade union leader Nicholas Gross and some members of the Sperr Circle. Moltke had had no connection with the July plot and had, in fact, been six months behind bars, and for the much lesser offence of forewarning a friend about to be arrested. He stood accused, he wrote to his wife, for the crime of being a Christian and for nothing else. Delp claimed that Moltke's crime was that of "re-Christianizing intentions", and of consorting with bishops and Jesuits. Delp was the first to face the jeering Freisler, who hated priests and Jesuits in particular. The outcome of

[46] Quoted in Annedore Leber, *Conscience in Revolt: Sixty-Four Stories of Resistance in Germany, 1933–1945* (London: Vallentine Mitchell, 1957), 185.

his trial was never in doubt, although, like Moltke, Delp had played no part in the plot to assassinate Hitler. In a farewell letter to his religious brethren in the Society of Jesus, Father Delp stated his conviction that being a Jesuit was the sole reason for his condemnation.[47]

Gerstenmaier and Steltzer were among the few who were spared the death penalty. Helmuth Count von Moltke, Theodor Haubach, and Nicholas Gross were hanged at Plötzensee on 23 January. In a final letter to his wife, Gross wrote: "How good God is, and how rich he has made my life. He gave me love and mercy and a loving wife and good children, and I shall be grateful for that for the rest of my life."[48] Father Alfred Delp was the last member of the Kreisau Circle to meet his appointed end, when, in the company of Carl Goerdeler and Johannes Popitz, he was hanged ten days later on 2 February 1945. The day after the three men surrendered their lives, Roland Freisler lost his when an Allied bomb struck his courthouse while he was presiding over a case.

The example of the German opposition to Hitler endures as an imperishable sign of hope, even if the concrete results were negligible. For all the salutary efforts of what was never more than a minority of courageous Germans, ultimately it was Allied military might, and Allied military might alone, that brought an end to Hitler's tyranny.

---

[47] Alfred Delp, S.J., *Prison Writings* (Maryknoll, N.Y.: Orbis Books, 2004), 163.
[48] Quoted in Leber, *Conscience in Revolt*, 50.

9

Problems of Vatican Diplomacy

Having met with failure in his bid to avert war, Pius XII never desisted in his efforts to assuage its effects. In January 1943, when the war was at its height, the pope addressed these words to President Roosevelt:

> It is Our undeviating programme to do everything in Our power to alleviate the countless sufferings arising from the tragic conflict: Sufferings of the prisoners and of the wounded, of families in fear and trembling over the fate of their loved ones, of entire peoples subjected to limitless privations and hardships; suffering of the aged, of women and children who at a moment's notice find themselves deprived of home and possessions.[1]

The president replied on 16 June 1943:

> No one appreciates more than I the ceaseless efforts of Your Holiness to prevent the outbreak of war in Europe in 1939 and subsequently to limit its contagion.[2]

The solicitude for all of humanity, regardless of race, religion, or nationality, was a primary concern of both world leaders, as is evident in their wartime correspondence.

[1] Pius XII to Roosevelt, January 1943, in Myron C. Taylor, *Wartime Correspondence between President Roosevelt and Pope Pius XII* (New York: Macmillan, 1947), 82.
[2] Roosevelt to Pius XII, 16 June 1943, in Taylor, *Wartime Correspondence*, 91.

The pope's many exertions on behalf of the victims of the conflict were, alas, often frustrated by the Germans. Hitler would tolerate no representations from the Vatican on any matter respecting the territories of the Greater Reich; and all other representations the Nazis habitually dealt with in a dilatory fashion. The scarcity of news coming out of German-controlled countries contributed to the general sense of helplessness. The Holy See depended for most of its information on Monsignor Orsenigo, the papal nuncio in Berlin, whose own sources of information were limited.

Papal speeches directed to ending the war did not go down well with either the Axis or, indeed, the Allies, as both factions were intent on waging war to ultimate victory. The Allied press evinced an indifference verging on hostility to peace talks. The pope was held to be defeatist, even when, in an address of 2 June 1944, on the occasion of the feast of his patron saint, Eugenio, he made allowances for the punishment of war criminals. Instead, Pius had to get used to being at the centre of what was virtually a propaganda tug-of-war, as the contending parties endeavoured to recruit him to their side.

It forever frustrated the pope and the Curia that even the most casual remarks could be seized upon and reinterpreted for a propaganda purpose. So it was the wise course of action for the pope and Vatican diplomats to be guarded in their discussions with foreign envoys. As is now known, Weizsäcker's dispatches to Berlin consistently misrepresented the views of the Vatican. His impulse was to protect the pope, but, as he himself tells us, German diplomats, fearing the Gestapo, habitually misled them in their reports.[3] The slanting of official dossiers was rife

---

[3] *The Memoirs of Ernst von Weizsäcker* (London: Victor Gollancz, 1951), 308.

in the Reich, where the desire to create the right impression took precedence over objective reporting. But the British minister Osborne was not averse to tailoring his reports to the Foreign Office, and for the same reason that motivated Weizsäcker—namely, to protect the pope. Anything the pope confided to Osborne might well inflame Mussolini or Ribbentrop if intercepted by their intelligence services; for it was common knowledge that the seals on the diplomatic pouches were regularly broken and the contents of the pouches scrutinised.

Vatican Radio broadcasts were coloured with an anti-Axis bias when recast by the BBC. Indeed, as Pierre Blet has intimated, the British did not stop at forgery if it suited their purpose.[4] The broadcasts on Poland early in the war were elaborated by the British to serve their own agenda, as Montini had to explain to Menshausen of the German embassy when he called at the Vatican to complain. Menshausen was back at the Vatican later that year objecting to American broadcasts, which were putting their own slant on information originally transmitted by Vatican Radio.

In his Easter message of 1941, the pope delivered a strongly worded criticism of the treatment of subject peoples by occupying forces, which could have meant only Germany and Italy. The broadcast incensed the Germans. Copies were confiscated by the Gestapo, and Goebbels demanded that Vatican Radio be silenced. Fearing that reprisals would be taken against German Catholics if he did not comply, the pope instructed the director of Vatican Radio, Father Filippo Soccorsi, to cease commenting

[4] Pierre Blet, S.J., *Pius XII and the Second World War according to the Archives of the Vatican* (Herefordshire: Gracewing, 2003), 103–4. See also J. Derek Holmes, *The Papacy in the Modern World* (London: Burns and Oates, 1981), 130; Owen Chadwick, *Britain and the Vatican during the Second World War* (Cambridge: Cambridge University Press, 1986), 146–47.

on the religious situation in Germany until further notice. The action displeased the British. The British had, as Alec Randall of the Foreign Office candidly admitted, reaped the greatest propaganda value by exploiting Vatican Radio.[5] Accordingly, a strong protest was sent from London and conveyed to the Vatican by Osborne. In reply, Maglione professed regret that the British could not refrain from altering or otherwise misrepresenting texts of Vatican Radio transmissions. He intimated that the British could have little cause for complaint insofar as they had brought the problem on themselves.

Axis hopes of enlisting Vatican support intensified when in June 1941 Germany attacked the Soviet Union. While the action was welcomed by the German hierarchy and by some French and Italian prelates, the contrasting silence of the pope angered Mussolini, who seems to have expected a papal endorsement of what he depicted as a war on atheistic Communism in defence of Christian civilisation. But the pope was not deceived by Mussolini's rhetoric; his attitude to Hitler's anti-Russian offensive remained distinctly cool.

Towards the end of June, the pope broadcast an address on radio in which he uttered not one word about the German invasion of Russia, much to Mussolini's chagrin. The broadcast disappointed Axis hopes that the Holy Father would give his blessing to this latest act of aggression by Hitler. When the Italian ambassador to the Holy See, Bernardo Attolico, raised the matter of Hitler's anti-Bolshevik crusade and the pope's singular lack of interest, Tardini reminded him that the pope had already condemned the errors of Bolshevism and that it was Germany, and not the Vatican, that had previously entered

[5] Holmes, *The Papacy in the Modern World*, 131.

into a treaty of friendship with the Soviet Union. Papen, now the German ambassador to Turkey, had his hopes dashed when he approached the apostolic delegate Roncalli with a similar request for papal approbation.[6] The Vatican made it plain that it could not condemn either Communists or Nazis without condemning the other, since any such action would, in the context of the war, be viewed as political. And, in any case, both systems persecuted religion and stood condemned for that reason. Meanwhile, the Vatican was daily being vilified in the Fascist press for its lack of enthusiasm for the anti-Russian campaign. Father Robert Graham remarked aptly, "Only a Pope calls a crusade, and the voice of Pius XII was spectacularly missing in June 1941."[7]

The activation of Operation Barbarossa against the Russians in the East focussed attention on American reaction, and the question as to whether aid should be sent to the Soviet Union. The American people with their prized freedoms and inbred suspicion of totalitarian regimes had to be convinced. As Roosevelt's representative at the Vatican, Myron Taylor, indicated, it was an issue that involved the fundamental attitudes of most of the world's peoples regarding some of their most cherished values and aspirations.[8] Roosevelt was resolved to give the Russian people all practical assistance. What he particularly wanted to know was whether he could rely on the support of American Catholics. Communist Russia had come under

[6] Lawrence Elliott, *I Will Be Called John: A Biography of Pope John XXIII* (London: William Collins Sons, 1976), 155–56.

[7] Robert A. Graham, S.J., *The Vatican and Communism during World War II* (San Francisco: Ignatius Press, 1996), 23. Father Graham notes the complete absence from official documents of any communication between Berlin and the Vatican on this matter.

[8] Myron C. Taylor in an editorial note in *Wartime Correspondence*, 57.

papal censure on several occasions. The pope's immediate predecessor, Pius XI, had been damning in his pronouncements on atheistic Communism, most recently and notably in the 1937 encyclical letter *Divini Redemptoris*, which was released within days of *Mit brennender Sorge*, Pius XI's missive directed against Nazism. Roosevelt accordingly instructed his personal representative at the Vatican to raise the matter with the pope.

Pius XII made no distinction between the respective ideologies and practices of Communism and Nazism. Both were godless, and both persecuted religion. He thought Hitler more to be feared than Stalin but that Communist Russia presented the greater long-term threat to religion. In the short term, although each regime had set its face against the Church, religious observance was high in Germany, where the churches remained open and congregations were generally unmolested. The pope did not share Roosevelt's sanguine opinion regarding the future of religion in Soviet Russia. Nonetheless he was able to reassure Mr. Taylor that while the encyclical *Divini Redemptoris* condemned atheistic Communism, it implied no condemnation of the Russian people, for whom the pope had nothing but paternal affection. The pope reiterated these sentiments soon after in an allocution and again in his Christmas message of that year. A pastoral letter was issued under the auspices of the U.S. bishops to allay any fears entertained by American Catholics. These gestures on the part of the pope went some way to assisting the passage of the Lend-Lease Act through Congress.[9]

Less than full agreement was obtained on the measures to be taken to protect the Jews. The transportation

---

[9] Roosevelt to Pius XII, 3 September 1941; Pius XII to Roosevelt, 20 September 1941; in Taylor, *Wartime Correspondence*, 39.

of European Jews to the territories of the Reich was, in the beginning, associated with forced labour. Jews, Poles, and other subject peoples, it was generally supposed, were being relocated to labour camps to work for Germany. Soon it became evident that many of them were being worked to death. Only gradually, accompanied by widespread scepticism, did news filter through to the West that Hitler was intent on the wholesale extermination of European Jews.

There was no certain knowledge of this satanic scheme prior to 1943.[10] In June 1942, acting on firsthand information on the clearing of the Warsaw ghetto, the *Daily Telegraph* broached the subject of the deliberate extermination of the Jews. The matter was also aired in several BBC broadcasts. Persecution was bad enough; but extermination was wickedness on a scale too incredible to take in. The reaction was sceptical, most people judging the report to be nothing more than anti-Axis propaganda. That summer, numerous rumours circulated in the West hinting at genocide. The U.S. State Department was aware of the rumours but dismissed them as unsubstantiated, as did the French. In August, an official of the Health Department of the SS, Kurt Gerstein, circulated a verbal report on the gassings taking place at Belzac concentration camp, which he had witnessed during an official visit. But Gerstein's revelations failed to arouse interest. The British Foreign Office dismissed them as atrocity propaganda. The general apathy that greeted his report preyed upon Gerstein's mind and contributed to his eventual suicide.

---

[10] Chadwick, *Britain and the Vatican during the Second World War*, 217; see also Pinchas E. Lapide, *The Last Three Popes and the Jews* (London: Harper Press, 2009), 139, and, especially, Guido Knopp, *Hitler's Holocaust* (Stroud, UK: Sutton, 2004), 272, quoting Helmuth Count von Moltke.

There were those who wanted the pope to do what Washington and London would not, and in the absence of reliable confirmatory evidence, could not do—that is, issue a public protest. Regretting that it was unable to pronounce on unconfirmed rumours, the Vatican pointed out that, in any case, the pope's position on the matter could be inferred from the condemnations he had already made in general terms. In December, Britain, the United States, and the Soviet Union issued a joint declaration on the Jewish persecution. The only way to help the Jews, it said, was to prosecute the war to ultimate victory over the Axis. A. A. Berle, the U.S. assistant secretary of state, explained this to a protest meeting in Boston the following May.[11]

Since the summer of 1942, information had been coming into the Vatican from its nuncios concerning the mass slaughter of Jews in German-occupied countries. Then, early in 1943, Bishop Preysing and the nuncio in Berlin, Monsignor Orsenigo, independently relayed news of the gas chambers of Auschwitz. About the same time, the British government submitted a dossier of evidence to Mussolini.[12] The situation in the General Government was described by Cardinal Hlond writing in one of the *Cahiers* at the beginning of the year. He alluded to the mass shootings and gassings taking place there and alleged that the killings were part of a design to extirpate completely the Jews of Europe.[13] Certainly by early 1943 there was information available on the genocide of Europe's Jews.

Yet, the reluctance to believe the evidence persisted. Escapees from the camps of Sorbibor, Chelmno, and

[11] Knopp, *Hitler's Holocaust*, 241.

[12] Nicholas Farrell, *Mussolini* (London: Weidenfeld and Nicolson, 2003), 365, citing Italian archive.

[13] Quoted in Henri de Lubac, S.J., *Christian Resistance to Anti-Semitism: Memories from 1940–1944* (San Francisco: Ignatius Press, 1990), 155.

Auschwitz, relating their experiences, were met with incredulity. They were judged to be mad or suspected of spreading Polish propaganda. As the accounts multiplied, the numbers of the victims represented were so high that government officials and newspaper editors thought them Jewish exaggerations.[14] Jews themselves could not accept the reality of large-scale exterminations until they arrived in the death camps, and sometimes not even then.[15] Why were so many people sceptical of the news coming out of the Reich? What convinced them it was propaganda? One reason was that they had heard it all before. The British had spread atrocity stories during the First World War, alleging that German soldiers butchered Belgian babies. The allegations were untrue, but they were widely believed. Now the same people were being asked to credit the Germans, the most cultured people in Europe, with operating gas chambers and crematoria to dispose of Europe's Jews. Even taking into account Hitler's recent record, who could believe such a monstrous thing possible? Hilaire Belloc warned against reading history backwards. With the benefit of hindsight, it is only now possible to comprehend the horror of the extermination process. At the time, it seemed inconceivable.

In April 1944, two Slovak Jews, Rudolph Vrba and Alfred Wetzler, escaped from Auschwitz and reached Bratislava, where they gave eyewitness accounts of the gas chambers and crematoria to the papal envoy, Monsignor Burzio. Burzio was appalled; he informed the pope, who was at the time in the process of drafting his famous telegram to Admiral Horthy. The escapees had claimed that plans were afoot to transfer Hungarian Jews, who up till

[14] Knopp, *Hitler's Holocaust*, 241.
[15] Martin Gilbert, *The Holocaust: The Jewish Tragedy* (London: Collins, 1986), 379.

then had been spared, to Auschwitz. The pope apprised Horthy of the situation. Horthy thought Vrba and Wetzler's report nothing more than atrocity propaganda, but he promised to do what he could and, in fact, was successful in curtailing the transports from Hungary. The information was communicated by the Vatican to other countries, giving rise to the protests sent to the Hungarian government by the king of Sweden, the International Red Cross, and other neutrals.

Vrba and Wetzler were subsequently interviewed by a panel of Jewish officials, to whom they related their grisly experiences of Auschwitz. They were not believed. Deeply disappointed, Vrba complained regretfully, "Human consciousness first had to be educated merely to take in the concept of mass murder on the scale of Auschwitz."[16] Vrba and Wetzler's written report on conditions in Auschwitz became known as the *Auschwitz Protocols*. After being translated into several languages, copies were sent to the British and Americans, as well as to the World Jewish Congress, the Red Cross, and the Vatican. Some excerpts from the *Protocols* were transmitted by the BBC, but the reaction in Britain was, as ever, sceptical. And the reaction was not confined to the general public; British intellectuals, including those on the left, were equally dismissive.[17]

The unwillingness to accept the truth about the extermination of European Jews prevailed to the last stages of the war and was markedly strong amongst Americans. American troops refused to believe in the existence of concentration camps.[18] An opinion poll conducted in the United States at the end of 1944 revealed that the majority

[16] Knopp, *Hitler's Holocaust*, 284.

[17] Nick Cohen, *What's Left? How Liberals Lost Their Way* (London: Harper Perennial, 2007), 248–49.

[18] Knopp, *Hitler's Holocaust*, 254.

of Americans thought that fewer than a hundred thousand Jews had been murdered by the Nazis.[19] American scepticism involved more than servicemen and the man in the street but persisted among the educated and among those whose business it was to be informed. Vatican expert Father Robert Graham, S.J., surveyed every wartime edition of the *New York Times* and found little information on or condemnation of the extermination of the Jews, and none at all when he came to review back copies of Eleanor Roosevelt's daily newspaper column.[20] Allied propaganda even, while sweeping in its condemnation of German atrocities, never mentioned extermination camps.[21] When, six months after the surrender of Germany, the military tribunal convened at Nuremberg, the general public was still unaware of the implications of Hitler's Final Solution.[22] The Nazis went to considerable lengths to ensure secrecy about the extermination process. In his testimony at Nuremberg, Rudolf Hoess, the commandant of Auschwitz, claimed that his wife had remained in ignorance of what took place in the camp until the end of 1942, when she asked him to confirm what had only then been brought to her notice. Hoess, whose chilling frankness and evident pride in his work stunned members of the tribunal, was giving evidence on the means employed in ensuring that Auschwitz remained isolated and its operations a secret.[23] Yet, even after Western correspondents entered Auschwitz on the liberation of the camp, they displayed an obstinate

[19] Ibid., 272.

[20] See the obituary on Father Graham by Felix Corley in *Independent*, 8 March 1997.

[21] Father Giovanni Sale, "Two Popes, the Nazi Party and the Second World War", *Universe*, 20 June 2004, 15.

[22] James Owen, *Nuremberg: Evil on Trial* (London: Headline Review, 2007), 8–9.

[23] Ibid., 201.

disinclination to be taken in by what they imagined was Russian propaganda.[24]

Despite the sense of uncertainty, Western diplomats residing in the Vatican wanted the pope to issue a ringing condemnation of Nazi atrocities. That he had protested on several occasions has already been made clear in the foregoing chapters of this work. In the first encyclical of his reign, *Summi Pontificatus*, Pius XII had launched into a scathing attack upon totalitarian regimes, while proclaiming the dignity of all men, whatever race they belonged to. Vatican Radio broadcasts at the outbreak of war were unambiguous in denouncing atrocities perpetrated against Poles and Jews. The Holy Father's Christmas message of 1942 referred to the hundreds of thousands who had been condemned to death solely because of their nationality or race; and these words were repeated the following year in the pope's widely publicised address to the College of Cardinals. In successive Christmas broadcasts the pope spoke in a similar vein.

Unfortunately, the pope's denunciations, though welcome, were judged to have fallen short of what the Allies required of him. But unless the pope were to supply ammunition for the Allies' propaganda war against the Axis, his words were always going to disappoint. Then, diplomatic manoeuvres in the Vatican calculated to get the pope on the Allies' side always came up against the issue of Vatican neutrality. The assumption of neutral or impartial status was not a political choice decided on by the pope but was intrinsically connected to the Church as universal. As Pius XII explained to President Roosevelt, "[T]he neutrality of the Holy See places the Pope above any armed conflict between nations, while committing him to a defence

[24]Knopp, *Hitler's Holocaust*, 306.

of the eternal, spiritual, interests of all men redeemed by Christ."[25] Pius XII might think that Nazi Germany was in the wrong, but he also knew that millions of German Catholics, few of whom were dedicated Fascists, were risking their lives fighting for their country. The Holy Father's paternal instincts extended to them as to everyone else involved in the conflict. And should the pope have risked alienating forty million German-speaking Catholics by siding with the enemy? Most Germans, he knew, found it difficult to make the distinction between Nazism and the Fatherland. Further, Pius XII never completely abandoned the hope that the warring factions might be brought to the conference table. In which case, he was the logical choice as mediator; for only a neutral can mediate a peace.

Osborne and the Americans noted that the pope never identified the Nazis by name and never specified the word *Jew*. They wanted the pope to forsake the language of diplomacy. They wanted him to name names; even though, as the former American diplomat Tittmann frankly admits, "The danger of error involved in descending to the particular amidst the heat of war passions was obvious."[26] For one thing, the Vatican could never be sure of the reliability of the information it received; and the Nazis denied every charge that was laid against them. The pope, not unreasonably, pointed out that if he did as the Allies requested and condemned the Nazis in explicit terms, he would also have to be explicit in his denunciation of Allied atrocities. When the Axis urged the pope to condemn the saturation bombing of German cities such as Cologne, which resulted in the deaths of noncombatants,

[25] Pius XII to Roosevelt, 19 July 1943, in Taylor, *Wartime Correspondence*, 95.
[26] Harold H. Tittmann Jr., *Inside the Vatican of Pius XII: The Memoir of an American Diplomat during World War II* (New York: Image Books, 2004), 119.

the British minister Osborne exerted every effort to prevent the pope from speaking out. Moreover, the pope could not name and condemn the Nazis without similarly stigmatizing the Bolsheviks for their crimes against the Poles. Certainly the British and Americans would have had no wish for papal censure to fall on their new ally, the Soviet Union. And would they have wished for an explicit papal condemnation when, in the later stages of the war, Russian soldiers were raping and pillaging their way across the countries they were meant to be liberating? Had the Pope used words of fire to condemn either faction, assuredly his words would have been seized upon by the other side and exploited to the full. Mr. Tittmann has admitted as much.[27]

In a letter addressed to Myron Taylor prior to one of Mr. Taylor's last visits to the pope, President Roosevelt wrote:

> I should like you to take the occasion to express to His Holiness my deeply-felt appreciation of the frequent action which the Holy See has taken on its own initiative in its generous and merciful efforts to render assistance to the victims of racial and religious persecution.[28]

It seems clear enough that the president was here referring to Jews. The correspondence between Roosevelt and the Holy Father, which commenced at the outbreak of war and ended only a few months before the president's death in April 1945, was, as in the foregoing passage, conducted always in general terms; and neither leader named names. In his 1941 Easter telegram to the pope, Roosevelt complains of "a transient parade of arms with nothing behind

[27] Ibid., 121–22.

[28] Roosevelt to Taylor, in 3 August 1944, *Wartime Correspondence*, 113.

it save confusion and corruption of a group which has lost all spiritual values, and solely lusts for power".[29] Is it possible not to know to whom the president was referring? Similarly, when the pope condemned the persecution of a people because of their race, no one at the time needed to be told that he had Jews in mind.

The significance of the Holy Father's condemnations may be inferred from the effects they produced. Sir D'Arcy Osborne, who held Pius XII in the highest esteem, thought the 1942 Christmas address clearly applied to the oppression of the Jews and said so in his report to London. Osborne further considered the pope's criticisms of totalitarian regimes "unmistakeable".[30] The historian Anthony Rhodes agrees that the 1942 Christmas broadcast provided "a clear enough reference to the Jews",[31] and he cites the opinion of the Italian Socialist Ignazio Silone, who thought that the pope spoke "with a force and nobility that makes him the spokesman of the human race".[32] In applauding the pope's defence of the Jews, the *New York Times* said the broadcast amounted to the verdict of a supreme court.

The clearest indication that the pope was speaking up for the Jews may be gauged from how the Axis reacted to his words. The Christmas broadcast of 1942 aroused the ire of Mussolini and caused Ribbentrop to threaten retaliation. The Reich Security Office observed of it, "His speech is one long attack on everything we stand for.... [H]e is clearly speaking on behalf of the Jews.... [H]e makes himself the mouthpiece of the Jewish war

[29] Roosevelt to Taylor, Easter April 1941, in ibid., 52.

[30] Quoted in Holmes, *The Papacy in the Modern World*, 155.

[31] Anthony Rhodes, *The Vatican in the Age of the Dictators, 1922–1945* (London: Hodder and Stoughton, 1973), 27.

[32] Ibid., 274, footnote.

criminals."[33] Publication of the pope's address was forbidden in Germany, and those who defied the ban had their print shops closed down.

Jewish reaction is no less edifying. Pinchas Lapide is the author of the definitive history of Pius XII's papacy from the Jewish side. Lapide is insistent that whenever the pope used the word *race* in his public addresses, it was a clear reference to Jews.[34] Rabbi David Dalin agrees. Rabbi Dalin is a historian of American Judaism and of Christian-Jewish relations. In his estimation, Pius XII's Christmas broadcasts of 1941 and 1942 set forth "a clear condemnation of Nazi attacks on Europe's Jews".[35] On learning of the death of Pius XII in 1958, Golda Meir commented: "When fearful martyrdom came to our people, the voice of the Pope was raised for its victims."

The pope was wise enough to appreciate that stigmatizing Hitler and the Nazis in a thundering public protest that some were calling for him to make would not help the victims of Nazism. Rather, by his inflaming Nazi passions, worse calamities would surely ensue; for it was invariably their practice to answer protest with reprisals. The encyclical *Mit brennender Sorge* led to an acceleration in the oppression of the Church in Germany; Vatican Radio broadcasts on Poland had to be suspended as they served only to increase the sufferings of the Poles; the Dutch bishops' protest provoked instant reprisals; episcopal protest in occupied France threatened to make matters worse for the Jewish community; in Germany, Jewish leaders restrained Bishop Galen from condemning the treatment of their

[33] Quoted in ibid., 272–73.

[34] Lapide, *The Last Three Popes and the Jews*, 251.

[35] Rabbi David Dalin, "A Righteous Gentile: Pope Pius XII and the Jews", Catholic League for Religious and Civil Rights, 26 February 2011, accessed 4 September 2015, at http://www.catholicleague.org/.

people, fearing subsequent reprisals[36]—the precedents are almost without number. "Whenever protests were made, treatment of prisoners worsened immediately", Sister Margherita Marchione has observed.[37]

Officials of the International Red Cross agreed with the pope and adopted the same policy.[38] Jewish leaders also agreed with him. Lapide comments: "I know of no authoritative Jewish accusation which equates papal reticence with inaction or reluctance to save Jews."[39] Lapide cites the case of Marcus Melchoir, the chief rabbi of Denmark, who was rescued along with most of the Jewish community in the Danish evacuation. Dr. Melchoir gave it as his opinion that if Pius XII had made an outspoken attack on Hitler, the fate of European Jews would have been immeasurably worse. This also was the opinion of Dr. R. W. Kempner, the U.S. deputy chief prosecutor at Nuremberg. Weizsäcker and his deputy in Rome, Kessel, knew it to be true, and both said so. "I know how our people react in these matters", Weizsäcker said.[40] Especially pertinent in this regard is the opinion of Tittmann, whose position in the Vatican gave him a unique insight into the events of the time. In his memoir, *Inside the Vatican of Pius XII*, Tittmann considers the question of whether there would have been fewer victims or more if the pope

[36] David Welch, *The Hitler Conspiracies: Secrets and Lies behind the Rise and Fall of the Nazi Party* (Shepperton, UK: Ian Allan, 2001), 118.

[37] Sister Margherita Marchione, "The Truth about Pius XII", *Catalyst* (March 1998), at Catholic League for Religious and Civil Rights, accessed 4 September 2015, http://www.catholicleague.org/. See also Gerard Noel, *Pius XII: The Hound of Hitler* (London: Continuum, 2008), 187. Noel quotes Monsignor Jean Bernard, bishop of Luxembourg, on how papal protest affected the treatment of inmates of Dachau.

[38] *The Memoirs of Ernst von Weizsäcker*, 270.

[39] Lapide, *The Last Three Popes and the Jews*, 265.

[40] See ibid., 247–48.

had spoken out in the way the Allies required of him. While admitting that there can be no final answer to the question, Tittmann concludes: "Personally, I cannot help but feel that the Holy Father chose the better path by not speaking out and thereby saved many lives."[41]

After the war, a considerable number of Jews converted to Catholicism, including the chief rabbi of Rome, Israel Zolli, who, in a tribute to Pius XII, took Eugenio as his baptismal name. Some have suggested that the conversions were prompted more by gratitude than by religious conviction.[42] If so, they bear eloquent testimony to the role of the Church and the papacy during the era of Nazi oppression.

[41] Tittmann, *Inside the Vatican of Pius XII*, 122–23.
[42] Ralph McInerny, *The Defamation of Pius XII* (South Bend, Ind.: St. Augustine's Press, 2001), 117.

SUMMARY AND CONCLUSION

The uniqueness of the Catholic Church is axiomatic and is easily explained. Her catholicity is three-dimensional: the Church embraces all nations, is present in all centuries since apostolic times, and possesses an enduring teaching that remains uncompromised by modernizing tendencies. The Church's visible unity is further manifested in the hierarchical character of her priesthood, centred on the pope in Rome. Thus it was only natural that the Catholic Church should emerge as the main spiritual bulwark against Hitlerism and that thoughtful and upright men everywhere would look to the moral authority of the papacy for guidance.

The year before the Beer Hall Putsch—Hitler's doomed challenge to established authority—racialism and extreme nationalism were repudiated, and the doctrine of the universal brotherhood of men reaffirmed, in Pius XI's first encyclical letter, *Ubi Arcano Dei*. Six years later, anti-Semitism, specifically, came under the ban of the Holy Office. The Church's strictures were repeated in the pope's Christmas message of 1930, and again, two years later, in the encyclical *Caritate Christi Compulsi* when, on both occasions, the National Socialists in Germany were celebrating spectacular electoral gains.

When the strident voice of Nazism was first heard in Germany, it was answered by the accredited representative of the Holy See, Archbishop Pacelli, and by responsible Catholic opinion, clerical and lay. Nazi sensibilities were affronted when, on the eve of the Hitler-Ludendorff debacle, Cardinal Faulhaber interceded with the Weimar government in the interests of its Jewish citizens. The Nazi worship of race was later denounced in a public address by the most senior Catholic prelate, Cardinal Bertram, and by the bishops collectively in a pastoral letter. Although the bishops shared in the resentment over the Versailles Treaty, and although some, at least, were supportive of Hitler in certain aspects of his foreign policy, the hierarchy maintained a spiritual resistance to Nazism that was uncompromising. Catholic newspapers, until they were suppressed, and influential laymen, until they were silenced, were fearlessly vocal in opposition. Members of the Catholic theological faculties, with few exceptions, were determinedly resistant to the lure of Nazism, which often found acceptance amongst their Lutheran colleagues in the same universities. Faulhaber, Galen, and several Catholic academics were foremost in exposing the pseudo learning of Rosenberg, whose blood-and-race outpourings were regularly denounced from Catholic pulpits—so much so that the Nazi leadership demanded the heads of the priests concerned. Protestant dissent hardened after pastors in large numbers deserted Hitler's official church to establish their own Confessional church, which abjured the poisonous tenets of the German Christian movement. Then in 1937 came Pius XI's assault upon the neo-paganism and anti-Semitism of the Hitler regime, and its abuses of the concordat, in the encyclical *Mit brennender Sorge*.

The Holy See made innumerable protests on behalf of Hitler's victims through the nuncio in Berlin, Monsignor Orsenigo. This was not generally known and is still not well known today. As the leading German cleric, Cardinal Bertram, privately and through diplomatic channels, made repeated protests to the Reich chancellery office.

Denied any say in the political life of the nation, the bishops, acting within the terms of the concordat, continued to denounce Nazi ideology from their pulpits and in their pastoral letters. In a single year, the year of the Röhm purge, Nazism came under attack in the sermons of Cardinal Schulte and Archbishop Gröber and by the hierarchy jointly in a published statement; and the regime's racial policy was expressly condemned by Bishop Galen in a pastoral letter of that year. The writings and speeches of Rottenburg's Bishop Sproll made him a marked man, and he maintained an outspoken opposition to the Nazi regime until 1938, when he was forced from his diocese and into exile. In Cologne, Hitler's henchmen vandalised the diocesan printing offices in a retaliatory action provoked by the pastoral letters of Cardinal Schulte. After his death in 1941, Schulte was succeeded by the worthy Archbishop Frings, who from his pulpit regularly inveighed against the oppression of the Jews. A redoubtable preacher against human-rights abuses, Bishop Preysing of Berlin set an example in his diocese by urging his clergy to speak out against injustice. His 1942 pastoral letter on the subject was smuggled out of Germany before being transmitted by the BBC. The Catholic bishops spoke out when other voices, those of German intellectuals and academics, for example, which might have been raised against Hitler, remained silent. "Only the Catholic Church protested against the Hitlerian onslaught on liberty", declared the Jewish physicist Albert Einstein from his exile in the United States and then went on to praise the Church unreservedly.

News of the hierarchy's opposition to Hitler spread abroad. Among the French Resistance, many drew inspiration from the German bishops' pastoral letters. The bishops were praised in the American press as much as they were reviled in the Nazi press. Bishop Galen's sermons found an echo worldwide; when duplicated, they became required reading for all Germans who opposed Hitler. To Galen's condemnation of the euthanasia programme must be added those of other members of the Catholic hierarchy and the courageous protests of many Protestant church leaders.

Bertram, Faulhaber, Gröber, and Preysing all hid or otherwise assisted Jews. Preysing and his colleagues, notably Margarete Sommer, who headed his diocesan rescue operations, arranged for Jews and other refugees from Nazism to flee Germany. In 1943, when the fact of the Holocaust became known, although doubt long persisted in the West, the Catholic bishops issued a joint declaration deploring the wholesale eviction and murder of Jews. It should be borne in mind that throughout this period, the Catholic Church in Germany had to fight for its survival, as faith schools and religious houses regularly became prey to Nazi zealots, priests were attacked in the streets and cast into prison, and bishops' residences were broken into and profaned.

The German opposition united Catholics and Protestants, and those who, while professing no particular religious faith, discovered in Christianity the prerequisites for German and European restoration. Of the Kreisau Circle, only Leber queried the central place given to Christianity. His fellow Social Democrats Haubach and Mierendorff both found Christ while interned in a concentration camp. Haubach kept a picture of Saint Thomas Aquinas above his desk, and Thomist philosophy informed his political thinking.[1] The publications of the White Rose were permeated with religious sentiments. The opening paragraph

[1] Ger van Roon, *German Resistance to Hitler: Count von Moltke and the Kreisau Circle* (London: Van Nostrand Reinhold, 1971), 126.

of the third leaflet, authored by Hans Scholl and Alexander Schmorell, perfectly encapsulates the Catholic theory of the state. It was taken for granted by all Germans who envisaged the rebirth of Germany after Hitler that Christianity would furnish the foundational principles; in the case of the Kreisau Circle, a combination of Christian and socialist principles was decided upon.

While serving as papal nuncio in Germany in the 1920s, Archbishop Pacelli made several outspoken attacks on Nazi ideology. He restated his opposition to Nazism in the 1930s when, as cardinal secretary of state, he addressed pilgrims at Lourdes and Lisieux and the congregation in Notre Dame, Paris, and when he spoke at the Eucharistic Congress in Budapest only months before his election to the papacy.

Summi Pontificatus, Pius XII's first encyclical as pope, contained a blistering indictment of racism and totalitarian dictatorships, earning him unstinting praise in the press of the free world. Vatican Radio broadcasts at the beginning of the war protested the inhuman treatment of Poles and Jews, until harsh retaliatory measures and the threat of worse to come forced the suspension of the transmissions. After the German assault in the West, broadcasts attacking racialism were beamed to France from the Vatican. Texts of Vatican Radio broadcasts were read and distributed clandestinely in France and elsewhere in occupied Europe, papal allocutions on racialism receiving an especially wide circulation in Vichy.

Several times in 1941, Pius XII spoke out in the interests of oppressed peoples under Axis occupation, a concern that preoccupied his Easter message of the following year. In his Christmas message of 1942, the pope raised his voice expressly on behalf of the beleaguered Jews of Europe. The *New York Times* praised the address unreservedly. Print shops in the Reich were closed down if they reprinted it. Pius XII's 1943 address to the College of Cardinals condemned the extermination of the Jews; the address was subsequently broadcast to the world by Vatican Radio. In his encyclical of that year on the Mystical Body of Christ, the pope referred to the love of Christ, which embraces all of humanity. Church leaders who spoke out against Nazi injustice—Cardinal van Roey in Belgium, for instance, and the bishops of Vichy France—had their protests endorsed by the pope, who ensured they were more widely publicised by having them broadcast on Vatican Radio or by ordering their inclusion in *L'Osservatore Romano*. When the Allies, with an eye to their own advantage, no doubt, wanted Pius XII to make ringing condemnations naming names, the pope wisely declined. He feared that Catholics and Jews would suffer greater calamities as a result. The evidence bears him out. Jews dreaded the consequences of such an action. Sympathetic Germans such as Weizsäcker knew that reprisals would follow. At least one Allied diplomat in retrospect has acknowledged the soundness of the pope's policy, a policy also adhered to by the International Red Cross.

In Slovakia and in Hungary, in the Balkans and in the occupied countries of Western Europe, whenever Jews were arrested and rounded up for deportation, ecclesiastical protest immediately followed. The papal nuncios, particularly in the countries of Eastern Europe, were relentless in their pursuit of government ministers and heads of state. In every case, they acted upon orders from Rome. As the pope speaks, so speak his legates. Due to Vatican intervention, the deportations from Rumania were stopped. This was not always possible in other counties, but delays and temporary suspensions of eviction orders resulting from Vatican pressure were often successful in enabling Jews to go into hiding, thus ensuring their survival.

Jews fleeing Hitler's executioners found a haven in church buildings and religious institutions, and in the homes of ordinary Catholics. Catholics cooperated with Jewish welfare agencies and, in occupied Western Europe, with Protestants in the work of rescue, particularly as it related to the welfare of children. Armies of priests and nuns became engaged in the manufacture of false identity papers, while leading churchmen, such as Archbishop Roncalli, signed thousands of baptismal certificates. For rescuing Jewish children, French priests were deported east. Large numbers of priests were shot or died in captivity for resisting Hitler, or simply because, to Nazis, they were objects of special hatred. Risking all, priests were foremost in the work of concealment and rescue, aided by courageous men and women among the Catholic laity, and often with the active cooperation of their bishops. Writing of Catholic priests in wartime Italy, the historian Philip Morgan notes, "[T]hey were the people sought out by fugitives of all kinds ... the go-betweens in prisoner exchanges, even truces ... the organizers of temporary ceasefires."[2]

Pius XII made repeated pleas directed to the avoidance of war, and when these failed, he laboured tirelessly to keep Mussolini from taking Italy into war on the side of Germany. World leaders praised his efforts, though they were unsuccessful. The Pontifical Relief Commission, which Pius XII set up to alleviate the devastation wrought by war, distributed food, clothing, and needed medical supplies. The Vatican Information Bureau, which employed a staff of hundreds, enabled two million people to be put in touch with loved ones missing or incarcerated as prisoners of war or in concentration camps. In Greece and

[2] Philip Morgan, *The Fall of Mussolini* (Oxford: Oxford University Press, 2007), 194–95.

in Rome the population was delivered from famine due largely to Vatican intervention. Vatican money, including Pius XII's personal fortune, was poured into welfare and rescue work, and millions of dollars were raised by American Catholics for that purpose. Friendly countries had to exceed their quotas of Jewish refugees when they arrived on their shores bearing documents signed by Vatican officials.

Papal intervention on behalf of Hitler's victims was appreciated by Jews as much as it was resented by Nazis; and after the war, Pius XII was honoured by the state of Israel. In September 2008, a conference of Jewish scholars and rabbis from around the world told his successor Pope Benedict XVI that Pius XII had helped to save nearly a million Jewish lives.[3] Alas, the truth is often obscured by an atmosphere of prejudice and hate for Rome. Even works that betray no particular animosity towards the pope and the Catholic Church repeat the demonstrably false accusation that Pius XII remained silent as the Nazis enslaved and murdered European Jews. Nothing could be further from the truth. Catholics need have no doubts about the role of the papacy during the Third Reich. Rather, they have every reason to feel proud. Two reigning popes and three future popes in significant ways offered resistance to Hitler. The facts are well attested. Wherever Nazism held sway, it found an unrelenting foe in the pope and the Catholic Church. Of that there can be no doubt, save in the minds of the misinformed and the prejudiced.

[3] Ed West, "Pope Benedict Defends the Role of Wartime Pontiff", *Catholic Herald*, 26 September 2008, 1.

ACKNOWLEDGEMENTS

I wish to record my appreciation for the help given me by members of my family, chief among whom are my wife, Maureen, and my daughter and amanuensis, Colette. To her I owe my warmest thanks, for her many exertions on my behalf, and not least for her unwavering support during the preparation of the manuscript and following its submission for publication.

It may be helpful to include a note on my use of papal encyclicals. Excerpts from the encyclical letters of Pius XI, *Ubi Arcano Dei*; *Non Abbiamo Bisogno;* and *Mit Brennender Sorge* have been taken from the collection edited by Anne Freemantle and published by Mentor Books, except for one brief citation from *Ubi Arcano Dei* which does not appear in Freemantle's edited text. This I have taken from *The Pope and the People*, a compilation of papal texts published by the Catholic Truth Society. For Pius XII's first encyclical letter, *Summi Pontificatus*, I have preferred Monsignor Ronald Knox's translation made for the Catholic Truth Society.

BIBLIOGRAPHY

Alvarez, David, and Robert Graham, S.J. *Nothing Sacred: Nazi Espionage against the Vatican, 1939–1945*. London: Frank Cass, 1997.

Bessel, Richard. *Germany after the First World War*. Oxford: Clarendon Press, 1993.

———, ed. *Life in the Third Reich*. Oxford: Oxford University Press, 2001.

Binchy, D.A. *Church and State in Fascist Italy*. London: Oxford University Press, 1941.

Blet, Pierre, S.J. *Pius XII and the Second World War according to the Archives of the Vatican*. Herefordshire: Gracewing, 2003.

Bosworth, R.J.B. *Mussolini*. London: Arnold, 2002.

Briody, Father Joseph. "The Vatican Pimpernel". *Alive* (September 2008): 13.

Burden, Hamilton T. *The Nuremberg Party Rallies: 1923–1939*. London: Pall Mall Press, 1967.

Burleigh, Michael. *The Third Reich: A New History*. London: Macmillan, 2000.

Caldwell, Simon. "The Student Who Took a Stand against the Reich". *Catholic Herald*, 10 April 2009.

Chadwick, Kay. "The Battle of the Airways: Wartime Propaganda". *BBC History Magazine* 2, no. 7 (July 2010): 50–54.

Chadwick, Owen. *Britain and the Vatican during the Second World War*. Cambridge: Cambridge University Press, 1986.

————. *The Christian Churches in the Cold War*. London: Penguin Books, 1993.

Cianfarra, Camille M. *The War and the Vatican*. London: Burns, Oates and Washbourne, 1945.

Ciano, Count Galeazzo. *Ciano's Diary, 1937–1938*. London: Methuen, 1952.

————. *Ciano's Diary, 1939–1943*. Edited by Malcolm Muggeridge. London: William Heinemann, 1947.

Clonmore, William. *Pope Pius XI and World Peace*. London: Robert Hale, 1937.

Cohen, Nick. *What's Left? How Liberals Lost Their Way*. London: Harper Perennial, 2007.

Conway, J.S. *The Nazi Persecution of the Churches: 1933–1945*. London: Weidenfeld and Nicolson, 1968.

Coppa, Frank J., ed. *Controversial Concordats: The Vatican's Relations with Napoleon, Mussolini, and Hitler*. Washington, D.C.: Catholic University of America Press, 1999.

Corley, Felix. "Obituary: Fr. Robert Graham, S.J." *Independent*, 8 March 1997. Accessed 4 September 2015. http://www.independent.co.uk.

Craig, Gordon A. *The Germans*. New York: Penguin Books, 1991.

Craig, Mary. *Man from a Far Country: A Portrait of Pope John Paul II*. London: Hodder and Stoughton, 1979.

Crofts, A.M., O.P. *Catholic Social Action: Principles, Purpose and Practice*. London: Catholic Book Club, 1936.

Dalin, Rabbi David. "A Righteous Gentile: Pope Pius XII and the Jews". Catholic League for Religious and Civil Rights, 26 February 2011. Accessed 4 September 2015. http://www.catholicleague.org/.

Delp, Alfred, S.J. *Prison Writings*. Maryknoll, N.Y.: Orbis Books, 2004.

De Lubac, Henri, S.J. *Christian Resistance to Anti-Semitism: Memories from 1940–1944*. San Francisco: Ignatius Press, 1990.

D'Entreves, A. P., ed. *Aquinas: Selected Political Writings.* Oxford: Basil Blackwell, 1959.

DiGiovanni, Monsignor Stephen M. "Pius XII and the Jews: The War Years as Reported by the *New York Times*". *Rutgers Journal of Law and Religion.* Accessed 31 August 2015. http://lawandreligion.com/sites/lawandreligion .com/files/DiGiovanni.pdf.

Dobschiner, Johanna-Ruth. *Selected to Live.* London: Pickering and Inglis, 1979.

Dumbach, Annette E., and Jud Newborn. *Shattering the German Night: The Story of the White Rose.* Boston: Little, Brown and Company, 1986.

Elliott, Lawrence. *I Will Be Called John: A Portrait of Pope John XXIII.* London: William Collins Sons, 1976.

Eyck, Erich. *A History of the Weimar Republic.* 2 vols. London: Oxford University Press, 1962.

Falconi, Carlo. *The Silence of Pius XII.* London: Faber and Faber, 1970.

Farrell, Nicholas. *Mussolini.* London: Weidenfeld and Nicolson, 2003.

Faulhaber, Cardinal Michael von. *Judaism, Christianity and Germany.* Translated by George D. Smith. New York: Macmillan, 1935.

Fischer, Klaus P. *Nazi Germany.* London: Constable, 1997.

Fogelman, Eva. *Conscience and Courage: Rescuers of Jews during the Holocaust.* London: Victor Gollancz, 1996.

Fontenelle, Monsignor R. *His Holiness Pope Pius XI.* London: Methuen, 1938.

Frain, John. *The Cross and the Third Reich: Catholic Resistance in the Nazi Era.* Oxford: Family Publications, 2009.

Frei, Norbert. *National Socialist Rule in Germany: The Führer State 1933–1945.* Translated by Simon B. Steyne. Oxford: Blackwell, 1993.

Freemantle, Anne. *The Papal Encyclicals in Their Historical Context.* New York: Mentor Books, 1959.

Friedlander, Saul. *Pius XII and the Third Reich*. London: Chatto and Windus, 1966.

Gallin, Mary Alice. "The Cardinal and the State: Faulhaber and the Third Reich". *Journal of Church and State* 12 (1970): 385–404.

Gilbert, Martin. *The Holocaust: The Jewish Tragedy*. London: Collins, 1986.

Gitter, Benno. *The Story of My Life*. London: Weidenfeld and Nicolson, 1998.

Goebbels, Joseph. *The Early Goebbels Diaries: 1925–1926*. Edited by Helmut Heiber. London: Weidenfeld and Nicolson, 1962.

———. *The Goebels Diaries*. Translated and edited by Louis P. Lochner. London: Hamish Hamilton, 1948.

———. *The Goebbels Diaries: The Last Days*. Edited by Hugh Trevor-Roper. London: Book Club Associates, 1978.

Graham, Robert A., S.J. *The Pope and Poland in World War Two*. London: Veritas Foundation Publication Centre, 1965.

———. *The Vatican and Communism during World War II*. San Francisco: Ignatius Press, 1996.

Graml, Hermann, Hans Mommsen, Hans-Joachim Reichhardt, and Ernst Wolf. *The German Resistance to Hitler*. Batsford: London, 1970.

Harrigan, William M. "Nazi Germany and the Holy See, 1933–1936: The Historical Background of *Mit brennender Sorge*". *Catholic Historical Review* 47, no. 2 (July 1961): 164–73.

———. "Pius XII's Efforts to Effect a Détente in German-Vatican Relations 1939–1940". *Catholic Historical Review* 49, no. 2 (July 1963): 173–91.

Harris, Mark Jonathan, and Deborah Oppenheimer. *Into the Arms of Strangers: Stories of the Kindertransport*. New York: Bloomsbury, 2000.

Harris, Robert. "Stepinac: War Criminal or Saint?" *Catholic Herald*, 3 October 2008.

Hassell, Ulrich von. *Diaries: The Story of the Forces against Hitler inside Germany*. London: Frontline Books, 2011.

Hauner, Milan. *Hitler: A Chronology of His Life and Time*. London: Palgrave Macmillan, 2008.

Heenan, John C. *Not the Whole Truth: An Autobiography*. London: Hodder and Stoughton, 1973.

Heiden, Konrad. *The Fuehrer*. London: Robinson 1999.

Helmreich, Ernst Christian. *The German Churches under Hitler*. Detroit: Wayne State University Press, 1980.

Hiden, John. *Germany and Europe, 1919–1939*. London: Longman, 1977.

Hitchcock, William I. *Liberation: The Bitter Road to Freedom, Europe 1944–1945*. London: Faber and Faber, 2009.

Hitler, Adolf. *Mein Kampf*. London: Pimlico, 1996.

Hoffman, Peter. *The History of the German Resistance, 1933–1945*. London: MacDonald and James, 1977.

Hoffner, Sebastian. *Defying Hitler: A Memoir*. London: Phoenix, 2002.

Holmes, J. Derek. *The Papacy in the Modern World*. London: Burns and Oates, 1981.

Horn, Daniel. "The Struggle for Catholic Youth in Hitler's Germany: An Assessment". *Catholic Historical Review* 65, no. 4 (October 1979): 561–82.

Hughes, John Jay. "The Pope's 'Pact with Hitler': Betrayal or Self-Defense?" *Journal of Church and State* 17 (1975): 63–80.

Humbert, Agnes. *Resistance: Memoirs of Occupied France*. London: Bloomsbury, 2008.

Jackson, Julian. *France: The Dark Years, 1940–1944*. Oxford: Oxford University Press, 2001.

John XXIII, Pope. *Journal of a Soul*. London: Four Square Books, 1966.

Johnson, Paul. *A History of the Modern World from 1917 to the 1980s*. London: Weidenfeld and Nicolson, 1984.

Junge, Traudl. *Until the Final Hour*. London: Phoenix, 2005.

"Just a Thought: She Saved 2,500 Children from Death". *Alive* (September 2008).

Kallay, Nicholas. *Hungarian Premier*. London: Oxford University Press, 1954.

Kedward, H.R. *Occupied France: Collaboration and Resistance, 1940–1944*. Oxford: Basil Blackwell, 1987.

Kent, Peter C. *The Pope and the Duce*. London: Macmillan, 1981.

———. "A Tale of Two Popes: Pius XI, Pius XII and the Rome-Berlin Axis". *Journal of Contemporary History* 23, no. 4 (October 1988): 589–608.

Kershaw, Ian. *Hitler*. Vol. 1, *1889–1936: Hubris*. London: Allen Lane, 1998.

———. *Hitler*. Vol. 2, *1936–1945: Nemesis*. London: Allen Lane, 2000.

———. *Life in the Third Reich*. Edited by Richard Bessel. Oxford: Oxford University Press, 2001.

———. *Making Friends with Hitler*. London: Allen Lane, 2004.

Knopp, Guido. *Hitler's Holocaust*. Stroud, UK: Sutton, 2004.

———. *The SS: A Warning from History*. Stroud, UK: History Press, 2008.

Krieg, Robert A. *Catholic Theologians in Nazi Germany*. New York: Continuum, 2004.

Kurzman, Dan. *A Special Mission: Hitler's Secret Plot to Seize the Vatican and Kidnap Pope Pius XII*. Cambridge, Mass.: Da Capo Press, 2007.

Lanckorońska, Countess Karolina. *Those Who Trespass against Us: One Woman's War against the Nazis*. London: Pimlico, 2005.

Lapide, Pinchas E. *The Last Three Popes and the Jews*. London: Souvenir Press, 1967.

Leber, Annedore. *Conscience in Revolt: Sixty-Four Stories of Resistance in Germany, 1933–1945*. London: Vallentine Mitchell, 1957.

Lewy, Guenter. *The Catholic Church and Nazi Germany*. London: Weidenfeld and Nicolson, 1964.

Lukacs, John. "The Diplomacy of the Holy See during World War II". *Catholic Historical Review* 60, no. 2 (July 1974): 271–78.

MacGregor-Hastie, Roy. *Pope Paul VI*. London: Four Square Books, 1966.

Marchione, Sister Margherita. "The Truth about Pius XII". *Catholic League for Religious and Civil Rights*. Accessed 4 September 2015. http://www.catholicleague.org/.

Marsden, Father Francis. "The Anti-Semitic Legacy". *Catholic Times*, 8 August 1999.

———. "Nazis Killed Catholics Too". *Catholic Times*, 9 April 2000.

Martinez, Mary Ball. "Pope Pius XII in the Second World War". *Journal of Historical Review* 13, no. 5 (September–October 1993): 26ff. Institute for Historical Review. Accessed 28 August 2015. http://ihr.org/.

Matheson, Peter, ed. *The Third Reich and the Christian Churches*. Edinburgh: T&T Clark, 1982.

McDonough, Frank. *Sophie Scholl*. Stroud, UK: History Press, 2009.

McElligott, Anthony, ed. *Weimar Germany*. Oxford: Oxford University Press, 2009.

McInerny, Ralph. *The Defamation of Pius XII*. South Bend, Ind.: St. Augustine's Press, 2001.

Mindszenty, Josef Cardinal. *Memoirs*. London: Weidenfeld and Nicolson, 1974.

Monk, Matthew, M.L.N. Couve de Murville, and Hugh Clark. *Edith Stein, Marcel Callo, Titus Brandsma: Victims of the Nazis*. London: Catholic Truth Society, 1997.

Moore, Bob. *Survivors: Jewish Self-Help and Rescue in Nazi-Occupied Western Europe*. Oxford: Oxford University Press, 2010.

————. *Victims and Survivors: The Nazi Persecution of the Jews in the Netherlands 1940–1945*. London: Arnold, 1997.

Moorhouse, Roger. *Killing Hitler: The Third Reich and the Plots against the Führer*. London: Jonathan Cape, 2006.

Morgan, Philip. *The Fall of Mussolini*. Oxford: Oxford University Press, 2007.

Niven, Bill. *Facing the Nazi Past: United Germany and the Legacy of the Third Reich*. London: Routledge, 2003.

Noakes, J., and G. Pridham, eds. *Nazism 1919–1945*. Vol. 2, *State, Economy and Society 1933–1939*. Exeter: University of Exeter Press, 1995.

————. *Nazism 1919–1945*. Vol. 3, *Foreign Policy, War and Racial Extermination*. Exeter: University of Exeter Press, 1995.

Noel, Gerard. *Pius XII: The Hound of Hitler*. London: Continuum, 2008.

O'Carroll, Michael, CSSp. *Pius XII: Greatness Dishonoured—A Documented Study*. Dublin: Laetare Press, 1980.

O'Connell, Gerry. "Letters Show Decency of Pius XII in Wartime". *Universe,* 20 June 2004.

Orlow, Dietrich. *The History of the Nazi Party*. Vol. 1, *1919–1933*. Pittsburgh: University of Pittsburgh Press, 1969.

————. *The History of the Nazi Party*. Vol 2, *1933–1945*. Pittsburgh: University of Pittsburgh Press, 1973.

Ottaway, Susan. *Hitler's Traitors: German Resistance to the Nazis*. Barnsley, UK: Leo Cooper, 2003.

Owen, James. *Nuremberg: Evil on Trial*. London: Headline Review, 2007.

Packard, Reynolds and Eleanor. *Balcony Empire: Fascist Italy at War*. London: Chatto and Windus, 1943.

Palmer, A. W. *A Dictionary of Modern History 1789–1945*. London: Penguin Books, 1969.

Peukert, Detlev J. K. "Young People: For or Against the Nazis?" *History Today* 35, no. 10 (October 1985): 15–22.

Phayer, Michael. "The Catholic Resistance Circle in Berlin and German Catholic Bishops during the Holocaust". *Holocaust and Genocide Studies* 7, no. 2 (1993): 216–29.

Pius XI, Pope. *The Pope and Catholic Action: Pontifical Letters*. London: Catholic Truth Society, 1935.

Pius XII, Pope. *Summi Pontificatus*. Translated by Msgr. Ronald Knox. Catholic Truth Society, 1939.

Poggi, Gianfranco. *Catholic Action in Italy*. Stanford: Stanford University Press, 1967.

The Pope and the People: Selected Letters and Addresses on Social Questions. London: Catholic Truth Society, 1950.

Porter, Anna. *Kasztner's Train: The True Story of an Unknown Hero of the Holocaust*. New York: Walker, 2008.

Portmann, Heinrich. *Cardinal von Galen*. London: Jarrolds, 1957.

Pridham, Geoffrey. *Hitler's Rise to Power: The Nazi Movement in Bavaria, 1923–1933*. London: Hart-Davis, MacGibbon, 1973.

Pulzer, Peter. *Germany 1870–1945: Politics, State Formation and War*. Oxford: Oxford University Press, 1997.

Randall, Sir Alec. *The Pope, the Jews and the Nazis*. London: Catholic Truth Society, 1963.

Rhodes, Anthony. *The Vatican in the Age of the Dictators, 1922–1945*. London: Hodder and Stoughton, 1973.

Ribbentrop, Joachim. *Memoirs*. London: Weidenfeld and Nicolson, 1954.

Ritter, Gerhard. "The German Opposition to Hitler". *Contemporary Review* 177 (January–June 1950): 339–45.

Roon, Ger van. *German Resistance to Hitler: Count von Moltke and the Kreisau Circle*. London: Van Nostrand Reinhold, 1971.

Rosenberg, Alfred. *Selected Writings*. Edited by Robert Pois. London: Jonathan Cape, 1970.

Sale, Father Giovanni. "Two Popes, the Nazi Party and the Second World War". *Universe*, 20 June 2004.

Scholl, Inge. *Students against Tyranny: The Resistance of the White Rose, Munich, 1942–1943*. Middletown, Conn.: Wesleyan University Press, 1970.

Scrivener, Jane. *Inside Rome with the Germans*. New York: Macmillan, 1945.

Sonnert, Gerhard, and Gerald Holton. *What Happened to the Children Who Fled Nazi Persecution?* New York: Palgrave MacMillan, 2008.

Speer, Albert. *Inside the Third Reich*. London: Weidenfeld and Nicolson, 1970.

Stargardt, Nicholas. *Witnesses of War: Children's Lives under the Nazis*. London: Jonathan Cape, 2005.

Taylor, James, and Warren Shaw. *The Penguin Dictionary of the Third Reich*. London: Penguin Books, 1997.

Taylor, Myron C. *Wartime Correspondence between President Roosevelt and Pope Pius XII*. New York: Macmillan, 1947.

Tinnemann, Sister Ethel Mary, S.N.J.M. "Attitudes of the German Catholic Hierarchy toward the Nazi Regime: A Study in German Psycho-Political Culture". *Western Political Quarterly* 22 (1969): 333–49.

———. "The Silence of Pope Pius XII". *Journal of Church and State* 21 (1999): 265–85.

Tittmann, Harold H., Jr. *Inside the Vatican of Pius XII: The Memoir of an American Diplomat during World War II*. New York: Image Books, 2004.

Tolansky, Ethel, and Helena Scott. *Pius XII*. London: Catholic Truth Society, 2003.

Vinen, Richard. *The Unfree French: Life under the Occupation*. London: Allen Lane, 2006.

Walker, Lawrence D. " 'Young Priests' as Opponents: Factors Associated with Clerical Opposition to the Nazis in

Bavaria, 1933". *Catholic Historical Review* 65, no. 3 (July 1993): 402–13.

Weizsäcker, Ernst von. *The Memoirs of Ernst von Weizsäcker*. London: Victor Gollancz, 1951.

Welch, David. *The Hitler Conspiracies: Secrets and Lies behind the Rise and Fall of the Nazi Party*. Shepperton, UK: Ian Allan., 2001.

West, Ed. "Pope Benedict Defends the Role of Wartime Pontiff". *Catholic Herald*, 26 September 2008, 1–2.

Williamson, David G. *Poland Betrayed: The Nazi-Soviet Invasion of 1939*. Barnsley, UK: Pen and Sword Books, 2009.

Winterbottom, Michael. *Pius XII: A Saint in the Making*. Cheadle Hume, UK: Universe Media Group, 2010.

Wistrich, Robert S. *Who's Who in Nazi Germany*. London: Routledge, 2002.

Woodward, E. L., and Rohan Butler, eds. Assisted by Anne Orde. *Documents on British Foreign Policy 1919–1939*. 3rd series. Vol. 5, *1939*. London: Her Majesty's Stationery Office, 1952.

———. *Documents on German Foreign Policy 1918–1945*. Series C (1933–1937), The Third Reich: First Phase. Vol. 1, *January 30–October 14, 1933*. London: Her Majesty's Stationery Office, 1957.

———. *Documents on German Foreign Policy 1919–1939*. Series D. Vol. 6, *The Last Months of Peace, March–August 1939*. London: Her Majesty's Stationery Office, 1956.

———. *Documents on German Foreign Policy 1919–1939*. Series D. Vol. 7, *The Last Days of Peace, August 9–September 3, 1939*. London: Her Majesty's Stationery Office, 1956.

———. *Documents on German Foreign Policy 1919–1939*. Series D. Vol. 8, *The War Years, September 4, 1939–March 18, 1940*. London: Her Majesty's Stationery Office, 1954.

Zahn, Gordon C. "Catholic Opposition to Hitler: The Perils of Ambiguity". *Journal of Church and State* 13, no. 3 (Autumn 1971): 413–26.

Zamoyski, Adam. *Poland A History*. London: Harper Press, 2009.

INDEX